I Surrender

Insights into How God Works His Plan for Your Life

Michael Springston

And what I found was better than what I was looking for

TRILOGY

Trilogy Christian Publishers
A Wholly Owned Subsidiary of Trinity Broadcasting Network
2442 Michelle Drive
Tustin, CA 92780

Copyright © 2020 by Michael Springston

All Scripture quotations, unless otherwise noted, taken from THE HOLY BIBLE, NEW INTERNATIONAL VERSION®, NIV® Copyright © 1973, 1978, 1984, 2011 by Biblica, Inc.® Used by permission. All rights reserved worldwide.

Scripture quotations marked (KJV) taken from *The Holy Bible, King James Version*. Cambridge Edition: 1769.

All rights reserved, including the right to reproduce this book or portions thereof in any form whatsoever.

For information, address Trilogy Christian Publishing
Rights Department, 2442 Michelle Drive, Tustin, Ca 92780.
Trilogy Christian Publishing/ TBN and colophon are trademarks of Trinity Broadcasting Network.

For information about special discounts for bulk purchases, please contact Trilogy Christian Publishing.

Manufactured in the United States of America

Trilogy Disclaimer: The views and content expressed in this book are those of the author and may not necessarily reflect the views and doctrine of Trilogy Christian Publishing or the Trinity Broadcasting Network.

10 9 8 7 6 5 4 3 2 1

Library of Congress Cataloging-in-Publication Data is available.

ISBN 978-1-64773-228-8 (Print Book)
ISBN 978-1-64773-229-5 (ebook)

This book is dedicated to my wife, Sharon, who has supported me and been the stabilizing person in my life. Thank you for being such a consistent, kind, and thoughtful mate.

I also dedicate this book to my mother, Erma Springston, who has worked with me tirelessly to produce the results that those who read will see. She is also the one who taught me the two most important lessons of my life: first, how to love the Word of God, and second, how to pray.

Lastly, I dedicate this book to Ellen and Ron Treadway. These two were the ministers that held forth the banner for me to follow over the years. Ellen worked with me also on this book. Ron is the most dynamic preacher that has ever earned the license to preach. Your wit and your ability to communicate was a blessing then, and it becomes dearer to me as the days go by.

Thank you to all those who read this book. I pray that God adds a blessing to your life.

Contents

Foreword 7
Preface 11
Introduction 13
The Training Ground and the Battleground 21
From Tipping Point to the Turning Point 31
In the Furnace of Affliction 45
The Revelation of the Eternal Jesus 57
The Revelation of the Personal Jesus 71
The Revelation of the Creative Jesus 83
The Revelation of the Life in Jesus 101
The Revelation of the Light in Jesus 117
The Revelation of the Illumination in Jesus 133
The Revelation of the Salvation in Jesus 155
The Revelation of the Glory in Jesus 175
The Glory of God Manifested in Jesus as Righteousness
    and Sanctifier 191
The Glory of God Manifested in Jesus as Shepherd
    and Healer 203
The Glory of God Manifested in Jesus as Banner
    and Provider 213
The Glory of God Manifested in Jesus as Peace
    and He Is There 227

The Glory of God in Jesus after the Resurrection 251
The Revelation of the Grace in Jesus 261
The Revelation of the Truth in Jesus..295
How to Relate the Revelations of Jesus Christ to Yourself...........319
Works Cited...327
Endorsements..329
Ways to Visit the Ministry of Mike Springston............................331

Foreword

"Does God still speak today? This question has remained the subject of much discussion and debate for much longer than my thirty-five years of Christian ministry. We are familiar with the remarkable biblical accounts of God conversing with Adam in the garden, instructing Noah to build an ark and calling to Moses through a burning bush. But what about today? The question is most often associated with hearing an audible voice. The truth is, God has the ability to speak to those who believe in Him, even if it's not through an audible voice. He communicates powerfully to us through His Word, persistent prayer, and the work of the Holy Spirit. The "why" of the original question is important. It relates to God's purpose and desire toward us. More than a religion or a set of rules, He wants a relationship with us through His Son, Jesus Christ. That relationship begins with a new birth and is followed by discipleship. The new birth is the miracle of the moment, but the making of a disciple takes a lifetime.

I have always been intrigued by Jesus's approach to discipleship. The first thing Jesus did was to invite a group of men who were curious about Him to "Come and see" (John 1:39).

Then He told them,

> Follow Me, and I will make you fishers of men.
> (Matthew 4:19 KJV)

In time, Jesus invited them to

> Take My yoke upon you and learn from Me.
> (Matthew 11:29 KJV)

By and by, He drew these men to himself.

> Abide in Me [remain in Me], and I in you. (John 15:4 KJV)

And then He told them, in effect, "Obey Me." He said,

> If you love Me, you will keep My commandments. (John 14:15 KJV)

> You are My friends if You do what I command you. (John 15:14 KJV)

What were His final words?

> And ye are witnesses of these things. And, behold, I send the promise of my Father upon you: but tarry ye in the city of Jerusalem, until ye be endued with power from on high. (Luke 24:48–49 KJV)

For the first disciples, and for us, this path leads us to a place of complete fulfillment and total *surrender*.

The book you hold in your hand is a must-read. The author of *I Surrender* relates his powerful testimony of God's unrelenting love and grace at work to preserve his life and prepare each step to bring about God's will. Though his own story and circumstances are unique, the wonderful truths and gripping insights he shares as a result of each encounter with the Lord and His truth will encourage and challenge you to pursue the Lord and His plan for you.

> Seek the Lord while He may be found, Call upon Him while He is near. Let the wicked forsake his way, And the unrighteous man his thoughts; Let him return to the Lord, And He will have mercy on him; And to our God, For He will abundantly pardon. (Isaiah 55:6–7 NKJV)

Mike Springston is my friend. What I want you to know about Mike is that he lives what he preaches. I've known Mike Springston for a relatively short time, but I've known him long enough to witness firsthand the love he has for the Lord Jesus Christ and His church. His preaching, teaching, and mentoring ministry reveals his great heart for people and his desire to see God transform lives.

Mike has been a minister of the Gospel and a football coach for well over forty years. He currently serves as the pastor at Family Fellowship Chapel in Mount Airy, North Carolina, and serves the many coaches in the football community as an offensive consultant. Mike's current ministry reaches the country through various methods as he is on radio, podcast, and YouTube. His driving philosophy is concurrent with the Word of God written in Mark 13:10, which states,

> And the gospel must first be preached to all the nations. (Mark 13:10 KJV)

Mike is the inventor of the modern-day spread offense and the run pass option offense. Both are used in the current game of football in some way or fashion within virtually every offensive system worldwide. Mike has coached at all levels of football and has developed his systems to match the skill level of the players who have played for him. Mike has been a head football coach at both the collegiate and the high school levels. He has also served as a consultant to the country of India during the beginning phase of their venture into professional football.

Mike's ministry has allowed him to preach and teach the Word of God in many states across the country. He has been an evangelist, church conference speaker, camp meeting speaker for youth, camp meeting speaker for the adult services, and has shared the Gospel through the Fellowship of Christian Athletes program. He is currently ordained by the International Pentecostal Holiness Church.

Mike and his wife, Sharon, live in Winston-Salem, North Carolina. Mike still teaches special education at the high school level, and Sharon is a retired nurse. Together they have three children: Paul, Chris, and Lisa.

> Bishop Michael S. Ainsworth
> Cornerstone Conference IPHC
> PO Box 150
> Browns Summit, NC 27214

Preface

Life in general has been very good to me. There have been opportunities that have come my way that have been exciting. I have searched for answers in the professional world and possibly even found a few. I have dealt with the troubles and defeats of life but never examined what those trials and defeats were attempting to teach me. I will share this thought with you to begin the direction of the book.

When I summed it all up and consider the journey of my life, what I found in the end of my search was far better than what I thought I was looking for during my years of trouble. My life took on new meaning the night I heard Benny Hinn speak concerning the revelations of Jesus Christ. The reason for that is detailed in this book. I hope, as you read, you will place yourself into the pages of this book and reflect on exactly why you were there and that your experiences come to life. When this occurs, as it did for me, I feel certain that you will locate the real direction God has attempted to channel your life.

In this book, I will attempt to define the revelations of Jesus Christ as they have occurred in my life. Also, as you read this book, I hope that you will see the ten revelations of Jesus Christ as given by the Holy Spirit to John. This book describes Him from the perspective of His position in the Godhead to His impact upon mankind. These revelations are essential to digest as they define the relationship of God to mankind from heaven's perspective.

This writing will also define the role and impact of the Word of God in relation to the office that He held in the Godhead. This role translated to men when Jesus became flesh and dwelt among us. It then translated to His office as the High Priest of His own sacrifice.

This book will also share the revelation of the individual whom God birthed for the express purpose of being the one who would be prepared to identify the heavenly revelation when He appeared. John the Baptist is a tremendous revelation in himself. The ten revelations of Jesus Christ found in the Gospel of John that describe Him as the King of Glory traces this King from eternity to glory, truth, and grace. Along the way you will see Him as a Person, Creator, Life, Light, Illumination, and Salvation.

This journey will take you through some insights into the scripture and life of Christ that are extremely revealing concerning the life and work of the Word of God. The Holy Spirit releases some wonderful thoughts and explanations concerning the Word of God that are exciting and bring new thought to his person, position, and purpose. Lastly, this book may define some of the ways that a Christian can become deceitfully drawn into what appears to be real and even good while they lose the impact of Christ upon their life, spirit, and ultimately endure the hardships of life. These moments and times catch men unaware as they simply are attempting to develop the best opportunities that may be available for their life. They do this never realizing the harm that is done to their spiritual life.

John, being led by the Holy Spirit, unveils the revelations of the Word of God so that we can clearly see from eternity to grace the impact of the King!

Introduction

Life is to be lived. That is a statement that is very true. However, life must also be reflected upon for what the events of one's life are attempting to teach the person.

At the tender age of eighteen months old, my life hung in the balance as I was diagnosed with pneumonia. I spent several days in an iron lung as the medical personnel of the day attempted to save my life. I have no recollection of any of the events, but my family remembers it well as their son and brother teetered between life and death. Death was one breath away.

At the age of seven, another major physical event occurred in my life. I was playing whiffle ball with my friends in a vacant lot near a busy street in Parkersburg, West Virginia. My team was at bat, and it was my turn to play catcher as I was up to bat next. The hitter fouled off the pitch, and it went over my head and into the street. Immediately I gave chase. I remember hearing my brother's voice scream, "Mike, stop!" It was too late. Down the street came a car at an extremely high rate of speed. I heard the tires screech, and the entire moment went into slow motion.

The car was a heavy Cadillac. As I approached the car, it lurched forward and up on its front tires. As I saw the car appear in front of me, it was in a skid. My eyes turned to the driver, and he was arm-locked pressing against the steering wheel. The car and I collided as I ran into the driver's side front fender. The force knocked me backward into the street. As I sat on the double yellow lines, there was no sound, no movement, and no pain. I simply was placed in a seated position. Shortly thereafter, I heard myself crying. I looked at the cars stopped and the drivers sitting as if they had seen a ghost. The driver of the Cadillac was still arm-locked on the steering wheel. A crowd appeared on the curbing all in a hush. Shortly my mother appeared through the crowd and picked me up and took me home.

The next day I found out some insight into this event that was shocking. The driver of the Cadillac was in an argument with his wife. The speed of his vehicle had exceeded one hundred miles per hour. The impact of the stop alone had severed the shock absorbers, and they remained in the gutter of the street. Death was one step away.

Then as a third-grader, I took a tumble in the basement of our family's store. Upon hitting the floor, the bottom of a Coca-Cola bottle lodged in my left knee. The pain was excruciating! Shortly my mother took me to the hospital where it was determined that glass from the bottle was lodged in my knee. The medicine at the time determined to use heat to cause the glass to rise from the wound. During the treatment, I began to spike an extremely high fever. For days on end, I lay in that hospital virtually lifeless. My mother would come to visit me and comfort me. I had a bed by the window, and I could see her walk to her car when she left. As a nine-year-old, I wondered if I would see her tomorrow.

The fever grew worse. They came into my ward and packed me in bags of ice to attempt to control the fever. My body temperature must have been off the charts. I do not recall the duration of these treatments, but I do remember the nightly assault upon my body as they gave me a barrage of shots. I remember one distinct moment when a visitor to our ward held a french fry. She turned to me and held it between her fingers. It looked so good. I had had very little food, and I would have loved to taste that fry. As she looked at me, I heard her say, "I wonder if he would like a french fry." Then she stopped and took a bite of the fry and said, "No, he is way too sick to eat." I remember turning my head and crying. Death lurked within just one degree on the thermometer.

As I review these events, I see a common thread. The thread is that something was attempting to bring an end to my life before it could have the chance to begin. There was always a physical attack that was so severe that death was just a breath, a step, or a degree away. But something or someone was obviously intervening and interceding at the critical moment. However, like most of us, I simply moved on to whatever came next with no reflection concerning why was I chosen to still be here when others were lost. That really is the question that must be pondered concerning not only my life but all of us who come out of the crises of life.

God would teach me this reflective ability through the life of a dear friend. God had placed in my life a man who would serve to be a friend, a father figure, and mentor. However, he seemed to consistently be in trouble. He was an awesome and intelligent man who had tremendous abilities, but he consistently seemed to find opposition. He was opposed by people, by church members, by his leadership, and by the betrayal of his health. He was a great person and a tremendous preacher. His oratorical skills were second to none. He could make you laugh, and he could bring you to tears within a few words. His creative ability to develop sermons was quite astounding as he served as a ghostwriter for many men who had great stature in their respective denominations.

One day, while praying, God began to deal with me concerning this wonderful man. As I prayed for him, I began to share with God some of the problems that I knew he was encountering. After a bit, the Holy Spirit spoke to me and said these words, "How many crises has he been through?"

I replied, "Well, Holy Spirit, I have known him for years, and I could not count the number of rough places he has been in."

The Holy Spirit then said something to me that was a revelation. He said, "I did not ask you how many he had been in. I asked you how many he had been through."

Now this was a statement that took on a whole different meaning. The message was quite clear. It is not how many problems and struggles you have been in that makes the difference. It is how many of those trials that God has brought you through!

After coming to the comprehension of what the Spirit of God was sharing with me, I called my friend and shared the revelation with him. Here is how the Holy Spirit showed me to do it.

I said, "Brother, I was praying about you and your situation today, and man, you have had a lot going on."

Naturally, he agreed.

I then said, "Have you ever taken a pen and begun to keep a list of the things you have been through?"

Naturally, he replied, "No."

I then said, "Take some time to do that, and I will call you tomorrow, and we will talk about it."

He agreed, and we hung up.

The next day I called him to discuss the problems. I asked him," How did it go?"

He replied, "I ran out of paper. But then I saw the point. It is not about what I am in that counts. It is about what I have come through. You know, God has been mighty faithful to me. He has delivered me physically many times. He has solved problems for me many times when I was total at a loss for what to do. I could go on and on, but I found my answer in the Twenty-Third Psalm."

> The LORD is my shepherd; I shall not want. He maketh me to lie down in green pastures: he leadeth me beside the still waters. He restoreth my soul: he leadeth me in the paths of righteousness for his name's sake. Yea, though I walk through the valley of the shadow of death, I will fear no evil: for thou art with me; thy rod and thy staff they comfort me. Thou preparest a table before me in the presence of mine enemies: thou anointest my head with oil; my cup runneth over. Surely goodness and mercy shall follow me all the days of my life: and I will dwell in the house of the LORD for ever. (Psalm 23 KJV)

When he got to verse 4, he stopped and shouted while as he saw precisely what David had said. He had walked through enough to know that the God that he served was a faithful and loving God. He had seen that in the middle of the trials and turmoil of life, God had set a splendid table in the very presence of his enemies for him to be fed, cared for, and to be satisfied by.

There surely is goodness and mercy available when we wade through the deception of the enemy to stop and reflect on what God has accomplished in our lives. The great news is that if He has done it once, He will do it again and again! The biggest lie the devil tells us is that we are in too deep and that there is no way out. Let's ask Abraham, Isaac, and Jacob about that. Let's have a meeting with Gideon to see if his number is not enough. Let's visit with David to see if he found out how to get out of trouble. Don't forget Job as he did not take the bait. This goes directly through the Bible. The people that God has chosen their story did not accept a lie as if it were the truth.

I was not exempt from this very issue as I have encountered opposition virtually everywhere I have been in secular work. The focus of people is on the destruction of those in power to enhance their personal ambitions. This is not just indigenous to the world of work; it is indigenous to people, whether they are saver or not. We must be cognizant of what these encounters are attempting to teach us. The importance of identifying the genesis of the problem and functioning in the spiritual domain concerning these problems is essential to having personal and spiritual balance in our lives.

The key to maintaining this balance is to recognize exactly what you have already been through. God is faithful, but it is imperative that we locate the points in time when we can place our finger on how He was faithful in a similar situation. We do know that Israel built altars for a reason as they journeyed to the promised land. That reason was to remember what God had done and where. It was also to serve as a talking tool for teaching the young ones to know when, where, and what God had done to deliver the promise to His people.

There has been a tremendous application that has been applied to my life from the pages of this book. I have shared the process as well as some of the procedures that I have gone through during my life's development. I believe that within the pages of this book, people from any walk of life can locate applicable material that they can readily identify as something that they could use to impact their lives.

Although my life has been spent as a football coach / teacher / preacher, the moments that have served to define my life are simply ones that as I wrote the book the Holy Spirit brought to my thoughts. The question then is this: "If you were defining your life and took a really close look at the times, places, and people that have come into your life, what have those events taught you? Have you, like most people, taken the issues of life dealt with them and moved on?"

So it is imperative that we evaluate the times, occurrences, and events of our life to see what message and lesson is attempting to be shared with us. This we know that God is a God who trains and chastises His people. We must look no further than into the book of Proverbs to obtain that understanding. With this knowledge, then is it possible that many important spiritual lessons have been missed? Is it possible that the life you are currently living is not the life for which you were intended to live at all?

The probability is that the God of the universe who created us in His own image has been working in your world through the events of your life to provide you with the opportunities that best fit His plan for your life. We, in our haste to not have trouble or crisis, have worked diligently to solve the immediate issues without considering the bigger picture.

This is the bigger picture as it appeared to me through the struggles that life has presented me: I was called to preach the Word of God. I was anointed to do so from my birth. The ministry is the location from where I do the most good for the most people. My natural abilities are connected to the requirements of the ministry. My natural ability to communicate and manage people are best used when I am working with spiritual things. My creative ability through the revelation of God has been of equal stature to the creative abilities that I produced in the secular world.

Although football and teaching had their high points and high moments, they did not satisfy my inner self. They served to some degree to hinder and distract my spiritual development. The players that I met while working in that area were great. Most of the coaches were quality people. The memories are awesome. But for me, it was not my calling. It was my profession. I did that for forty-plus years, had good success, and have a great reputation coming out of the business. But it was not what I was called to do.

So you are thinking, "How does this relate to me? I am in the profession for which I am trained, and I am unable to change what I do. I have bills, obligations, and debts that require my financial attention. It is virtually impossible for me to totally have a career makeover at this point in my life."

This is so very true. The answer here is that I am not suggesting you change your lifestyle, work, dwelling place, husband, children, friends, or any of those areas that you have designed into your life. What I am suggesting is that you begin to evaluate yourself against the revelations of John chapter 1. I am also suggesting that you begin to ponder the events of your life to see the avenues and opportunities for which they may have afforded you another opportunity. Having evaluated these, you can then begin to meditate upon what God was trying to do with you during that time. This will lead you to see if what God was doing for you then, and He may still be opening a door for you to pursue a course that can be a benefit to you and your loved ones. Most importantly, this open door may place you inside the ultimate calling of your life. I am sure you will agree with me that such reflection, meditation, and determinations would be well worth the peace that will follow.

This procedure may cause you to reflect upon some of life's major spiritual questions. It may cause you to evaluate what you believe and whom you have surrounded yourself with in view of your belief system. It may lead you to locate and build a better you based upon better beliefs. It may solve some of the hard spots in your life as you learn to better deal with people and work through problems. How does this occur? Well, the character and nature that comes from the ten revelations of Jesus Christ begin to impact you. When they do, two things will occur. First, a transformation will begin inside of you. Secondly, a transfer will take shape as your thoughts begin to become more directed into spiritual things.

This may cause you to rekindle your need for a relationship with Jesus Christ. As you evaluate yourself, it becomes very difficult if you do not have an evaluative measure. This is a great spot for the entrance of the Word of God and a study of the life and character of Jesus Christ. When you do this self-reflection, it may become important to remove my stories from this book and replace them with your own. The personal nature of this will allow you to see the revelations that are in Jesus as they apply to you. Remember, this is your story, and it is personal.

As I conclude this section, I desire to pray with you.

Father, in the name of Jesus, open the pages of this book to the heart and spirit of the reader. I ask You to all them that reflect upon the memories of their life, for them to see the times when You were working to direct their paths. Lord, we know that our steps are ordered by the Lord. Today, Lord, we surrender to You, Your direction, Your instruction, and Your leading. We receive what we believe concerning Your ability to work in us and to bless our ways. Lord, we know that You are working all things for our good. We receive that today. It is my desire to serve You and to hear from You concerning my future. Again, I surrender to You. In Jesus's name. Amen.

May God bless you as you surrender to Him. He will direct your paths. He will lead you through the valley of hardship. You must have keen awareness of how He is directing you and what He is placing in your path to perfect your relationship to Him and to your world.

The Training Ground and the Battleground

It was fourth and eighteen with the ball on our own forty-nine-yard line. My quarterback, who was a true freshman from Huntington, West Virginia, had just been tackled for a big loss. This, of course, is a cardinal sin when you are trying to drive the field in the two-minute drill.

I had finally gotten my chance to be a head football coach at the collegiate level. I was hired at West Virginia University Tech as the head football coach in March of 1999. I had been a very successful offensive coordinator and a well-respected assistant. Many would say that I am the pioneer of the modern-day spread offense. So I knew what good football was supposed to look like. My first team at West Virginia University Tech did not really resemble a good team. This game which I reference was not a championship game. It was not the storybook year that some coaches have the opportunity to write about. Nope, it was game 10 of ten. My troops were great kids, and they showed up for work every day, but they had not won a single game.

I took them to church during that first year at Maranatha Fellowship in Saint Albans, West Virginia. When we were introduced to the church, the pastor asked me how many games we had won during that 1999 season. He had asked us to stand to be recognized and my crew of fifty-some kids stood. When I answered the question with the response that we had not won yet, he waved his hand and in a most Christian way shouted, "My Lord, sit down." My kids and I were embarrassed. He made up a story to make us feel better, but the damage to my kids had been done.

The season progressed, and in week 9, we thought we had won a game, but we dropped a pass in the end zone and lost a squeaker. By the way that was the thirty-fourth loss in a row for this program. Did I mention that this school had only won four games in the entire decade of the nineties? Did I share that I had been the offensive coordinator of a team that led the nation in offense in 1990 at WVU Tech? That team had won three of those four games the school won from 1990 until the 1999 season. The decade had not been good to WVU Tech.

I had moved on from Tech after the 1990 season to become the offensive coordinator at Glenville State College. I had been hired to bring our spread offense to Glenville. The head coach was a highly intelligent man. He was quick to see the advantages of the spread system. Since that year, the spread offense has become the standard of offenses used predominately in college football. As I was told by a run-and-shoot pioneer after our first and only meeting, "keep it alive." So I think that what I designed and developed at Tech and Glenville has far exceeded just "keeping it alive" as this offense is now the industry standard for football.

Now, back to 1999, we were getting better! On the last week of the year, we were playing Concord University. This was our final chance to end this streak and move into the off-season with positive feelings. We had played a great game to this point, but their punter had backed us up against our own goal line. When we were forced to punt, they did an excellent job of creating a short scoring drive to go ahead by six points.

Now we faced the dreaded fourth down and long distance just to maintain possession. I called time-out, and I set the play in motion. The call was ram sixty smoke z chain x post. This was the perfect call for what they were doing in their two-minute defense. We were in maximum protection. That means we were protecting with the five down linemen and the back. We had four out in the route. The formation had three receivers to the right and one receiver to the left. The outside receiver to the right would run to the first down marker and then run across the field. The next inside receiver would run his route deep down the numbers, and the third receiver would run up the hash marks. The single receiver to the left would run a post.

I SURRENDER

When the ball was snapped, everything was in place. Concord did as I had predicted. All that was left was for our protection to hold up long enough for our outside receiver to get to the first down marker and my quarterback to throw him the ball. I watched as everything that I had planned worked to perfection. As I saw the receiver turn wide open, I ducked my head to move toward where the ball would be spotted and call the next play. Then it happened.

A roar came up from the fans! I distinctly remember thinking to myself that our quarterback must have been sacked and our chances to win were over. But as I looked, I saw the ball flying through the air. Again, my heart sank as I knew that this ball would miss the receiver that I had intended the call to go to by a mile. Suddenly, I realized that this ball was going deep, and it was in play. The problem was that there were two Concord defensive players in the area and none of my players. If Concord batted this ball to the ground, they would win, and old number 35 would follow us back to Montgomery, West Virginia.

I cannot provide you with an explanation as to why what happened next occurred. But it did, and it impacted the entire future of the program at our school. I had been hired to appease the alumni. They had put some money on the table to save the football program. I was their handpicked guy to ensure football's future at Tech. I am not sure of this, but my one assistant and I may have been the only ones on campus who wanted football.

As the defensive back approached with the intention of intercepting the ball, another defensive player came to the scene. The middle field player arrived first. The ball slipped through his hands and bounced off his facemask. The outside defender went for the ball as well. As the ball had done to the first defender, it went through his hands and off his face mask. The two defenders collided as the ball began to tumble back into the field of play.

Now, do you remember how we had dropped a pass the prior week to lose our thirty-fourth in a row? Well, that young man was probably our most gifted player. He was a dual-sport athlete. He could run and in general had really good hands. As the ball tumbled up in the air and eventually began to fall toward the ground, I saw our receiver turn on a burst of speed. As I watched, it became apparent that he had a chance to catch the deflection, and there were no defenders to tackle him as they had knocked each other down while trying to intercept the ball. Edwin caught the ball about thigh-high, and into the end zone he went. We had a lead with under a minute to go.

Old number 35 was not posted against my boys that day. The embarrassment of losing was drawn to a close. We had won the first of what would become many at Tech. The program took on a whole different atmosphere. Although almost ten years later, the program would be dropped, it did not happen under my watch.

Can you imagine the euphoria that our team felt? Some of these kids had never won a game on a college football field. My defensive coordinator, who has gone on to accomplish tremendous things in college coaching, began to hug me. He wept on my shoulder. It was a great moment, but he was a tobacco user, so you can imagine what my white vest looked like when he was done. The home fans remained in their respective seats to watch our players celebrate. It was a magical moment. Unfortunately, like every magical moment in my coaching career, there was always a sudden stop at the bottom. A distinct let-down of emotions that always left me extremely unsatisfied.

Since the first time I stepped on a football field with a whistle around my neck, there had been an unpeaceful coexistence operating in me. When they began to refer to me as coach and my expertise and understanding of the game now had to be performed, an unholy alliance was formed that impacted most of my life.

I do not know how it happened; it just did. The weight of competition, trying to win as I had been accustomed, and then having to train others to do what I had always done relatively naturally is a heavy burden. Of course, there was the expectation by all stakeholders to win even though their stake had little to do with their wallet.

My professional life and my spiritual life were at odds with each other. The battle within raged as I tried to fulfill the requirements of being a coach in an era where winning was the only real thing that mattered. The methods were far less important.

Now, I could go to church, preach, and feel as normal and comfortable as I had ever felt. I was anointed, insightful and interesting. That was puzzling to me. But if that were true, then I must be okay spiritually, and my life must be on track. Surely, if God would use me to tell others of Him, I must be doing okay, right? I consoled myself with those thoughts when anxiety set in.

Later in life, I found out that the ministry in God's eyes is an office. His calling to that end is without repentance. So when I preached, the office of preacher or teacher came forth as if I had put on a glove. In essence, I had, but this ability had no reference to the unpeaceful coexistence that raged within my inner man. No, my spiritual life was being suppressed by my professional life. But when I stepped into the office for which I was called, God would do awesome things and say awesome words through me. In myself, I was fooled and deceived by not understanding the calling and office of ministry. I do not know whether this is relatable to any of you, but to me it became a revelation that has had implications that have legitimately changed my life.

I am sure that in the eyes of my players, they never saw or considered the struggle that went on inside of me. I desperately wanted to succeed to such an extent that even though I was preaching, witnessing, and leading others to Christ, I was becoming a superficial and shallow Christian. I did not say that I couldn't preach; I could. I did not say that I lived or walked in open sin; I did not. But my intimate relationship with Jesus was cold and somewhat indifferent.

Almost anytime and over most any situation in which I thought things were not going the way I wanted or the way I prayed, I was willing to throw my works in the face of the Father. If it got tough, hard, adversity struck, or when my professional life became difficult, God and I were in a huge argument. Did He not know what He was supposed to do for me? Did He not know what I was doing for Him? Yes, and yes.

He also knew what I was trying to do for myself, and that in reality transcended anything that I would or could do for Him. I had become so professionally minded that I was absolutely of no spiritual good. This was so but not to the naked eye. You see, there was a place in my heart that even I wouldn't go. Why? Because it would force me to reveal the real Mike Springston. Lord only knows, I did not want that. I wanted everyone, including myself, to be just fine and dandy with the way it was. If I could remain behind the mask of being a Christian coach and ensure that all outward appearances were in good shape, I could go on in my mind indefinitely.

Was I a sinner in deep depravity? Was I a fraud from a Christian's perspective? No and no. What I was would be defined as a cold Christian who had allowed the deception of the devil to infiltrate my professional life, and in so doing, the profession became the real God of my life. That, my friends, was the place in my heart that I would not and did not want to go. God's calling transcended my ambition, my profession, and my future. Read on, please.

I have been a football coach for most of my life. Sports was a very easy thing for me when I was a kid. I enjoyed the competition, and most of all, I enjoyed winning. Most of the time, during my high school days, we did just that. In all three sports, we were able to win. It was fun, it was exciting, and the girls seemed to like winners.

When I was injured as a college player, it became apparent that my desire exceeded my ability when I was competing at the upper levels. So continuing as a player was not going to happen.

At a young age, I knew that I would grow up to become three things. I would be a teacher, a coach, and a preacher. By the time I was twenty-two, I had done all three. While a player at West Virginia Institute of Technology, I was a quarterback on the football team and a pitcher on the baseball team. I was not the star that I had been in high school, but I was pretty good. Certainly not good enough to play beyond the small college level, but good enough to compete there and win.

I began coaching at West Virginia Tech after an ankle injury. I found it to be an awesome experience. I had always been a leader as that trait was required of the positions that I played in sports. I also found that I enjoyed the inside parts of the game that others overlooked. The details of how to execute techniques and how to work a team into a cohesive unit was an intriguing part of coaching.

I had been a guy who loved the game and studied the game with a great intensity. Obviously, the more you study, the more you learn, and the more you learn, the more experiments you feel comfortable attempting.

In 1982, while at Linden McKinley High School in Columbus, Ohio, I was an assistant on a bad football team. The kids were awesome, but not richly talented. Eight years later, I implemented an experiment that would change the face of the football world. In a football rich state where Woody Hayes's influence ran very deep, we went to a spread no-back offense. Yes, you heard that correctly. In 1982, we began the spread. We won three ball games at the end of the year predominantly because nobody knew how to defend the formation. It was fun, entertaining, and the players experienced success in football for the first time. Little did I know the eventual impact that this season would have upon my career and the world of football.

I left Columbus in 1987 to go to New Mexico to work with a fabulous man of God. He had been the pastor of the Frebis Avenue Church of God, one of the largest churches in the denomination. He was going to be the state overseer in the State of New Mexico, and I was going to work in evangelism. It was exciting.

After a little more than a year, I had the chance to go back to coaching at the University of Texas at El Paso. I did so and enjoyed the season at UTEP. Although we were not very good, the teams we played were, and some of the players in the Western Athletic Conference were awesome. For instance, Brigham Young had the Heisman award winner in 1989. Pretty good stuff! While I was there, we played Lamar University, and I suddenly was looking at my team from 1982. Their formations were somewhat different, but they ran a system called the run-and-shoot and used it in certain game situations.

Shortly after the 1989 season, I received a call from an old friend of mine and was offered and accepted the offensive coordinators job at West Virginia Institute of Technology in Montgomery, West Virginia. It was here that the modern-day spread offense was designed and executed to perfection. We led the nation in total offense. Statistically, for that time, we were off the charts. Our quarterback, Jerry Lucas, led the nation in personal total offense. It was a most successful season on offense, but as a team, we were not very good. As an up-and-comer in the coaching profession, my focus was purely on what we could do on offense. If we won 51–50, great! If we lost 51–50, well, I didn't like to lose, but I could console myself with the fact that the system was humming.

I was in demand professionally and took a lot of jobs thinking that, surely, I would land a head coaching job and my career would be headed for great things. Well, it never really did happen that way. Almost everyone wanted what I knew. I was expendable once I taught them the offensive system. That was never more apparent to me than the year I spent working at Glenville State College. I may, at some point, write a book concerning these sort of things, but this book will not follow in that direction.

So we invented the modern-day Spread at Tech in 1990. I went to Glenville State College located in Glenville, West Virginia, during the 1991 season. While there, we used the modern day spread again and led the nation in offense. This offensive system was great to me and generally great for my career.

I did receive that head coaching opportunity I craved. It was back at dear old Tech in 1999. By the time I returned to Montgomery, the program was in shambles, showing five total wins during the decade of the '90s. Rocked by coaching changes, poor administrative decisions, and financial issues, Tech hired me to be the head coach. I later found out the purpose for hiring me was to prove to the alumni that the program could not be saved even by their handpicked guy. The administration was wrong. Way wrong!

During years second to fourth, we competed well and finished second in our league three years in a row. We defeated the conference champion twice during that stretch. This was done with minimal support from the administration. There is another book to be written concerning this time in my career, but not now.

I left Tech after the 2004 season and went to be the head coach at the University of Charleston. This was a start-up program. It became a fund-raising expedition to help save the institution. We did that well as our players paid a couple of millions into the school bank. The school is thriving even now. However, my career and my life were miserable. Ultimately, it was a poor decision on my part to take the job. There were other opportunities, but if I took the UC job, Sharon and I didn't have to move. I came out of there as quickly as possible. The university knew that I was leaving, and to save face, they made it appear that I had been relieved of my duties. This was absolutely not the truth, as I had informed the president of my intentions in August of 2005. At the end of the day, I was able to leave UC. That ultimately was the goal.

Then in 2008, my dear friend, Dean Hood, offered me the offensive coordinators job at Eastern Kentucky University. This university had been a traditional college powerhouse. I accepted the position. Sharon and I moved to Richmond, Kentucky, with great anticipation. Our team in 2008 was a mix of interesting kids. Our quarterback, Allen Holland, had been the Ohio Valley Conference Player of the Year in 2007. But he was coming off shoulder surgery and was unavailable to us during our first spring. Shortly thereafter, it became clear as to why they nicknamed him the "Big Biscuit." He ballooned up to 265 pounds at six feet tall. Allen was by no means a runner. He also was coming off the shoulder surgery, so he had to be protected as he was the only legitimate quarterback on our roster. Allen was a tremendous player and has become an awesome college head football coach.

Our normal offensive system would not work if that meant Allen had to be a runner. So we reverted to a style of play that we had used at Parkland High School in Winston-Salem, North Carolina, in 2007. We gave it a name and called it Read Pass. Allen would often refer to it as the perfect play. By the way, if you follow football, you have heard this system referred to as the run pass option (or RPO) offense. Yep, we invented that system also in 2007 and unveiled it at the collegiate level against the University of Cincinnati in the opening game of the 2008 season.

That team at Eastern Kentucky University won my one and only championship ring. I cherish it to this day. We lost in the national playoffs to the eventual national champion, Richmond Spiders. Nevertheless, another groundbreaking invention is the one that to this day creates more sleepless nights for defensive coaches than the casual fan can imagine.

Shortly after I left EKU, I sat on my couch and witnessed the Iron Bowl miracle where Auburn ran a missed field goal back to beat Alabama. Yes, that is what the casual fan remembers. Not me! Auburn was behind and needing to score. Alabama had done a great job on defense most of the day. Then it happened. The Auburn quarterback placed the ball in the belly of the running back. It was obvious to me that he had a defensive lineman in his sight and was determining the defender's reaction so that he could make his response. The quarterback pulled the ball and headed for the perimeter of the defense.

Just as designed, Alabama began to run defenders to tackle the man with the ball. Elementary, my dear Watson, unless you have a secondary pass play attached to the initial play call. Auburn did! The quarterback threw a pass to a wide-open receiver down the left sideline, and Auburn scored to go ahead. I ducked my head, laughed, and shed a tear all at the same time.

Here I sat and watched one of the most iconic events in sports history, and I had designed the play system that made it happen. That was not bad for a guy who had been told by his school counselor that he was not smart enough to go to college. If he did go to college, he had better major in physical education because that would be the only thing he had any chance to pass and who was told by the adults in his world that he had a million-dollar arm and a ten-cent brain. That guy had designed the system that the world had watched give Auburn one of the most thrilling wins in college football history.

I get a chuckle as I sit and watch and listen today at the multitude of coaches attempting to take credit for the system. The truth is a counterfeit that will always resemble the real; regardless of how much they beat their chest and attempt to take credit, there are those who know the truth. There is a statement that goes like this, "Imitation is the highest form of flattery." Gentlemen, I am flattered!

How did all this occur to me? Well, as you will see if you stay with me in this book, God has had His hand on me, my life, and my mind from the beginning. Here is an example of what I'm saying.

I remember our offensive line coach, Carson Jeffers, at EKU telling his wife, "I don't know how we could have survived at EKU had God not shown Coach Springston a revelation of offense."

From Tipping Point to the Turning Point

After the 2010 season at Eastern Kentucky University, Sharon and I came home to Winston-Salem. I was hired to begin the football program at Walkertown High School in the Winston-Salem Forsyth County School district. It was a wonderful time with the kids and their parents. Probably the greatest experience of my life in that regard. Our football team began with thirty-six great young men. Only five of them had experienced the game of football. We taught them how to play the game, beginning by learning how to sit in a chair. As the process unfolded, we taught them how to fall and get up without injuring themselves, how to get dressed appropriately, and all the nuances of the great game of football.

Our team developed nicely, as did our community support system. The stadium would be full for both our home and away games. We raised money easily and took care of our players extensively. The coaches and the players experienced tremendous success over the four years that we were together. Many of those kids went on to play at the next level. They have found academic and football success. That makes the time, effort, and struggle to develop a program worthwhile.

Without going too deeply into the makeup of the Walkertown situation, when I look back on the experience, I have identified a clue to my time at Walkertown that probably caused me to leave. What was that? Not everyone is happy about others' success. Also that kids are not always the main priority of the school or the school system.

During the summer of 2014, I was coming home from practice when I noticed a strange click in my throat. That click would turn my world upside down. I noticed a growth on the left side of my neck shortly after I recognized the click in my throat. Because it was football season, I paid absolutely no attention to it. I went on with the season. Our program was rolling. We were in our first varsity season and were on our way to a playoff bid. The season ended with our record showing eight wins and three losses. A great start to football at a new school!

During the month of October, I became sick from what was later diagnosed as carbon monoxide poisoning. One of my players had it far worse than I did. We both rebounded and continued. How did I get this poisoning? My director of athletics would not allow us to practice on the game field when the time changed that year. So we had to bus our players thirty minutes to a rented baseball facility for practice. On this day, he had not scheduled us a bus for the trip. The only bus available was one bus with what we later learned was a leaking exhaust. By the way, this leak had been reported long ago and not been repaired. So we traveled and practiced. I became ill and went to the doctor on Saturday after the game that Friday evening.

Then November came, and I fell ill with the flu and again went to the doctor. While I was being x-rayed, the doctor mentioned to my wife the possibility of my having cancer. She mentioned it to me, and I responded emphatically, "No, I do not have cancer!'

As the next few weeks rolled along, we eventually lost in the playoffs. But a bilateral lump had appeared. Now I could not wear a button-up shirt, and I resembled Frankenstein. In December just a bit before Christmas, my daughter, Lisa, came home. She is a nurse practitioner and was specializing in brain and bone cancer at that time. She came in the door, walked directly to where I was sitting, and said, "You need to see a doctor immediately." I laughed and said that I would. Her reply was a bit bossy! She said, "I'm serious, you need to get to a doctor right now!' Having had a very healthy life in general, I paid very little attention to her directions. Anyway, I was a faith man, and God would surely take care of me.

The lumps continued to grow. Now they looked like handles on either side of my neck. But my faith was in the healing power of God. I realized that this was unnatural, but I prayed, and I waited for God to do something. In January of 2014, I finally was able to get in to see a doctor. He referred me to a specialist, and the roller coaster began for real.

Upon entering the doctor's room, I saw a very tall man who had an air of confidence about himself. As you know, I kind of like that in people.

He looked at me and said, "Let me have a look in your mouth." He did. Upon the conclusion of his very brief examination, he declared, "You have cancer!"

I laughed and said, "Where is it?"

He said, "I don't know, but I know you have it!"

Again, on the inside, I was saying, "Yeah right! How can I have something that you can't see, feel, or identify?" I was in complete denial of the possibility that I could have cancer.

After two more appointments and various needles being placed directly into the lumps, the pathologist and the confident doctor were stumped. He continued to declare that I had cancer, but he could not locate it. On the third appointment during the first part of February 2014, he snapped his gloves on his hands, and with a look that told me that if he had to stick his finger down my mouth into my stomach, he was going to find something that confirmed his diagnosis.

After my choking, nearly vomiting, and tasting the sweet taste of latex gloves, he emerged with a gleeful statement, "I think I felt something!"

Naturally, I replied, "You think?"

As he fell back into his chair, he said, "Maybe I did, and maybe I just want to feel something. Nevertheless, at the place where I think I have felt something, we have a real problem in doing a biopsy in that area. There are three ways to do it. The first way is that we go in through your neck. The problem with that is that we rarely are able to close the hole which must be made. The second way is to crack your face down the middle and go in that way."

As you might imagine, I put a stop to both options rather quickly.

Then he described a third method using a robotics surgeon. There was one in our region, and he was at Wake Forest Baptist. The doctor said he would see how quickly he could get me in. Within a week or so, I was given an appointment and scheduled for the surgery.

After another week or so, I received the call from the doctor. I will never forget his words. After a few pleasantries, he told me the analysis of the biopsy.

"Mike, you have cancer!"

My mind began to spin. How could this be? I believed God. I have preached faith and the healing power that is in Jesus's name all over the country!

Then he said, "If you do exactly what we tell you to, this cancer has a high success rate. We can get you through this."

I asked him two very important questions. Why they were important, I do not know, but these are the two questions I asked.

"Will I be able to sing again, and will I be able to whistle again?"

Why? I don't know. I have always enjoyed both while I drove and when I preached. But I am somewhat average in both. His response was that he could not answer that question. However, some were able, and some were not.

I returned to my classroom in a daze. It appeared that my belief system had a flaw in it. I knew, however, that the flaw was not in my Heavenly Father. I was convinced that if there was an error, it was to be found in me! I went to my administrator and shared with him what the diagnosis was. I told him that I expected to miss three days of work. What an unaware comment that was! My prescribed treatment was for thirty-five rounds of radiation and three rounds of chemotherapy. That, to the uneducated, does not sound too demanding. So March came along, and I entered treatment orientation. I showed up at the cancer center very unaware of what was about to be done.

They placed me in a tube, which was terrifying. I did not like that feeling at all. I told them I needed out of that contraption. A nurse asked me if I had taken or brought with me the medicine. I did not know what she was talking about. After a bit, they brought me a pill that changed everything. My fear left, my anxiety subsided, and into the tube I went. They then did a most unbelievable thing. They put a hot piece of plastic against my face and molded it to my skin. This device would serve to hold me motionless during the radiation treatment. I felt like the guy in the movie *Silence of the Lambs*. It was awful! My brain knew it, but my body did not care!

The next day I began chemotherapy and radiation. I took my Bible and a headset to the chemotherapy appointment. I would read and listen to harp music. Because I knew that was how David calmed Saul when he was uneasy. It really works! These appointments lasted eight hours. It was a war against boredom with many trips to the restroom carting lines, tubes, and bags. What a mess!

Radiation began after the infusion. I seemed fine. We went to Red Lobster after it was all over, and I noticed no physical changes. The next morning, I went to work. I began to feel queasy in the stomach, but I made it through the day. Little did I know what lay ahead. The following morning began the onslaught of fifty-five days of brutality! I was sick. I was vomiting. I could not comfortably lie down, nor could I comfortably sit up. My body was in total rebellion!

The radiations were done five days a week for thirty-five treatments. They would put that mask on me, and I would hear the bolts clamp me to this most uncomfortable stainless steel table. The machine would go around my face from spine to spine and back two times. The duration was between twenty-two and thirty-eight seconds. There were thirty-two regions that had to be radiated, sixteen on the right side and sixteen on the left. There was no feeling associated with the treatment. Other than being tied to a table, it did not seem so bad. Of course, unless your nose began to itch! Then it was devastating.

The sickness from the chemo worsened. I did not desire food at all. I had a food port installed in my stomach and a drip port installed in my upper right chest. These would serve to be both a blessing and a curse. After seven days of radiation, my mouth and throat began to close for anything that needed to enter from the outside. As you can imagine, there was no stopping the flow of internal elimination that seemed to want to break loose all the time. I began to be fed through the tube as I could not swallow any longer. My speech was extremely limited also.

I was continually nauseated. The chemo and the food that the insurance company gave me to use were really making me unable to function at all. I lost twenty-seven pounds in seven or eight days. Who cared? Not me, just keep a bucket close by! About this time, my saliva was beginning to coagulate. I could not dispel the fluid short of removing it by hand. It was scary to sleep as I thought sure that I was going to drown in my own secretions.

One night, while lying in the bed, I did what I did regularly, which was to pray. Now, I want you to know that I did not miss one treatment. I did not cut short anything the medical personnel instructed me to do. I went through it all! Day by day, moment by moment, and treatment by treatment—it was brutal! But I prayed, nevertheless, that God would deliver me from this evil thing called cancer! I went through it all. This night as I prayed, I heard something in my spirit, and this is what it said.

The voice of God spoke so clearly into my spirt and said, "For I know the thoughts that I think toward you, saith the LORD, thoughts of peace, and not of evil, to give you an expected end."

We know that as Jerimiah 29:11.

I remember distinctly saying in the weakened condition of my voice, "You are thinking of me! I am thinking about You! Where have You been? Do You see the condition that I am in?"

My spirit quieted as I heard His voice declare the words of the God of the universe, "I know the thoughts that I think toward you!"

My spirit leaped with joy! God was thinking about me! Surely, deliverance was on the way! He was speaking!

"My thoughts are of peace! They are not of evil. My thoughts are to give you an expected end!"

Man, that was great news. I was going to have an end that I expected to happen. I was going to live!

My personal revelation of the God of the universe was that life was mine, peace was mine, and evil was encompassed in the peace of a blessed ending. Now I could live with that! I clung to those words

I SURRENDER

for the next thirty or so days. It always amazes me how God works ahead of the problem. Why? Because the real ride of brutality was about to get underway in a big way, and God had already spoken! The treatments continued, as did the sickness associated with them. I was unable to get out of bed. When I did, my wife had to pick me up. I could not even bath or shower myself. This once vibrant and strong man could not walk across the floor. I had to walk with a walker! But the revelation of God had declared that I was coming to an expected end.

While taking my second chemo run, my pastor, Tim Wolfe, came in to visit with me. We were chatting, and out of the blue, I heard myself ask pastor Tim this question.

"Pastor, do you think that there is any way that I could get some sort of license in the IPHC?"

His response was quick and sure. "Of course, you can, Mike. Those guys on the board are all friends of mine. As soon as you are ready, I will take you down there myself."

That conversation literally changed the course of my immediate future! I felt as if God was turning my attention toward a different calling. Shortly, I would see that my feelings were correct. Many around the situation did not understand the revelation of God. Prayers were going heavenward from everywhere, but in Winston-Salem, North Carolina, there was just treatment after treatment. I had a word from God concerning the outcome, but not a word in sight that would lessen the brutality of the process! I was sick! My body did not interact with any kind of food. My bowels were locked, and my saliva was coagulated greater than ever! It was a scary time.

The first time I went into the hospital, it was because I was dehydrated. I did not enjoy the stay at all. But I did find a machine that gave me some relief. It was a machine designed to suction fluid. I used it to help eliminate the coagulating saliva that I thought was going to choke me if I went to sleep. The machine was awesome, and we found a company to provide us with one at home.

At this time, we were keeping our daughter's dog while she went to Hawaii on her honeymoon. Cameron had her strange quirks, but she was a great dog. One night while lying on the couch trying to sleep, I became extremely cold. Suddenly, I saw Cameron leap toward me. While in the air, she turned and banged me in the chest with her hips. This action by this awesome dog might have saved my life! Evidently, I had gone into convulsions, and Cameron went to work. She lay on me to warm me, and in a few minutes, Sharon came to see what was going on. From 1:00 AM until 4:00 AM, I received an ice bath from my mother and my wife. The fever finally broke, but I was exhausted!

The next morning, Sharon indicated that we needed to go to the hospital. Emphatically, I said, "No! I do not want to go back there."

A quick phone call to Lisa, and preparations were underway for me to go to the emergency room. It seemed like forever! I was cold, and they would not give me any blankets. Finally, two doctors walked into the room and declared the diagnosis to Sharon and me.

They said, "He needs to be admitted immediately. He has four blood clots in his lungs. We need to get a filter in him before he passes one of these into his heart."

So there you go, back in the hospital!

I thought, "What stupid blood clots? I am breathing fine. Well, maybe they will give me a warm blanket up there."

Off to the cancer unit I went after what seemed like the rest of the day in the emergency room.

Sharon went home for the night. With the suction machine, I could sleep a little bit. But the next morning around nine o'clock, I was lying on my right side when the door opened and Sharon walked in. As she passed the foot of the bed, I turned to my left side. The move caused a rebellion in my stomach. I began to have another violent episode of vomiting! After that, I could tell something was wrong. The nurse in Sharon kicked in, and she was busy doing something with the tray.

Soon the door opened, and another nurse came in, then the rest is a blur. I can tell you what I remember. I remember seeing my daughter and her new husband in the door. I remember his face looking like he had seen a ghost. I remember a horrible odor that was breathtaking. I remember being yelled at to put something somewhere. I remember going into an elevator. Did I mention the fact that the odor was enough to choke you to death? My thoughts were that this hospital smelled awful! How could they allow this place to smell that bad? However, it seemed to follow me everywhere I went. Inside the intensive care unit, things were in a frenzy. Doctors and nurses were rushing around with worried looks on their faces. I lay there wondering why in the world the place had such a terrible odor.

I looked up at the monitor to my left, and I saw a bunch of numbers that I recognized. The first number was 199. That represented my heart rate. The second number was 62/35. That represented my blood pressure. The third number was 65. That number represented the oxygen in my blood. None of those numbers were very appealing. With the flurry of activity going on around me, I could see outside in the hallway as the nurses and doctors came in through the curtain. Outside in the hallway was my wife. I so wanted to let her know that I was all right. But I was not able to communicate. Then I noticed my dear pastor, Tim Wolfe. Again, I wanted to tell them, "Don't worry, I'm okay." Unable to do so, I lay back and watched the action.

They had two poles working various fluids into my body. They came and went at a pace that was almost too quick to comprehend. I would have loved to have been able to put the entire room on pause and ask them one question: "Does it smell like this down here all the time?" But that was not possible. I made a promise to myself that somebody was going to hear about this when they get through! After a while, a man walked into the room. He had a pained look on his face. I could tell that he had smelled the bad smell that was in the hospital and came to see if it was in this room. After a minute, he inspected my area. He then did something that shocked me to my core. He lifted the sheet that covered me, and he quickly turned his upper body away.

At that second, it became painfully obvious to me that the odor in the room belonged to me as I had evidently lost control of myself sometime between the room and ICU. Now that was ultra embarrassing! Here are the parts of which I have no recollection.

Evidently, I had vomited blood. This was obviously a major problem. As they inspected the fluid in the bowl, evidently, I went into convulsions. They must have been violent. I began to call for my mother and carry on to the extent that the rapid response team had to be summoned. At this point the attending personnel were on the cusp of calling a code blue. Going down the hall they were yelling at me to put the oxygen back in my nose. I could not figure out what they were saying, so I put it in my mouth. They quieted down.

Of course, the next thing I knew was that I was in ICU. To them, I guess, it did not look good. To me, all I wanted to tell everyone was that I was fine. "Don't worry about me! I'm going to be just fine. I had a revelation from a conversation with the Lord. I was in good shape."

I have to say the medical people are as focused and as tough as nails. I had gone into a condition referred to a being septic. My body was in total rebellion against itself. After they had stabilized me, the cleanup process began. It was at that moment that I had to come to full appreciation of the seriousness of this situation. It is often said that the loss of control of body functions is an act that occurs just prior to death. I had been right up close and personal with that event.

Upon conclusion of the cleanup and refreshing the air in my room, I was able to have a few visitors. My wife, my mother, and my pastor came in for a few minutes. I assured them that I was in good shape. Shortly thereafter, a surgeon came into the room and informed me that first thing in the morning, I would be going to exploratory surgery to locate something that was causing the bleeding. I told him that it was my throat. He said that was a possibility, but we would see in the morning.

The next morning, I lay in the bed waiting for them to come and get me for surgery. The curtain opened, and in walked my attending physician. Doctor Pashel was a Christian Jew. What a gracious and kind man! He had lived through cancer on a couple of occasions. He was always so upbeat! What he did then took me by surprise, but it was such a comfort and blessing to me. As he came around the bed, he reached down and scooped me up in his arms. As he held me close, he whispered in my ear, "Thank God, Mike, I thought we had lost you."

I looked at him, and he was crying tears of joy. So was I. We both knew the God that had been ultra faithful in delivering me from the grip of the enemy, which was death.

After he left, they came to take me to surgery! They wheeled me into the operating room, and there was a nurse whose husband was the booster president from Walkertown High School. They completed the observation, and I found myself back in the room. They informed me that the doctor would be around in a bit to tell me his findings.

He entered the ICU room with a smile and said, "I think you were correct. It had to be your throat. We looked all over the throat and the stomach, and we found no open bleeding." Then he said these words, "We did find a scar that we could tell was very recent. Strangely enough, that scar was completely healed. It did not even present a scab. That had to be it. It was totally healed though. You should be fine!"

I was not shocked by his news. God had totally healed me! There was no doubt about it. He was bringing me to an expected end, even if I was the only one expecting it! The rumor of my demise was highly unlikely! The next four days were spent in ICU. During that time, I had some visitors from Walkertown. After they left, word was sent that the rumor was floated that I was not going to survive and they needed to prepare to hire a new coach. That was a most premature call!

To my surprise, Dean Hood, who was my dear coaching friend and my former boss at EKU, unexpectedly came from a recruiting trip in Ohio to be with me in the ICU. I was ever so appreciative of his visit. He had been a such dear friend for years. The morning before he left, he really cheered me up as only Hoodie could do. He was sitting at my bedside when I woke up that third morning. I greeted him and asked him how long he had been there. He told me that he had been on the unit long enough to walk around. Holding his coffee cup, as he always did, Dean then made this comment.

"You know," he said, "I have walked around this unit, and I want to tell you something."

I said, "What?"

He said, "As bad as you look, there are others in here that look worse than you do!"

He was serious, but I had to laugh. Dean, we love you and appreciate you and your family.

Finally, they moved me out of ICU and back onto the floor. I was so ready to go home. Then I had another visitor who had come to confirm the rumor concerning whether I was going to make it back to coaching or not. Our principal sat down in my room with very little to say. He stayed about fifteen minutes and left.

I was still short one round of chemo. I prayed diligently that I would not have to do that round. My white blood count was holding at a solid 1! If it did not elevate, there could be no further treatment. If there was no treatment, I had to remain in the hospital. My wife and the doctor agreed that we would wait and take the treatment. I will never forget him looking me directly in the eyes and saying, "Mike, if we don't complete the treatment, this thing could come back."

My wife interjected, "We do not want that! Finish the treatment!"

I would have argued if I could, but the last thing I wanted was to go through this again. They finished the last chemo run on Tuesday, and I went home on Wednesday. Glory to God.

Here was the strange fact of my lowest events. Every time I would go into a deep physical hole, I would rebound, and some element that had been adversely affecting me became immediately better. Whether it was my strength or my voice, I would come back and be able to do something that I could not do before this awful event. Oral Roberts always told those whom he prayed for, "If you believe God has touched and healed you, do something with the affected area that you were not able to do before." That advice fit me perfectly.

Shortly thereafter, a mandatory meeting was held at Walkertown High School. I called the principal and asked if I needed to be there. This was just a few days after I had visitors from the school in ICU and his being in my room at the hospital. He responded in the affirmative. I pulled myself together and went to the meeting. The responses on the people's faces were a look of terror. I had to be paraded in front of the parents so preparation could be made to replace me. No problem. I would be back. I had God's revelation on it! By the end of May, I was back to work. Weak and tired, I was intent on getting back to the team, the players, and the parents. I am sure this did not please the administration.

Our football season was excellent. We won the school's first football playoff game. We then ended our season in a close loss to the number 1 team in the state at our level 34–28, a 9–3 ending in our second year of varsity competition. We had begun a football program from scratch with kids that had no football background. We had averaged thirty-nine points a game for two years in a row. A job well done, in my opinion. We had built a strong parent organization, a strong fund-raising operation, and an extremely loyal fan base. Our kids were well disciplined and well behaved in the building. I am proud of what we did at Walkertown High School.

I left nineteen starters in the program. As a single A school that year, we had ninety-six players involved in the program. It was the right time to turn it over to someone else. My life was ready for the next chapter. Leaving Walkertown and returning to Parkland High School to teach was a breath of fresh air for me.

Shortly after my arrival at my new job, my pastor, Tim Wolfe, called to enquire concerning my availability to meet with the examining board to begin the process of ministerial licensure. He had done exactly as he said he would. He drove the route to Greensboro on the morning of the scheduled meeting. His last words to me were, "If there are any problems, you come and get me." There were none, and I was approved for consideration into the ministry.

I enrolled in the Biblical Ministries Institute and three years later was ordained as a minister in the International Pentecostal Holiness Church. I will forever be grateful for a man such as Tim Wolfe. He not only is a great person, but he is an outstanding pastor, leader, musician, and preacher. Of the many men that I have known who have the title of reverend and have ability, Tim Wolfe, in my opinion, is the prince of preachers!

Within a few months, I was asked to pastor a church in Mount Airy, North Carolina. God began to identify Himself in such a mighty way. The more I read and prayed, the more revelation He brought forth. With the idol of football out of the way, God began to do a wonderful thing in my spirit. My ability to communicate, teach, and preach the Word of God became extremely anointed. Study became so deep, and the insight, concepts, and ideas flowed to and through me as never before. The Holy Spirit would literally overtake my thoughts.

One day in prayer, again I heard the voice of the Holy Spirit. This is what He said:

"I am going to make the Word of God as apparent to you as football was. When you read and see the Word, you will identify the revelation in the Word just like you have in football."

Man, that was a lot for me to grasp. I know football. I understand the game. How was He going to expose the Word of God to that degree? Well, all I can tell you is that this is exactly what He has done. He has expressed and exposed insight into the Word of God that I have never heard or seen. He still speaks to those who are listening and in tune to his voice. This book is one of those revelations about the revelation of Jesus Christ!

As I close this chapter, I want to speak a few words to those who may find themselves in a similar situation as the one where I found myself. For me it was cancer; for you it may be another physical, mental, or emotional battle. Regardless of what the circumstances may be in your life, the underlying foundation that will cause you to be able to survive and thrive is none other than the person of whom this book is written. A foundation of faith in the Son of God, coupled with an intimate personal relationship, will provide you with help that the writer of the book of Hebrews said would come in the nick of time. I found this to be true. I believe you will also.

In the Furnace of Affliction

A Message from My Mother

The other day my ninety-six-year-old mother handed me this paper. She asked me to read it and see if I could see myself in the writing.

My mother is a prolific writer. She spends most of her days with the Spirit, the Word of God, and a pen and paper. She is a most inspired person who has tremendous insight into the Word of God.

Isaiah 48:10 is the scripture associated with this writing. Let's look at it.

> Behold, I have refined thee, but not with silver;
> I have chosen thee in the furnace of affliction.
> (Isaiah 48:10 KJV)

Life is certainly a mystery. We live it, look back on it, try to fix it when we can, and then we die and leave it. We rise, it seems only to fall; we gain only to lose and try only to fail. It's all a scrambled mystery. And we ask why God doesn't prevent us from making foolish mistakes that seem to destroy us. After all, aren't we trying our best to serve Him? Why doesn't He see our need?

Well, let's be honest. He sees, knows, hears, and acts upon our needs. But sometimes what we think is our need really isn't our need at all. It's our desire, which cuts across and circumvents God's purpose. We fail to consider that our ways are not His ways, and He is "slightly more intelligent than we are." Does that mean that because He is so intelligent, He is trying to punish us? No! He's trying to refine us!

We seem to forget, if we ever knew, that God is dealing with extremely flawed human beings. We are born into a broken covenant. The world around us is full of wrong thinking, living, and acting, and it is influencing every inch of our lives. We live in our selfishness as if God and everybody else owes us, and what we don't understand is that God and everybody else owns us. Our response is to try to break free.

It is not in mankind to want to be beholden to someone else's demands. We have a sense that something is missing. We don't know what it is. So we set out to find the missing link. However, we do not really know exactly what we are looking for. So we use all the thoughts, resources, and abilities within our control to identify that certain something that will allow us to feel fulfilled. We gain and lose and drive ourselves with purpose and intention in search of the thing that is missing.

Our purpose, process, and pursuits often turn out to be absolutely the incorrect discovery. We realize that when we approach the crossroad of decision, that would lead us to where we thought we wanted to go. This is the place where a wrong decision can be made that will cause all the work that has brought us to this point is lost. Inevitably, the best laid plans of mice and men conclude in a turn toward the trap!

There is a scripture which rings so true. Solomon wrote it from his own experiences. He said,

> Except the lord build the house, they labor in vain that build it; except the lord keep the city, the watchman waketh in vain. (KJV)

This says that we labor in vain and fall into despair when we leave God out of the effort. The worst-case scenario is that the world crashes in on us and falls to ashes at our feet. This is what we build, and then we ask a lot of questions and have no answers, and God gets the blame. But you did not ask before you built.

We make moves without advice or discretion. We seem to believe that because we are who we are, we're going to make it work.

We have heard the story that people often tell about out working others and that if you work hard enough, good things will happen. So bold-faced and bare-knuckled, we dive into our venture with the best of intentions and the highest of hopes. Fact check here! Our work ethic, our desire, and your best are not always good enough. Many great men have stepped into a role, a job, a marriage, or a financial venture with the best of intentions only to fail miserably. Coaching is the easy profession to consider when thinking of this.

The opportunity to fail does not only apply to the young; it applies to everyone who does not take God at His Word and take him and His Word seriously! God is not obligated to those who do not obligate themselves to Him. He will tell us what to do, but He will not make us do it. Then when we have fallen far enough into problems, we will reach a place where we will wish we had listened. We need to step lightly on our future before we destroy it!

God designed every human being with a purpose and equal opportunity. Lose control of your purpose, and you may lose control of your future. No one was designed to sin. That is a given. We were designed to love God with all our being in whatever role we play in life. That's why Jesus came. He was to enter the heart of the young, to teach them by their teachers, the first teacher being their parents, to live above sin and degradation. The process was to include and involve the church and the home, and these two were to so influence the environment that a godly influence was to be present and surround the life of all men.

Please don't forget that before each of us was sent into the arena of education, the parental guidance was to take place for five or six years. So parents had the first shot at preparing and shaping the future of their children. But when we came to the age where we could make decisions, we became responsible for our own actions, our own path, and all our own choices. So you can readily see that God is not responsible for our dilemma.

Did we live by the rules of conduct, did we ask for leadership, or did we deliberately choose to do what we wanted to do for whatever the reason we chose to do it? If the answer to the first two questions is an emphatic "no," then we will proceed to the next question. If the answer to the last part is an emphatic "yes," then it is very highly probable that you are headed for trouble and that in abundance, and therefore, you are headed for the furnace of affliction.

It is here, in the furnace of affliction, that we are forced to face the truth about ourselves, where we are, and what brought us to this point. We have the chance, and at times it appears it is a fleeting chance, to deal with the question, "How did I get here?" When this opportunity presents itself, there is the moment in time when the opportunity for change exists. Only when opportunity meets and couples with desire does any monumental effect occur.

It is at this crossroad, if we learn from our experiences and truly examine how trusting ourselves, our wants, our lusts, and our desires has worked out for us, that we intersect with the possibility of transformation.

It is when we draw these vital conclusions and assess ourselves that we can chart a new course for a better life. "What is that life you ask?" Some would say that life includes God and the church. As a friend of mine used to say, "There is some truth in that." But it does not reflect the full truth.

For the transformation to proceed, we must submit ourselves to God, crucify ourselves, and live by the faith of the Son of God. That sounds like a lot. But if we make the decision to live for Christ and allow Him to live in us, there is a glory that ensues that allows us to locate the thing we have searched our entire life to find!

> I will keep him in perfect peace whose mind is stayed upon me. Peace I leave with you, my peace I give unto you that your joy may be full! I am come that you might have life and that life more abundantly

It so obvious that the things that we wanted and sought for are not the important things. The important things are only found in our relationship to God! That is the purpose for which man was designed. Any other pursuit is outside the realm of his designation and not included in his destination for us.

Many people, however, go from the furnace of affliction to the grave. They live a life full of trouble and turmoil with no real lasting peace. They laugh and have moments of pleasure but no lasting and intense position of peace in the middle of life's storms. Then there are those others who live the same life, experience the same circumstances, and those issues of life refine them. They live in peace and find rest. They overcome the situations of life with grace to grace. They are refined and experience the purpose of the divine design of their Creator.

All go through the fire. Some see it as an experience which created the devastations of life. Bitterness, anger, fear, and doubt are the results of their time in the furnace. Then there are those who understand that the furnace refines the actual person that is inside of them. It serves to draw them closer to God, to walk more deeply in their faith, and to express a deeper expectancy and hope in the righteousness of Jesus Christ.

Here is reality, and we all can use a dose of that regularly. That, my friends, is "life!" The beautiful experience of life only comes when that life is lived by men who are "sheltered in the arms of God." They come out of the furnace of affliction to praise, testify, and worship the God who allowed them to be in the furnace in the first place because it was in that furnace that the fourth man appeared!

So where do we begin to fix a broken life? Where do we begin to rededicate a life that has strayed into serving personal wants and personal goals? The answer to that is found in 1 Peter 5:6.

> Humble yourselves therefore under the mighty
> hand of God, that he may exalt you in due time
> (1 Peter 5:6 KJV)

Lord, may we do just that. I thank You for the truth. I humble myself and ask You to make me ready for the moment when you exalt Your servant to minister to others or for the moment when I hear those awesome words:

> Well done, my good and faithful servant. (KJV)

Either way, I surrender myself to You! In Jesus's name! Amen.

So this section of the book began with my mother asking me, "Read this and see if you can identify yourself." Unfortunately, I can do so all too well! I identify a man who was deeply engrossed in his personal goals and ideals. I see a man who made God the scapegoat for every situation that did not go his way. As my friend, Charles Mckey, says, "I was pimping God," in a lot of ways for the purpose of professional gain.

Yes, my dear, I see myself! My own desire to excel and succeed in the game of football exceeded any life of depth and intimacy that I could have with the Lord. Why? Because during the months of July through December, the only real thing on my mind was winning! I was inundated by the pressure and the expectation of winning. As one of my illustrious alumni once said to me, "I am with you, win or tie!" Another administrator informed me one day that my job depended upon whether the players that I recruited remained in school! So it was my responsibility to win, to keep students in school, to handle discipline in such a way that athletes stayed in school and in most cases teach classes. This placed a conscientious employee under a huge amount of pressure!

So yes, I saw myself in this writing. I am certain that as you read this section, you see yourself as well. It is probable that we all are saying, "Of course, I attempt to keep God in His proper place. I try to pray and go to church. I make every attempt to live correctly. But there are the demands and pressures in life."

We all must agree that the demands of work and the demands of family in our culture, as well as the expectations of employers, can become overwhelming. It was for me, even though I had preached around the country and ministered to a lot of people during my preaching/coaching career. I would venture to say again, we all see ourselves in this teaching.

The question is, "What can we do about this?" Well, having failed miserably in my attempt to coordinate my spiritual life and my professional life, I can only make remarks from hindsight. We do not have the opportunity for replays in life. Nor do we have the chance to simply try it again. No, we are relegated to one take! I seriously doubt that there would be many flawless movie or theatrical performances without the forgiveness of a retake. Life does not offer a retake, nor does it offer much forgiveness. As a matter of fact, in our dog-eat-dog society, we are left extremely vulnerable to mistakes of any kind. We have the Roman Coliseum mind-set. If you are in the arena and do not win now, you really have no legitimate value.

With that in mind, here is what I have found as I moved on from coaching. First, I still hold a full-time position as a schoolteacher. I still am the lead pastor at a church, so my life has no less demands than it did before. I have just developed a better process for dealing with the demands of the various positions that I fulfill.

What I have established is a different set of priorities. What follows is by no means meant to be stated with an attitude of look at how great I am. As I have been most forthcoming with my personal deficiencies. It is meant to be shared with a look at how God reinvented my relationship with Him in a real and tangible fashion. It came when I was willing to do the single thing that always separates those that find depth in God. "What is that?" you ask. It is to pay the price of time. When you are willing to spend time with God, He is always willing to help you order your priorities. He will do the same for you!

First, I begin my day with focused prayer. I spend at least two hours and sometimes more, praying through the Tabernacle that God instructed Moses to build for the children of Israel. This ordered sequence of prayer has revolutionized my ability to maintain a direction and stay on track while in prayer. This so influenced me that I began to develop this process for the people at the church where I pastor. All these messages can be found on my YouTube site at Mike Springston FFC.

After beginning this prayer, I began to listen to people pray and realized that prayer really was a rambling statement with little content and less purpose. This order distinctly impacted my ability to pray, which ultimately took the focus off myself. What a revelation that became. I stopped using God as crutch and began to actively seek Him. My intimacy escalated beyond my wildest imagination. I was able to pray with a plan concerning everything and everyone that was a part of my life. It is awesome! When I finish, I feel totally complete and ready for my day.

Someone would ask, "Do you do that every day?" The answer is, only on the days that end in *Y*. There is such a deep sense of peace and a total sense of refreshing that I cannot even think about beginning my day any other way. My messages have helped me connect the Tabernacle to the New Testament. This has further enabled me to understand prayer and enhanced my intimacy with the Lord. Second, I spend time reading and writing on the Word of God. The entire book has been opened to me because of my time of intimacy with the Lord. The book you are about to read is the result of my time spent in prayer. Every word in this book comes from the breath of the Holy Spirit. Where did I find him, and how did I locate him? In prayer!

The question is, "If you have been preaching all over the country, and you are a Pentecostal preacher, then you had to have been baptized in the Holy Spirit with the appropriate evidence, correct?" Of course, I had been filled with the Spirit, and of course, I have experienced the gifts of the Spirit in my ministry. Then, "Why did you have such a struggle with the demands of life?" Because the demands become overwhelming, and I tended to focus on what is the most pressing need that I, physically and emotionally, faced.

Also, the demands of life generally hold a process and plan. We tend to organize the things that must be done. The expectations of the demands cause us to do deep inspection into the methods required to do a good job. It was not until I placed the same organization, expectation, and inspection upon my spiritual life that my eyes began to open. The wisdom, revelation, and knowledge of Him began to flood my spirit. When this occurred, the other issues of life that had seemed to put me in bondage began to take a subservient position. They began to get in line, but no longer were they standing at the front of the line! I was able to sleep less and get up refreshed and ready to "work" with the rest of my day!

The words that most people would use here is to "deal" with the rest of the day. Prayer, reading, Bible study, meditation, and writing have enabled me to "work" with my day. What a different mind-set!

So the Holy Spirit that was in me when I traveled and preached expressed Himself in relation to the office of which I was called. The Holy Spirit always honors the office of the ministry. Therefore, my ministry and my professional life became as separate as my spirit and my flesh. This is, and was, a hard lesson to learn.

As I went through the furnace of affliction, I began to realize that the problems with my life were simple. They were my inability to harness myself. With this revelation, I was now in position for God to set me on a different course. He did that through the teaching of some extremely anointed men of God who shared their insight and poured into my life without even knowing they were doing it. When I heard them speak on the Tabernacle and its significance toward man approaching God, it supercharged my spirit. I began to understand how to approach God and be in His presence. That was a life-changer for me.

Yes, it is documented that I went through personal sickness as well. But I also was afflicted in my professional life. It was that affliction that drove me to being upset, angry, in doubt, in fear and discontent with God. Why? Because I did not have a clear understanding of why everything in my life did not always come up roses. I imagine you sometimes wonder that too. If you do, go to YouTube and begin my series on the Tabernacle, and you will locate your answers.

Thirdly, I had to deprioritize myself. I had to realize that the guy that I used to be had to die! My personal goals, wishes, desires, and opinions had to be crucified with Christ. I had to live a new life after the faith of the Son of God. That meant that I had to surrender myself to become a servant. I had to surrender my control and accept the leading and guidance of the Holy Spirit.

Now I could do that when I preached. I could listen and hear the voice of the Holy Spirit as He, through me, instructed his people. I had to be able to do that in my moment by moment walk with the Lord. Paul said that we were to walk in the Spirit so that we would not fulfill the lust of the flesh. This was what I had to do. The way I learned to do that was through prayer, study, meditation, and writing concerning the Word.

I can tell you how deeply this process has changed me. The furnace of affliction has enabled me to step over the hurtful words of people and go on, regardless of the snide remarks or the criticism that used to infuriate me. Now the Holy Spirit serves to calm my spirit with the peace that passes my flesh's understanding. These actions do not happen when I preach. They happen when I live! However, the Holy Spirit directs and orders my steps around the minefield that the enemy places in my path.

Often, these mines are set by other Christians. This is sad but true. They, unwittingly or on purpose (only the Lord knows) live a life so infiltrated by the world that they don't pay attention, at times, to what they say or how they speak to people. Why has this transformation occurred? Because I have located the most precious of treasures.

> Again, the kingdom of heaven is like unto a merchant man, seeking goodly pearls: who, when he had found one pearl of great price, went and sold all that he had, and bought it. (Matthew 13:45–46 KJV)

Here it is! I have found the pearl of great price that is worth abandoning everything else so that that pearl can be kept!

Paul again identified this concept in 2 Corinthians 4:7.

> But we have this treasure in earthen vessels, that the excellency of the power may be of God, and not of us. (2 Corinthians 4:7 KJV)

It is the treasure that is in us! It is Christ in us. It is the effects of the Holy Spirit abiding in men. It is the anointing! This anointing is greater than gold! It is also greater than the pearl of great price! It is the most important ingredient that heaven shares with mankind. This anointing pervades every aspect of life when prior proper planning that involves prayer and the Word of God are enforced in the lives of men.

This was and is the divine design that God intended for mankind. This is the relationship of communion that God intended for us to share with him. So out of the furnace of affliction, God has brought me to the knowledge, wisdom, and revelation of Himself.

Before we get into the other nine revelations in this book, I want to share one more vital piece of information. I pastor forty people. I do not have a mega church, nor do I have a church that everyone is rushing to attend. No, God has become real to a man who, in the world's view, has done nothing spectacular in the church world. He has no platform on which to stand to say to the world, "Look at me and do what I do, and you can have what I have!" Nope, I do not relate to those who appear to be what the church world is looking for. But what I do possess is a deep relationship with the Master. I also possess this most critical ingredient. The Spirit of the Lord through His anointing resides in me!

I have told you how it comes and how to receive it. How the world perceives your success is the problem with the pressure that you feel to succeed. When your relationship is translated to the anointing through the means earlier related, you will find that all that matters is the maintenance of the anointing. The Spirit of God that flows through you as you walk this life daily with His Spirit will be so overwhelming that nothing else matters!

The Revelation of the Eternal Jesus

It was the spring of 1974 and the day of our beloved high school athletic coach's birthday. There was no doubt that he meant the world to our community. He was the head coach in all three major sports. As such, he was probably the most recognized person in our town.

It was baseball season, and I was the pitcher for our program. I was in the middle of a great season. Our team was doing well, so all was right in the world.

Coach's birthday was a big deal to us. We planned a surprise birthday party for him at his house. The plan was for me and my best friend to lure him away from the house by taking him to a new ice cream store that had just opened in our sister city. As we arrived at the store or got close, I was supposed to say that I hope he had brought the money. My partner in this deception was to reply, "I didn't bring money, I thought you were supposed to bring the money."

When we tried the plan, Coach quickly said, "Don't worry about it, boys, I have the money."

We winced because we knew what was planned, and we knew he would eat a big banana split. Oh well, let's eat!

Well, the real story happened on the ride to the store. My partner and I were both Christians. Coach, as great of a person as he was, had never made a profession for Christ. We knew this to be so because we had been told by our pastor that he had tried to speak with him on this issue. So we opened the conversation by sharing with him how much we loved and appreciated all he did for us. We told him some of our stories concerning our relationship to Christ. He listened intently, and after a while, he stopped us. His next words had chilling implications, as you will see shortly.

He said, "Boys, you guys know how much I think of you and all the kids. I really appreciate what you are saying, and I am glad Christianity has meant that much to you. I think it is great to believe in something. You know, it's strange that as recently as Sunday, the preacher had this same conversation with me. I told him the same thing I will tell you. I don't have time for that stuff. I am too busy coaching."

I asked him, "What did he say to you?"

Coach's response in hindsight has left an indelible print upon my life. He said, "Well, the pastor told me that a ball was going to send me to hell."

I told him, "If that's where all the balls are going, I guess I'll just go there too."

How do you combat such a statement from such a respected man when you're seventeen years old? We didn't even try. We went on with our plan for the birthday party. Anyway, there would be other days and other opportunities. Maybe his heart would soften in time.

There were not!

One week later, on Wednesday, we were at practice when Coach told me to get my running in and head for home. I was supposed to pitch the next day, so I did not have to participate in the fielding drills that were going to finish the practice.

A few days earlier, we had played North Hampton County, and an incident had occurred by a player making a gesture that was perceived as being made toward the coach. It was not done directly, nor was it not just an off-the-cuff response, but their coach, who was friends with ours, saw it and reported what he thought he saw to our coach. We had a brief meeting that was used as a teachable moment and moved on to the next phase of practice. He did not make a big deal of it, and the player apologized—no real harm in the matter. The players went back to finish the practice routine as always.

As for me, I was on the mound the next day. I would complete a bit of running, and I was through for the day. So as Joe Nuxhall the Hall of Fame Broadcaster for the Cincinnati Reds would say, "I rounded third and headed for home."

I was relaxing when the phone call came. I answered, and it was my best friend on the line. In his voice was a seriousness that I had heard too many times. I would describe him as the prankster of the group. He could make up a ridiculous story, tell it with a straight face, and make you believe every word of it.

He began, "Springy, Coach is in the hospital."

Naturally I said, "Come on, man, I just left you guys a couple of hours ago. I am not going for it!"

But I noticed a more persistent tone in his voice, and when he began to share the details, I knew that this was no prank.

Here is the story. When I left, they did infield and outfield, as we always did. Coach was standing on the second base side of the pitcher's mound hitting outfield. Our catcher was beside him. They were throwing to third base. When our third baseman threw the ball back to the catcher to continue the drill somehow, he didn't throw it far enough, and it hit coach in the head. He spun around and went down. He got up and said he was okay. But then he did something I have never seen him do: he hit a ball to left field over the fence. Now the fence was less than 275 feet away, but he was so good with this drill that this had never happened before. This single detail made me know that something was wrong.

I said, "Yes, that is very strange."

My friend's concerned voice then said, "Then the next thing I know, I'm getting a call telling me there is an ambulance at the coach's home. So what do we do?"

I said, "We need to get to our teammate and tell him before the rumors get started and make sure that he is okay."

We found him and explained what we knew and tried to make sure that he knew that this was just an unfortunate accident. We tried to assure him that everything would be okay. He was a great kid and a super athlete. He loved coach just like the rest of us.

Unfortunately, it was not okay!

After a brief stay in our local hospital, they transported our beloved coach to Durham, North Carolina, where he would be admitted into the Duke University Medical Center. There he was diagnosed with having broken his skull in four separate places.

He would eventually pass away from the injuries. After twelve blood clots and multiple surgeries, our beloved coach and friend departed this world in October of 1974. I can still hear those chilling words.

"If that's where all the balls are going, I guess I'll go there too."

Without warning, eternity met a man who was healthy, vibrant, and had everything in life ahead of him. He was unprepared. He would one day stand before the eternal Jesus who had died for him, loved him, and extended Himself to Him only to be met with a rejection for something temporal and material. I was there one week earlier when preparation was extended and refused. It is such a sad commentary but one that motivates me to push forward in my faith. We buried our coach, and life went on. But my life would be altered for good. I was a quality baseball player but was never again able to perform at the level that I had prior to that event. The ball was a weapon, and my life was in danger.

Man will face the eternal God in only one of two ways. We will face him as a lamb upon the cross, or we will face him as a lion upon the throne. I choose to face the lamb. Please do not avoid or put off your moment of instruction. Where you spend eternity is too big of a risk to leave to happenstance. More importantly, with whom you spend your eternity will depend upon how you view the eternal Jesus Christ. If you view and value Him and His eternal Person, then there will be a life spent under His dominion and in His domain. If you choose otherwise, you are doomed to spend life in the presence of other created beings who have lived their lives without recognition of the eternal God. You will be among those who share the consequences of eternal separation. I would add the eternal existence for any created being who finds himself in that place and in that condition will go there over the greatest efforts of the very Christ whom they rejected.

John begins his gospel with the identification of Jesus Christ as being eternal. This fact is of vital importance to the believer in that the connection of Jesus to the Godhead is critical for understanding His role and purpose in the redemption of man. As the eternal Son of God, He had the seed of eternity that would enable Him to live in a world full of sin; be fashioned as man, which legitimized His sacrifice; and live a life that allowed Him to become that sacrifice. Let's look at the way that John described this part of Jesus.

> In the beginning was the word, and the word was with God, and the Word was God. (John 1:1 KJV)

From the beginning, there have been three that bear record in heaven—the Father, the Son, and the Holy Spirit. In John chapter 1, the introduction of the Word is related to the reader. Here is how the revelation of Jesus Christ came to John.

1. He, Jesus Christ, was from the beginning. This meant that He was eternal! He is, and He was. He said of Himself in John 8:58,

> Jesus said to them, "Truly, truly, I say to you, before Abraham, was, I am." (John 8:58 KJV)

Hear Isaiah refer to Him in Isaiah 9:6.

> For a child will be born to us, a Son will be given to us; and the government will rest on his shoulders; and his name will be called wonderful, counselor, Mighty God, Eternal Father, Prince of Peace. (Isaiah 9:6 KJV)

Then see how Paul identifies Him in Colossians 1:17.

> He is before all things, and in him all things hold together. (Colossians 1:17 KJV)

It is clear from the scripture that Jesus is an eternal being. It is also clear that Jesus is an equal part of the eternal Godhead because John was moved to say so when he said,

And the word was God. (KJV)

The book of Hebrews is full of revelation concerning the eternal nature of Jesus.

2. His position was revealed to John.

"He was with God" is the way it was revealed to John.
Again, the book of Hebrews is full of the revelation of His position in eternity

> Without father, without mother, without descent, having neither beginning of days, nor end of life; but made like unto the Son of God; abided a priest continually. (Hebrews 7:3 KJV)

> Who is made, not after the law of a carnal commandment, but after the power of an endless life. (Hebrews 7:16 KJV)

> For those priests were made without an oath; but this with an oath by him that said unto him, the Lord sware and will not repent, Thou art a priest for ever after the order of Melchisedec. (Hebrews 7:21 KJV)

> But this man, because he continueth ever, hath an unchangeable priesthood. (Hebrews 7:24 KJV)

> For the law maketh men high priests which have infirmity; but the word of the oath, which was since the law, maketh the Son, who is consecrated for evermore. (Hebrews 7:28 KJV)

> Jesus Christ the same yesterday, and to day, and for ever. (Hebrews 13:8 KJV)

He is the High Priest from eternity, and He will continue to be the high priest forever. The involvement of men in the plan of God does not change nor inhibit the position from eternity to eternity that Jesus holds. His involvement with men and His sacrifice simply make Him the High Priest of His own sacrifice. When they placed the purple robe upon Him in John 19:1–2 while He was in Pilate's judgment hall, this action by the Roman soldiers designated Him as the High Priest of His own sacrifice. They did not know what they were doing, but there could not be a sacrifice without a High Priest. We know that from the activities that occurred in the Tabernacle. Therefore, He is the Prince of Peace because He is the offering, He is the mediator, and He is the ultimate officiate over the activity in the heavenly Tabernacle!

3. The Holy Spirit revealed to John that the Word, Jesus Christ, was God.

The Holy Spirit revealed this truth to Paul in Philippians 2:6–9.

> Who, being in the form of God, thought it not robbery to be equal with God: but made himself of no reputation, and took upon him the form of a servant, and was made in the likeness of men: and being found in fashion as a man, he humbled himself, and became obedient unto death, even the death of the cross. wherefore God also hath highly exalted him, and given him a name which is above every name. (Philippians 2:6–9 KJV)

Isn't it awesome that John heard and spoke a revelation concerning Jesus and then the Holy Spirit confirmed that revelation through the voice of a second person?

Paul sees His position this way.

1. He had the form of God knowing He was the Word of God from the beginning. He knew that he could rob nothing

from the Godhead regardless of the state in which the plan of God placed Him.
2. He made Himself of no reputation among the men to whom He would come. He lowered Himself by status to become a servant.

Now notice this. Let me stop here a second and address the way God saw mankind. Paul says that Jesus lowered His status to that of servant, the concept being that men were designed to be a servant of God. Jesus came into the world to that end. Somehow, we have missed this phrase in our current Christian culture. The form of a servant indicates the adjustment from divine to the likeness of men. When He became man, He became what man was supposed to be from His creation, which was a servant of God and not a servant of Himself.

3. He was made the in likeness of men.

He took on the shape of man. His physical stature was such that He had nothing visible that man did not possess. His demeanor was made to be what man had been designed in the garden to be, a servant. So when Jesus was identified by John through his threefold revelation in John 1 as eternal, with God, and was God, Paul's revelation agreed with John. John then proceeded to expand upon the revelation that the Holy Spirit provided Him and took Him into his reason for being in the flesh. I want you to notice this. The reason Jesus was in the flesh is the exact reason for our being in the flesh since we are to be servants of the living God first and last!

4. He was a humble servant.

He lived His life not seeking His own will, way, ideas, directions, or thoughts. He operated according to the following scriptures, which are stated in his own words:

> Then answered Jesus and said unto them, verily, verily, I say unto you, the Son can do nothing of

> himself, but what he seeth the father do: for what things soever he doeth, these also doeth the Son likewise. (John 5:19 KJV)
>
> I can of mine own self do nothing: as I hear, I judge: and my judgment is just; because I seek not mine own will, but the will of the Father which hath sent me. (John 5:30 KJV)
>
> For I have not spoken of myself; but the Father which sent me, he gave me a commandment, what I should say, and what I should speak. (John 12:49 KJV)
>
> Then said Jesus unto them, "When ye have lifted up the Son of man, then shall ye know that I am he, and that I do nothing of myself; but as my father hath taught me, I speak these things." (John 8:28 KJV)

Jesus said that what He did was what he was told to do. He was humbled to the likeness of men by the design of God. By divine decree, He was sent to dwell among men for servanthood. He was a servant first, last, and always for the completion of the plan of God.

5. He was obedient unto death.

There is no question as to what the plan of God called for the one in the likeness of men to do. For Him to do this, He had to be able to function in two critical character traits.

First was servanthood. The second was to complete and to specifically obey, and He had to know that obedience was to ultimately mean death. He was a part of the plan from the beginning. He knew that the Holy Spirit would also be included in His earthly mission. He knew the limitations of the man and the likeness with which He was shrouded. He knew that there would be an encounter with the evil one. He knew the Jews and their stiff-necked disposition.

6. Wherefore, God hath highly exalted Him.

He has exalted his heavenly position as being with God and being God. He has exalted the work completed in the flesh as being a humbled and obedient servant. He has given him a name which is above every name, and that name is Jesus. Why do you suppose that is the case? Why would it not be the Word? Here is the reason. In that name, Jesus, all of Isaiah's titles are included. At that name of Jesus is the humbled and obedient servant. Through that name is the sacrifice for sin for all mankind. Through that name is the mediator for man's separation from God. Through that name is the High Priest that will minister the blood as the Tabernacle's spiritual official. In that name the heavenly host sings, "Holy, holy, holy and worthy is the Lamb."

The Word that is now Jesus represents the people of God's creation in the throne room of God today. His representation from there is according to Colossians.

> And ye are complete in him, which is the head of all principality and power: in whom also ye are circumcised with the circumcision made without hands, in putting off the body of the sins of the flesh by the circumcision of Christ: buried with him in baptism, wherein also ye are risen with him through the faith of the operation of God, who hath raised him from the dead and you, being dead in your sins and the uncircumcision of your flesh, hath he quickened together with him, having forgiven you all trespasses; blotting out the handwriting of ordinances that was against us, which was contrary to us, and took it out of the way, nailing it to his cross; and having spoiled principalities and powers, he made a

> shew of them openly, triumphing over them in it.
> (Colossians 2:10–15 KJV)

It is no wonder that this Jesus is exalted. Look at what He has done!

> And ye are complete in him, which is the head of
> all principality and power. (Verse 10 KJV)

He has made us complete in Him because He alone is the head of all in order of time, placement, or rank. He rules completely as the principle ruler. In other words, He is Adonai!

> In whom also ye are circumcised with the circumcision made without hands, in putting off the body of the sins of the flesh by the circumcision of Christ. (Verse 11 KJV)

We are cut in our heart with a cut that is made in our spirit. For all of us who by grace through faith have heard of Jesus, identified what Jesus did on the cross for us, acknowledged our sin and confessed Him as Lord, this spiritual cut took out all the sin that separated us from God. It was the act of force by which the cross interacted with our spiritual man. It was enacted and enforced by Jesus through faith.

> Buried with him in baptism, wherein also ye are risen with him through the faith of the operation of God, who hath raised him from the dead. (Verse 12 KJV)

We are immersed into Him by being covered by His own blood and by the accomplished work of the cross and the resurrection. All this is the design and plan of God for man through the works of Jesus while He was among men. We are immersed, covered, risen with

Him because God was faithful to His own plan for us, which He worked through the Word, Jesus Christ, the Eternal One!

> And you, being dead in your sins and the uncircumcision of your flesh, hath he quickened together with him, having forgiven you all trespasses. (Verse 13 KJV)

Jesus Himself, by means of our faith in Him and His work, has quickened or made alive your spiritual man so that your flesh is now under subjection to the newly born spiritual transformation that has occurred on the inside of everyone who believes.

Jesus has made the dead man come alive within Himself by what He accomplished on the cross. He has forgiven sin and any slide, slip, or error that you may do. In other words, He has personally supplied the fifth part of the sacrifice on our behalf.

> Blotting out the handwriting of ordinances that was against us, which was contrary to us, and took it out of the way, nailing it to his cross. (Verse 14 KJV)

He obliterated, erased, and tore apart your sin for pardoning you totally. He wiped sin out completely for any man who believes upon the eternal Word whose named Jesus. All the five offerings associated with the Old Testament sacrifices were nailed to one cross.

> And having spoiled principalities and powers, he made a shew of them openly, triumphing over them in it. (Verse 15 KJV)

He has destroyed every rule, influence, authority, and jurisdiction that has ever stood to oppose God. He is exalted above everything, anything, and anyone and has been so since the very beginning.

He alone came with the capacity to complete this work. He alone came with the ability to be filled with the Holy Spirit for operating in the divine plan of God. This infilling allowed Him to destroy every evil work that had been perpetrated for the years after the fall. Now, eternity comes on the scene in the form of heaven's Word, and the time of the separation of God within man's spirit is drawing short.

The truth is, all hell knew that He was coming. Unless they were not listening to the prophetic input by the Holy Spirit through the Old Testament, it was impossible for the principalities and powers to have missed the clues. What they did not put together was how the divine plan would function. Paul shared that with us here:

> But we speak the wisdom of God in a mystery, even the hidden wisdom, which God ordained before the world unto our glory: which none of the princes of this world knew: for had they known it, they would not have crucified the Lord of glory. (1 Corinthians 2:7–8 KJV)

So He has destroyed the opposition and made men free from all sin and all trespass. What a great and mighty God!

It is important to notice that once He had won and accomplished His works, He was not through. As every great warrior and every great winner who has fought the enemy into submission, Jesus exposed those whom He vanquished. Why was this done? It was done for the entire spiritual community to see that the enemy was completely subdued. Any resistance that the enemy would provide would be done so toward a people who by faith would already have the way of escape. The Word of God, Jesus Christ, would be their complete and total way of dealing with the devil. They would never again look to themselves for help, strength, power, or peace. They would defer to the exalted one. In Him and because of Him, everything that has a name bows its knee to the one who won the war! So the eternal Son of God completed a plan designed before the foundation of the world to reconnect man to God. Those in the earth could not know it. Therefore, they could not combat it. They were co-orchestrators of the plan. Jesus, the eternal Son of God, has accomplished and to this day continues to accomplish the divine operation of the will of God.

> Jesus Christ the same yesterday, and to day, and for ever. (Hebrews 13:8 KJV)

The Revelation of the Personal Jesus

In 1981, my son, Christopher, was five years old. I was living in Charleston, West Virginia, and I was coaching at West Virginia State College. Christopher had a lot of little friends in the neighborhood, and they all loved to play football. One day his little friends showed up at the door and asked if Christopher could play ball with them. I told them he could if their parents were there with them. They said they were, and off they went. My last instruction to them all was to stay away from that hill that was on the backside of the playground. They assured me that they would and that their parents would be watching them.

In about fifteen minutes or so, the two children reappeared at my door. The young man was extremely excited. He attempted to tell me that something was wrong. He stuttered and stammered to the extent that the little Asian girl had to push him aside.

When she was on center stage in my doorway, she calmly declared, "Chris fell over the hill, and he's stuck in the mud and can't get out!"

I leaped to my feet and took off! The hill where they were playing was at least a twenty-five-foot drop. Storms had eroded the mountain, and the ground had given way. It was a complete mud hole, and who knows how deep it was. When I arrived at the playground and looked over the hill, Chris was in trouble. Fortunately, he had landed on his feet. He had gone after a loose ball, just like his daddy had taught him, and rolled over the hill. He was up to his calves in mud, and it was as fluid as quicksand. Down the hill I went.

Mud is mud, regardless of your age, size, or strength. I walked as far as I could and could get no closer than to lay on top of the mud and touch the tips of his fingers. Over the next few seconds, I lost even that contact as Chris was being pulled under by the suction of the mud and the looseness of the dirt. This was a most critical situation as in a very short period, he would be engulfed and under the mud. Chris never seemed to panic. I am sure I did, but I had no time to digest the situation. This required absolute action to find a way to save that little boy. I strained with every ounce of my being and could not latch onto him enough to loosen him from the friction of the mud that was quickly attaching to both of us.

I got a stick and reached to him. He grabbed the stick, but it was not strong enough to pull him out of the mire that he was in. It seemed that I was helpless to rescue my own son. Out of the blue, I saw a man. I did not know him. I had never seen him before, and he did not speak to me. He began to walk toward us. It appeared that he was unaffected by the mud as he drew closer and closer.

In just a few seconds, he reached down his hand and grabbed Christopher's arm. I was then able to reach out and grab him as well. We pulled him from the clay. The suction was so hard that it pulled his clothes right off his body. His pants, undergarments, and shoes remained entombed in that mudslide! Now we had to get out of this mess together. It was a chore of major proportion, but we made it out—both of us covered in mud but alive and well. I believe that I thanked the man, although from that day until this day, I have never seen him again. I went looking for him after it was all said and done, but no one seemed to be able to identify the man who came and saved my son.

When I got Chris home, I put him in the tub and began to clean him up when the Holy Spirit spoke into my heart. This is what He said, "This is exactly what I did for you. When you were lost and undone and you needed a Savior, I sent My Son to pull you out of the miry clay."

I began to weep as I knew that this could have turned out much differently. Had Chris fallen in headfirst, my life would have changed instantly as he could not have survived. But he, by the grace of God, did not. God had taken this situation and used it to be a great personal lesson concerning an awesome personal God!

In reality, I am sure that we do not have the full understanding of the power of sin. God opened my eyes that day to the power and the potential of the grip of sin. It was harmless, it was seamless, and it was an accident, but once I had time to sit back and consider what might have been, it was most alarming. We never do that with sin and the potential consequences of being involved with sin. We often walk around the border of sin until we can taste and smell the results, but we feel that we are strong enough within ourselves to handle it. We are not! There must be someone that must intervene for us just as this man intervened for Chris and me.

Jesus is that person. His identity in you is the only shield that you possess when it comes to overcoming sin. If you take care of the shield and develop your relationship with the shield, He becomes extremely personal and your ability to get out and stay out of the mud and mire of sin is possible. But we must reconcile ourselves to the deceitfulness and the potential captivity of sin before we become desirous to avoid sin and its conventions altogether. He personally reached way down for me! I was lost and unprepared to meet the eternal God. But then in Jesus, He reached down His hand for me! What a revelation of the personal nature of an eternal God!

As you will see during this chapter, Jesus held a distinct office with distinct duties in heaven. There was a personal relationship between the Father and the Son. Their activity was such that the heavenly atmosphere was supercharged by their Spirits. It is, therefore, not surprising that he would be described as a personal Savior to and for mankind. Paul showed us this in Colossians 1:27,

> To whom God would make known what is the riches of the glory of this mystery among the gentiles; which is Christ in you, the hope of glory. (Colossians 1:27 KJV)

Let's look at how John describes His personal nature.

> The same was in the beginning with God. (John 1:2 KJV)

Here Jesus Christ is seen as a personal part of the Godhead. According to Paul in Philippians 2, He was equal with God. There were no distinguishing features that separated the three members of the Godhead. However, there were distinguishing roles for each to produce for the benefit of the universe. This scripture identifies the Word as Jesus. It tells us that he was from the beginning in order, time, and rank with God. Then it shares with us that Word was with God. The word *with* then describes a nearness to or ascension to the position of order, time, and rank. The word was very personal to God, and His position identified the personal nature of His existence.

Notice that He was eternal and He was personal to God in the form of the Word. The same could be said concerning the Holy Spirit on both accounts. Now as John unfolds the revelation, He does so through the Holy Spirit. This revelation extends beyond the position that the Word was placed in heaven. The question is why. The answer is that Jesus would become the personal possession of every person who would believe on Him.

> I am the good shepherd, and know my sheep, and am known of mine. (John 10:14 KJV)

He would become the personal possession of every believer. This is just as it was in heaven. He was so connected to the Godhead that His person and His nature were undistinguishable from the other two when the Word came to earth; the plan was to identify the Father and His nature to man. Then to fill man with the nature and character of the Godhead.

> He came unto his own, and his own received him not. (John 1:11 KJV)

Here again, we have another occurrence of the personal nature of Jesus. As we have defined earlier in this writing, Jesus holds a very personal relationship to all three worlds.

Let's explore these relationships. First, the Word of God holds a personal relationship to God and to the Godhead. His office is essential to the plan and design of God. Paul says in Philippians 2:5–7,

> Let this mind be in you, which was also in Christ Jesus: who, being in the form of God, thought it not robbery to be equal with God: but made himself of no reputation, and took upon him the form of a servant, and was made in the likeness of men: the Word of God did not think it robbery to be equal with God. (Philippians 2:5–7 KJV)

As Paul shares, He was in the form of God. This is a very personal position.

When I see myself in the mirror, I see my Father. I see the vision of his looks, his hair, his chin, and so forth. Why? Because he and I are extremely personal to each other. He is the progenitor of my life. It was his seed that crated me. How else should I appear? When Paul recorded these words, what he was sharing was the total identification that Jesus had with the father. When you saw the Godhead, they were inseparable in image but marked by the office, which belonged under their purview.

God was the planner, designer, and orchestrator. The Son was the Word of God with power and authority to speak creative words that set the course of the design of God in motion. The Holy Spirit was the activity of the Godhead. He was the mover and shaker that would take the picture found within the words and put them into a structure that was tangible. This concept becomes very clear when we listen to Luke in Acts chapter 1 and verse 2 define the relationship of the ascended Jesus to the apostles through the activity of the Holy Spirit. The process becomes very clear.

Second, Jesus held a personal relationship to His creation Lucifer. That is clear when we read the recorded scripture in Matthew's gospel concerning their personal interaction.

> Then was Jesus led up of the spirit into the wilderness to be tempted of the devil. And when he had fasted forty days and forty nights, he was afterward an hungered. And when the tempter came to him, he said, if thou be the Son of God, command that these stones be made bread. But he answered and said, it is written, man shall not live by bread alone, but by every word that proceedeth out of the mouth of God. Then the devil taketh him up into the holy city, and setteth him on a pinnacle of the temple, and saith unto him, if thou be the Son of God, cast thyself down: for it is written, he shall give his angels charge concerning thee: and in their hands they shall bear thee up, lest at any time thou dash thy foot against a stone. Jesus said unto him, it is written again, thou shalt not tempt the lord thy God. Again, the devil taketh him up into an exceeding high mountain, and sheweth him all the kingdoms of the world, and the glory of them; and saith unto him, all these things will I give thee, if thou wilt fall down and worship me. Then saith Jesus unto him, get thee hence, Satan: for it is written, thou shalt worship the lord thy God, and him only shalt thou serve. Then the devil leaveth him, and, behold, angels came and ministered unto him. (Matthew 4:1–11 KJV)

Here it is clear that the Holy Spirit was involved in the preparation for this meeting as He led him to the wilderness and into the realm of fasting. The necessity of this preparation was because this was a moment in time when Jesus would be on His own totally to represent the Godhead and the plan of God. He would stand not in the power of his physical self as it had been depleted from lack of nourishment, but He would stand in the power of the Spirit of

God that resided within Him. It was this spiritual attachment that decided the day.

The words of Satan speaks immediately to the real point of this encounter.

> If thou be the Son of God, command that these stones be made bread. Here is why.

If Jesus identified Himself as the Son of God and not the Son of Man, then He would have no legal grounds to become the sacrifice for the sin of man.

Satan had to challenge that position instantly. If he could establish this relationship, then the plan would have been null and void. Do you see how Jesus answered the question? He refers to Himself as man! His personal relationship in the form in which Satan saw Him was as man. Therefore, He was capable of being the legal sacrifice for the sin of man. What an awesome response and a most welcome one for mankind!

Man was to live by the words that proceeded from the mouth of God! What reference do you see here? The Word of God was referencing His instructions to Adam. These words were no doubt identified by Satan. They had a much deeper meaning than just to refer to how man fed His body. He was saying to the word *creation* in essence:

"We would not be here if man had listened to the words when you did this in the Garden of Eden! I am here now to uphold the words of My father. Somehow it is evident to Me that Satan resonated with that response and recognized the relationship to Eden. Furthermore, Satan, you would not be here if you had listened to the Word of God and maintained your created position. This entire meeting would have been avoided had you, Adam and Eve, understood the words that I have just spoken in response to your inquiry!"

We could have had the glory of heaven for our benefit. Man could have had the Tree of Life for his benefit, and the creation of God could have flourished under his dominion. When the Word of

God is not the bread that feeds the creation, the benefit of the power in that Word is lost!

The second temptation is the temptation of Jesus's soul. This conversation dealt with Jesus casting Himself down, and God in His love for the Son, would surely rescue him. With the overriding concept that God has promised to take care of you, and if that be so, you should put God to the test. Satan has alluded to the problem that he had encountered with God. He had put God to the test, and God with immediacy made sure that his deeds were not tolerated. Jesus immediately identifies the connection. This is how he answered:

"You tempted God with your high-minded rebellious personality. When you did that, you set a precedent that had to be addressed, not only addressed but your comments demanded swift judgment. Now you tempt Me with the same. I was a part of what happened to you. I know the simple answer to this question. If you tempt God, you do not have to cast yourself down, he will do that for you. Had you not done this, we would not be having this conversation!"

Satan had made a boost that heaven could not allow. Paul gives us the reason why in Romans 1:24–25.

> Wherefore God also gave them up to uncleanness through the lusts of their own hearts, to dishonor their own bodies between themselves: *who changed the truth of God into a lie and worshipped and served the creature more than the creator, who is blessed for ever. Amen.* (Romans 1:24–25 KJV)

This was what was being offered in heaven to its inhabitants. They were given the possibility of choosing to worship the creature more than the Creator. God would not allow it in heaven, nor would he allow it in the life of Jesus. Jesus brought Himself and His soul under subjection to the plan of God and replied that God is not in the business of having the creature be in control.

It seems to me that Jesus's reply was much like ours when people ask stupid questions. We reply with, "Huh? How could you, of all people, ask such an unaware question! How in the world did you miss that answer? It seems simple to the knowledgeable." On the other hand, the fool does things that he knows have worked for him in the past with the undereducated.

Look at how the undereducated responds to things that they really do not comprehend. This is the same type of conversation the serpent had with Eve. But Eve was a created being just as Satan was. When he said surely God has not said that you will die, he perverted the understanding and interpretation of the words spoken to Adam, which were only shared with Eve. The difference between Jesus and Eve is readily identifiable here as Jesus responds to the question.

The Word of God, whom we know as Jesus, here identified Himself as man, did not have a mediator to define for Him the purpose and intent in which the instruction was given. Jesus knew the Word because He was the Word. Eve only knew the instruction from Adam's interpretation and her ability to understand while being subject to her flesh. So Jesus responds by quoting the scripture. His physical self may have been weakened, but His spiritual self was full of, well, Himself and his words!

Referring to Deuteronomy 6:13, Jesus puts a quick end to this temptation.

It is an awesome understanding which I am sharing at this point concerning this scripture. Jesus had no intention of doing the following:

1. Jesus had no intention of interrupting the plan for which he entered the world. The least of which was to expect God to reveal Himself to the very one whose intention it was to steal his throne.
2. Being a King in his own right.
3. Setting up a kingdom absent of the kingdom that had been designed by the Godhead.
4. Bowing his knee to His own creation.
5. Ever coming into opposition with the divine design of God for Himself and ultimately for mankind.

Thirdly, Satan presented the kingdom to Jesus. Here, he appeals to the spirit man that was in Jesus. Now bear in mind that the kingdom belonged to Satan. He not only possessed it but also the spirits of men who dwelt in this world. Since Jesus was a man, He had the power to do what He said He would do. He had been given that authority from God as a part of the Godhead. Again, the response of Jesus identifies with the activity that occurred in heaven and the root cause of this conversation. Jesus told the devil the same thing that the Godhead had shown him when they cast him down and out of heaven.

There is but one God to worship and to serve. Don't you think that these words were highly recognizable by the devil? I am sure that he thought every answer sounded so familiar to him, the Word of God as being his only directive. God is not to be messed with when it comes to His position and control. Now, there is no one else who can be worshipped but God alone. So he is compelled again to flee from the presence of Jesus just as he was compelled to exit heaven. Yes, he had a personal encounter with Jesus that left him with answers that were ultimately the same as what he had been told in heaven. But not knowing the plan of God, all he could do was get out of there and use what he had at his command to continue to attack Jesus.

Jesus's response sent the devil away. From the position where He could see the known world and from where He had full view of all the things that were created, Jesus maintained the position for God. Satan seated Him in His correct position. He was unaware that the place where he set Him soon would be the place from which He would retrieve from Him. There was no one who could possess this position but the God who created it. Jesus was in the correct place all along. The devil, upon hearing the words of worship and allegiance, had to retreat. He left him for a season according to Luke 4. Do you know that it is strange that when Eve fell to the serpent, it is not recorded that he returned to her? Why would he since he took with him what he had come to claim?

It is apparent that the devil knew that there was more work required to break the Son of Man. Although we have no record of any further personal appearances, we have many instances defined for us where he entered the spirits of men to attack Jesus. Why? Because he controlled the spirit of men, and they lived in his domain.

I hope I have defined the fact that this encounter was of a personal nature between Satan and Jesus. The questions were far too pointed not to surmise the relationship between the two. Although Jesus did not appear to Satan in the form that Satan had remembered, He did have the content within Him that made this encounter extremely uncomfortable for Satan. Satan, no doubt, had seen the spirit appear and heard the voice of God at the baptism of Jesus. This left him with no option but to enquire concerning His origin.

Jesus, the obedient servant of God, handled the situation with great grace. But on the third trial, the power within His words were obvious! Get thee hence! This was power and authority. Do you suppose that Satan heard a voice that he recognized? It could be so. One thing we know—he got out from where he was and did not reappear to Jesus in the same recognizable form again. It must also be said that Jesus remained the same person that Satan encountered for the duration of His ministry. He had no reason and no way to be anything different than He already was. He was the Son of Man, and He would be so until the resurrection!

This scripture then shares with us the personal nature of Jesus to the heavenly angelic beings. They came to minister to Him. Matthew does not record what it was that they ministered, but he does say that they offered a ministry to Him. I am sure that they waited upon Him, spiritually fed Him, and brought Him a message of glad tidings from the Father. He had been in a personal encounter and had overcome the devil. Heaven had to have been rejoicing as their champion had satisfied the legal responsibility required to continue to the cross.

The third place that it is personal is within the heart of man. I will not spend much time here as I have described this earlier. The purpose for mentioning this again is to give respect to Matthew's gospel that saw Him as the Son of Man. Jesus's relationship to man had to be defined. The Son of Man is a prophetical term that is used in Psalms, Ezekiel, Daniel, and other places in the Bible to apply to the coming Messiah. So when Jesus refers to Himself in this way, it is completing three important works.

First, it ties Him to the prophetical person who was described by the Old Testament prophets. Second, it ties Him directly to the people whom He had come to rescue and save. Thirdly, it makes Him eligible to become the legal sacrifice that was required to redeem mankind. In this capacity only could He become the substitute that man needed for sin. Only by this means could He be considered as the Lamb. When measured according to the Levitical standards that the Jews knew as the requirements for the substitution offering, Jesus had to be perfect man. He had to be without spot or blemish. In other words, as the Son of Man, He had to be sinless. This sinless state had to be identifiable in the deeds of His flesh, in the works of His inner man, as well as in the intentions of His soul.

This paints an even clearer picture as to the meaning behind Satan's questions as he probed him in all three areas. The results were that Satan found an unmatched nature and an unparalleled character. He had found the perfect Son of Man! There was nothing else to do but to make every attempt to use what Paul referred to as the wiles of the devil to find a weakness in His nature and character which he could not expose in Matthew 4.

So the enemy used inroads to attempt to get into his mind, will, and emotions. Through hardship and trial and through religious bigotry, the ministry of Jesus was attacked. Also, by means of interpersonal misunderstandings and by accusations, the people were led to attack Him. Jesus stood and withstood the attacks and was deemed by God to have upheld the highest standard known to man! He, the Son of Man, was, in fact, the righteousness of God. Now this reference was not new as it had been conferred upon Abraham. In both cases, the one given this title was given so in reference to their ultimate faithfulness.

The Revelation of the Creative Jesus

I had gone to bed one evening during the late spring of 1982 and had fallen off to sleep. I was awakened from my sleep by a strong urge to pray. I began to pray and spend time with the Lord. Suddenly, I felt a closeness of the Spirit of God that I had not sensed before. Then a conversation between the Lord and I ensued. The Spirit spoke clearly and expressly with instructions concerning my coming weekend. I was supposed to go and preach at the Ebenezer Baptist Church in Handley, West Virginia, on Sunday morning. I was excited to do so as I had been there many times and preached revival there on one occasion. I had a dear friend who was the new pastor, and I was sure it would be a good time.

The Holy Spirit began to instruct me. "Mike, I want You to call Jack Steward at the Smithers Church of God and tell him you want to come and preach for him."

I responded by reminding the Spirit, "I barely even know Brother Steward, he won't allow me to come and preach."

The Holy Spirit became even more specific. "You tell him you are friends with Tommy Frye. He knows him, and he will allow you to come."

So I said, "Okay, I can do that."

After this I was sure that I had concluded this conversation. I also was sure that somehow, I had made these connections and determinations on my own. Oh well, it was a good plan. I was going to be there, and I had Sunday evening open. Why not see if he would have me?

I had met Brother Steward and attended his church a time or two when I was in college. But surely that was so long ago that he would not remember me. Anyway, I could call him. What's the worst that could happen—he'd say no? So what? I tried to go back to sleep. Shortly the Holy Spirit made his presence known again.

"Mike, when you get there, I want you to do two things."

I said, "What is that, Lord?"

The Holy Spirit then gave me instruction that was shocking, unnerving, and very uncomfortable. "I want you to wash his feet."

"What? Can you say that again?"

"I want you to wash his feet!"

My mind went crazy. I had seen that done before, but I certainly had never done anything like that. I would not know where to start! I told the Lord so. Quickly, I determined that I was in a dream and that this was not real. I would go back to sleep, and when I woke up, I would realize that it was a dream. But there was no sleep. My spirit churned and burned as if I were pregnant with something, and I just could not be comfortable. Out loud, I heard myself say, "No, I can't do that. This is crazy. How in the world would I even broach the conversation with him? Anyway, I see no way that this is from God."

After a while the Holy Spirit returned. The night was waning away, and I had to go to work the next morning. Again, the same conversation. I finally realized that "no" was not an acceptable answer and that no was going to send me to work without sleep. So I agreed to do what He said. The Holy Spirit then gave me his final instructions.

"When they turn the pulpit over to you, you have the musicians play and allow the people to worship. When you do, wait for Me, and when I tell you to preach, I will do a great work."

Well, as you can tell, instructions numbers 1 and 3 were quite easy. But number 2 was probably the most uncomfortable request, directive, or instruction that I had ever been given under any circumstance.

I agonized over this whole situation. Finally, drawing the courage to call Brother Steward, I heard the phone ring, thinking maybe he wouldn't answer, and I could report to God that I had tried but he wasn't home. No such luck! Brother Steward answered, and I introduced myself and told him of my acquaintance with Tommy Frye.

He remembered me and shared kind words about Tommy. I then got down to business.

"Brother Steward, I'm preaching in Handley on Sunday morning and was looking for a place to preach on Sunday evening in your area."

I was prepared to move forward with the script when he abruptly stopped me. He had a deep Southern West Virginia drawl, and when he said my name, it came out as "Maack."

"Well, Maack, let me check my calendar. I'll be right back."

He returned shortly and said, "Brother Maack, come on over. We would love to have you."

Oh, my blessed God! I was sure that he would say no. I was sure that I could report back to God that I had done what He told me to do but I was met with a "no room at the church" sign. Surely, He would understand that. Now, I had to make preparation mentally for an event that I had never done. More importantly, I had to find a way to communicate my intentions. Wow, this was hard!

I went and preached at the first church, and it had gone without a hitch. The people were great, the service was great, and the anointing was rich. Now I had five hours to get up the mental fortitude, otherwise known as the nerve, to walk into a man's office, whom I had not seen for years, and ask him to pull his shoes off and allow me to wash his feet. Service time was set for seven o'clock on Sunday evening. I arrived at his office just prior to 6:00 PM. Perspiring and nervous, I approached the door. Unsure of exactly what I was going to do once on the inside, I knocked, and his wife came to the door and invited me in.

She was a delightful lady with a bounce in her step. She also was an incredible pianist. She said, "Follow me, Brother Steward will be in shortly."

I sat down, and it seemed like an eternity when Brother Steward hobbled through the door on the arm of his wife.

"Brother Maack, it's so good to see you. I'm so glad you're here."

I replied in kind. After a few pleasantries, I felt myself duck my head, and I said, "Brother Steward, I don't know exactly how to tell you this, so I'll just have to try the best I can. I was awakened a few days ago with strange instructions from the Lord. I do not know why, and I am not sure how to say this other than to just tell you. I need to wash your feet."

Graciously, he replied, "Well, Brother Maack, I'll wash your feet, and you can wash mine."

What a relief! He then called his wife and explained to her what we were going to do. He asked her to prepare the water and the towels. She hurried off to do so.

I was nervous, and I'm sure that showed. We carried on conversation concerning my morning service, and then his wife reappeared with the water and the towels. We were really going to do this. I was very uncomfortable. She placed everything as the pastor instructed. I removed my shoes and socks.

Brother Steward looked at his wife and with a depth of love that was so palpable you could have cut it with a knife, he said, "Honey, will you be so kind as to remove my shoes and socks?"

I watched as she delicately took off his shoes and then pulled up his pant legs. She took off his socks and revealed two legs that were as visibly dead as any corpse that I could imagine. Dead, from the knee to the bottom of his foot, black and dead! I was shocked to say the least. I'm sure my eyes showed my shock.

With his gracious way, as she finished preparing him, he obviously recognized my nerves, and he said, "Now, Brother Maack, I'll wash yours first, and then you can wash mine."

He did so with a beautiful rhythm to his prayer. He spoke in a most precious language as he washed and dried my feet. Now it was my turn. I knew this was why I had come. I knelt in front of him and began to pray. I felt the Spirit of the Living God in my hands and in my language. It was awesome. But I was holding dead flesh as I was praying over his legs. I later found out that the doctors had told this wonderful man of God that these legs would soon have to be amputated.

I finished and looked at those legs, and not one thing looked different—black and dead. But I had followed the instruction of the Holy Spirit, and something good had to happen! He thanked me, and his wife returned to take the water and the towels away. In just a few minutes we would be heading into the sanctuary for the evening service. Church started, and there was nothing special. After thirty minutes, he got up and introduced me to his people. They had probably seventy-five or so in attendance that evening.

Now, folks, I had been through two of the three instructions and survived, so orchestrating the third part would not be too difficult. I stood up and gave the instructions just as the Holy Spirit had said. They graciously complied. Man, was that music awesome! Soon they began to worship. People began to shout and run the aisles. It was old-time Pentecostal power flowing through the sanctuary of the living God! After twenty minutes or so, the Holy Spirit gave me the go-ahead. I preached, and we had an awesome altar service with testimonies. The church had been revived!

Afterward Brother Steward took me to eat. As we spoke, he shared with me the trials that this church had endured. The building had burned to the ground, the morale was low, and the people were desperately in need of a move of God. He shared that they had been in prayer for such a move for some time, and God had heard and answered in the service that night. What a charge of the supernatural power and presence of God. For me, I felt blessed and left walking on cloud nine. That was the end of that. Back to the real world I went. My teaching and coaching jobs were my day-to-day cross to bear. No preaching engagements in sight.

During the next year, I moved to Columbus, Ohio. During the camp meeting season of 1983, I went back to West Virginia for the West Virginia Church of God State Camp Meeting. This was quite an affair. It was held at the Beckley Raleigh County Fairgrounds. The arena was a huge place that could probably hold eight thousand or more people in a double-tiered setting. I had gone with my sister, Ellen, and her husband, Ron Treadway, who was a longtime Church of God pastor. It was fun to be with them and to be in camp meeting. The music was awesome, and the worship was great. The service ended after a couple of hours, and everyone was headed for the exits. The noise of that many people in a closed environment, as you can imagine, was loud.

Then I heard a voice from the crowd. It was undeniable and extremely recognizable.

"Maack, Brother Maack?"

I knew Jack Steward was in the house. How he saw me is a miracle in and of itself. My eyes rushed around the arena. From my vantage point, Brother Steward was at the farthest point away from me. I was moving in the opposite direction of the flow, but he waited for me. When I arrived to the area where he was standing, he was in the balcony, and I was on the main floor. The distance was not too great, so we could talk comfortably. Then he did something that absolutely sent me backward.

He said, "Brother Maack, Look! Look!" He pulled up his right pant leg, and I saw with my own eyes a leg that was as pink as the skin on a newborn baby! He dropped that pant leg and exposed his left leg. It was a pink as a newborn baby. I began to cry.

He then said, "Brother Maack, God healed and saved both of my legs, and I did not know how I was ever going to let you know. I saw you across the room, and I knew that I had to get your attention. Look what God has done."

In just a minute he had to leave as his contingent was on their way out. But he and I parted rejoicing in the power of God that healed his legs and saved him from being a double amputee. I had witnessed the eternal God become personal to a man that needed a miracle. Then I had seen that same God become a Creator to a man whose body parts were long past dead.

Jesus is the Creator. I was there when the man was prayed for and when his feet were washed. God gave me the great fortune to view His creative power in this man's life. Brother Steward was a faithful servant to a faithful God who exhibited His ability to create life from death within this man's body. He went on to continue pastoring. He was blessed by the creative power that is in Jesus Christ to stand upon two healed legs for the duration of his ministry. I doubt that anyone would ever convince me that Jesus is not a Creator. Why? Because I can only tell you what I have both seen and heard!

Jesus was the creative force whose words were designated to be the activating concepts by which the Holy Spirit operated. He is the Creator of the universe; the earth past; the earth present; the angels, which includes the devil; the creation of man; and the new birth, which creates a new spirit within man. His role as Creator is extensive and must be understood to bring complete perspective to the divine design of God, which includes the defeat of his enemy, Satan, death hell, the grave, and the deliverance of mankind.

> All things were made by him; and without him was not anything made that was made. (John 1:3 KJV)

There is no question that the Bible teaches that the Word (Jesus Christ) is the Creator of all things.
Let's begin by looking at Genesis 1:1.

> In the beginning God created the heaven and the earth. (Genesis 1:1 KJV)

The role and operations of the Godhead will unfold as it relates to the work of the Word in creation as we move through this verse. By beginning with this statement, we would think of God as a separate and single individual. We would see Him operating independently in the plan of creation. The Bible, however, does not teach this as such. The Bible identifies the person who completes the act of creation. That person is the Word of God. The Father's role was the design of the operation of God that reflected His will. Once that plan was designed and produced, the distinct completion of each act was delegated to an entity related to the Godhead. All three executed their specific roles in the creation of the world as we know it and man as we recognize him.

The actions associated with the creation, then, are actions and words that come from the Word of God whom we identify through the Gospel as Jesus. The execution of these words then became the role of the Holy Spirit. He was the one to move the structure around and put it into the setting of which the divine design of God had planned for it to be stationed.

> And God said, let us make man in our image, after our likeness: and let them have dominion

over the fish of the sea, and over the fowl of the air, and over the cattle, and over all the earth, and over every creeping thing that creepeth upon the earth. So God created man in his own image, in the image of God created he him; male and female created he them. (Genesis 1:26–27 KJV)

So the speaking portion of creation is the role of the Word of God who we know as Jesus. The "us" part then consists of the inclusion of the separate roles that the Godhead would produce as participants in the design, the speaking, and the adding structure and foundation to both the design and the words.

All three played their role perfectly, and all things were created by the operation of the will of God. So the Word created man in His image. What image was that?

It is essential that we see man as we perceive the roles of the Godhead that created him.

1. Man has the capacity of the Father to design and plan.

There is no doubt about this. Man has been the greatest inventor. He has been the greatest of problem-solver. He has been the most wonderful innovator who is driven often by necessity.

The problem with man is that he possesses these great qualities with a fallen spirit if he is absent of the salvation of God.

No man can dispute the presence of the personality of the Father in man. Genesis 1:27 tells us so.

2. Man has the creative power of the Word (Jesus) in his own mouth.

It is not debatable that man is a communicator. Nor is it debatable that man instructs, directs, and teaches through the same capability that the Word used to speak and that the Holy Spirit used to formulate the structure of all things.

Again, the problem for man in general is that man is speaking from the position of a fallen spirit. So those words are as apt to devise mischief as they are to motivate good.

3. Man can take direction, instruction, and teaching and to produce an outcome.

There is no debate about this. When learned men using words that create pictures in the mind of man do so, the outcomes are things such as the combustible engine, the telephone, the light bulb, and a lunar landing module!

Again, the problem is that the spirit of man is operating from fallen Seven Spirits that have been flawed from the moment that Adam watched Eve not fall dead upon eating the fruit of the Tree of Knowledge. Adam did not see her die because it was not physical death that the Word was referring to when he made the statement concerning death in Genesis 2:17. Adam did not know what to look for as he had never seen death. He did not understand the significance of death and the cost that disobedience would quickly cost him. Shortly, thereafter, however, he found out the cost.

Man has been functioning from that day until Jesus was seated at the right hand of God under the shroud of that decision. Now man, by grace through faith, can be quickened back to life in man's spirit because the Word who created him has completed the entire divine process for our reconnection to God. He is the Creator!

> Thou hidest thy face, they are troubled: thou takest away their breath, they die, and return to their dust. thou sendest forth thy Spirit, they are created: and thou renewest the face of the earth. (Psalms 104:29–30 KJV)

This is referring to the office and work of the Word of God (Jesus). The Word of God sent forth the Spirit in creation to renew the face of the earth from the despicable shape that it was in prior to Genesis 1:1.

> I will praise thee; for I am fearfully and wonderfully made: marvelous are thy works; and that my soul knoweth right well. (Psalms 139:14 KJV)

David is in deep appreciation for the way in which he was made. When he says that he was fearfully and wonderfully made, he is referring to the grand divine design of the Father. When he refers to the marvelous works, he is referencing the work of the Word in speaking him into existence. When he states that his soul knows well, he is relating to how the Holy Spirit controls his soul. He is identifying the work of the Holy Spirit upon his inner man that influences how his mind, will, and emotions function in relation to his inner man. Again, we can see the distinct operations and functions of the Godhead upon man.

> Who hath delivered us from the power of darkness, and hath translated us into the kingdom of his dear Son. (Colossians 1:13–16 KJV)

Those who believe have been delivered through the creation of a new heart. He has turned away the darkness on our behalf. We will speak more about this during a subsequent revelation concerning Jesus. For the second revelation, we need to know that He is the one who, through His obedience and humility, made a provision for the creation of a new heart in man.

> In whom we have redemption through his blood, even the forgiveness of sins: those who believe have forgiveness.

The blood is the agent that creates in man a new spirit. Who is the image of the invisible God, the firstborn of every creature? Here we see the Word of God in His eternal and personal image. He was the Word that was made flesh!

> For by him were all things created, that are in heaven, and that are in earth, visible and invis-

> ible, whether they be thrones, or dominions, or principalities, or powers: all things were created by him, and for him. (KJV)

Notice how Paul has unfolded Jesus.

- He was the one who delivered and translated man from darkness to light.
- He was the one who bought man back by His own blood. He did so because of who He was being the image of—the invisible God.

In other words, He performed his role within the Godhead. He was the first begotten of every creature, meaning He was the original formation of the new man whose spirit was in contact with God.

4. Then Paul identifies Him in His creative role.

He told us what he was to us and how He impacted man in verses 13–15. Then he went even deeper to establish His divine role in the reconnection of man to God. Here he connects Jesus to all three worlds—earth, heaven, and the spiritual world. Notice what Paul says here in the second half of verse 16.

> Visible and invisible, whether they be thrones, or dominions, or principalities, or powers: all things were created by him, and for him. (Colossians 1:16)

The spiritual world was every bit as much part of His creation and under His authority in his role as the Word. The things that we cannot see are, regardless of what they are or where they are, were created by Him. It is important to note that when those things in the spiritual world were created, they were not created as fallen beings. They were created to complete a role within the framework of the divine economy.

Their sin caused them to be separated from God and their original purpose. What was their original purpose? Paul tells us that it was for Him. The thrones, dominations, principalities, and powers were designed to fulfill a role in the heavenly economy under the authority of the Word of God. Due to the rebellion of Lucifer, however, a third of those prepared to fulfill their original purpose left the kingdom of God to follow the deceiver. They lost their original position and purpose. It is with this understanding that we now know why it is that when they saw Jesus, the Word of God, that they identified and recognized Him.

The question that lingers then is, "Were they privileged to the knowledge of what the Godhead designed in relation to man?" The answer is no! First, their role was not in the execution of the relationship to anything beyond their specific role in the heavenly economy. Secondly, the need for the plan of God to be exposed was unnecessary until the rebellion and casting down of those rebels occurred. Thirdly, there was a world that existed prior to the world that Genesis 1 identifies as the one created by the Word of God. This was the area where the rebellion was cast down to according to Jeremiah 4:23–26.

So the plan and design of God was formulated without the knowledge of any of those who rebelled. More importantly, however, is that the beings that were created were created under the authority of Jesus. He exhibited this authority continually throughout the Gospels. Since He was able to express His complete authority over every principality, power, ruler, and throne, it is vital to understand that this dominion has not been relinquished by any man who has received Christ. Paul said it was so in Colossians 1:27.

> To whom God would make known what is the riches of the glory of this mystery among the Gentiles; which is Christ in you, the hope of glory. (KJV)

This is the Word of God is in us! He is personal to us! He is the Creator of a new spirit that is made the righteousness of God for us!

Let's look at another piece of scripture that defines Him as Creator.

> God, who at sundry times and in divers manners spake in time past unto the fathers by the prophets, hath in these last days spoken unto us by his Son, whom he hath appointed heir of all things, by whom also he made the worlds. (Hebrews 1:1–2 KJV)

I want you to notice how the writer communicates verse 2.

1. He has spoken to us by His Son. This is the role of the Word of God. We identify this from the text beginning in Genesis 1. It is with this speaking in Genesis 1 that time, space, and place took form to become the universe that now exists.
2. The Word of God has authority over all worlds. God has made Him the heir to everything that is created, which is what Paul related in Colossians 1.
3. He made the world. Here is a reference to the world that initially was made for Lucifer and his angels. This world had to be reconstructed after Lucifer's rebellion. After the war between Michael and Lucifer and their angels, God purged heaven and cast Lucifer and one-third of the angels into this domain. This casting down caused darkness and destruction to become so prevalent that the earth lost its form and became void according to Genesis 1:2. The difference now between the heavenly world over which the Godhead held authority and the span in which the rebellion was placed was that there was no source of time or reference to structure. Therefore, the Bible refers to Satan as the prince of the power of the air.

> Wherein in time past ye walked according to the course of this world, *according to the prince of the*

> *power of the air*, the spirit that now worketh in the children of disobedience. (Ephesians 2:2 KJV)

Then, of course, after the time lapse between Genesis 1:1–2 and the second sentence of Genesis 1:2 includes the Spirit of God's action upon the waters. Now, Genesis 1:3 is enacted to be the beginning of the first day when light came into visibility. This is the calling into being again of the structure that we refer to when we reference the world created in the beginning. That world was created with time, place, and structure. Again, verse 3 is the reconstructed earth that was made to include mankind.

So the world prior to Genesis 1:1–2 and the world that includes Genesis 1:2–3 and the rest of the story of creation are those both created by the Word of God and those in which the Word of God has absolute and complete authority! Praise God for this insight! We can know that in everything, if we develop and maintain Christ in us, then His authority which is in us will give us what Jesus promised. We are more than overcomers in Christ Jesus.

Consider John 16:33.

> These things I have spoken unto you, that in me ye might have peace. In the world ye shall have tribulation: but be of good cheer; I have overcome the world. (KJV)

He brought the authority of heaven to earth! He, by grace through faith, indwells man's spirit. He speaks peace to our inner man. What does He say?

> Be of good cheer, greater is he that is in you than he that is in the world!

Glory to God! I am a joint heir with the Creator of the universe, and He resides in me. Peace belongs to me, and the Creator of me said so!

> Nay, in all these things we are more than conquerors through him that loved us. (Romans 8:37)

In whatever situation I find myself, I have Him! I have His words, I have his peace, I have his cheerful attitude, and I possess His dynamic authority over His own creation! I am God's man! Why? Simply because He loved me! I am more than a conqueror because I did not have to fight in the war for my own soul. I did not have to go to the cross and die for my right to be connected to the Creator God.

All I had to do was to believe on the Son of God, and by grace through faith, He has saved me and reconnected me to Himself! I am more than an overcomer because of what Jesus did for me in the nine works that surround the message of the cross.

1. What He did for me in the garden
2. What He did for me on the cross
3. What He did for me in the utter most parts of the earth
4. What He did for me in the resurrection
5. What He did for me when He showed Himself among men
6. What He did for me in the ascension
7. What He did for me by being seated
8. What He did for me by sending the Holy Spirit into the earth for my benefit
9. What He does for me as the High Priest over His own sacrifice

All nine of these are why I am more than an overcomer.

1. I did not bleed for my will to break; He did it for me, and now my will can be His will.
2. I did not physically die upon the cross, but my spirit man can be crucified with Christ and my body can be brought under subjection to the finished work of the cross.
3. I did not go into the region of the damned to retrieve the keys of death and hell; He did and, therefore, I am no lon-

ger held captive by the spiritual death and the condemnation of hell.
4. I was not the first fruits of the resurrection, but because He was, and I believe in him, the grave has no sting for me, and I will be called from its clutches just as He was.
5. I was not there when He walked among men and they saw Him physically, ate with him, and handled him, but Paul says that He is in me and is my hope of glory due to my belief in the cross.
6. I did not see Him ascend into the Shekinah glory of God that Luke referred to as a cloud, but His ascension and my faith allows me to be accepted in the beloved and given entrance into the throne room of God.
7. I was not there when He sat down, but His seating gives me an advocate with the Father. It gives me a mediator and an intercessor. Further, His presence there assures me that I will always locate help from Him in time of need.
8. I was not there when He promised the Holy Spirit. Nor was I there when He sent, from the portals of glory the Holy Spirit into the earth, but I heard Him say to the disciples that those who believe because of their words are blessed. Then I heard the Holy Spirit preached and taught by the apostles that any man could be filled with the Comforter and live life under His direction. I heard, I saw, and I received, and I have never been the same.
9. I am not in the Tabernacle in the Holy of Holies to see it, but I know that He is overseeing my sacrifice just as the priest did in the Tabernacle in the wilderness. I am satisfied with the fact that what He is doing on my behalf is totally accepted by the Father, and that makes me a totally accepted child of God from heaven's point of view!

So the cross has made me more than I ever dreamed in the spiritual world. It has provided me more access, more authority, more power, more presence, and more blessings than I could have ever imagined when the sinner that I was found the grace that He is! I am an overcomer in the greatest way.

> Ye are of God, little children, and have overcome them: because greater is he that is in you, than he that is in the world. (1 John 4:4)

So the Word, who is the Creator, created for me the nine works of the cross. Those created works provide for me a new spirit of wisdom, revelation, and knowledge that can only come through Jesus Christ.

> That the God of our Lord Jesus Christ, the Father of Glory, may give unto you the spirit of wisdom and revelation in the knowledge of him: the eyes of your understanding being enlightened; that ye may know what is the hope of his calling, and what the riches of the glory of his inheritance in the saints. (Ephesians 1:17–18 KJV)

My eyes become open to what He has both called and designed for me to be. There are great riches in what He has called, designed, and died for me to be! These works become the glorious inheritance for every saint of God. These are the promises of the cross that I may, in fact, know! I may know what He has done for me and that I may through the spirit see it clearly. I may live in my glorious inheritance, and from the moment I receive Jesus, my eternal existence begins! This means my eternal prosperity and inheritance is usable and spendable today because of the nine works of the cross!

John addresses this further in verse 10.

> He was in the world, and the world was made by him [Creator], and the world knew him not. (Verse 10 KJV)

Now, John, the writer of this gospel, again recognizes Him as the eternal Creator. But it is the second portion of the scripture that catches my eye.

The world knew him not!

What a sad indictment on the state of confusion that man was in. That comment drags itself into view in the world in which we now live.

Look at our world and its chaotic atmosphere. We have so many different religious ideas. We believe everything to nothing in our current culture. We see God through so many different lenses that the message is at best garbled. It is a sad condition when a man who had never seen Him and really had very little to go on could so easily identify both the truth and the life that was Jesus Christ. With all the revelation of the Bible, with all the revelation of history, and with all the revelation through various print mediums, we still fail to identify the two elements John saw. He was Truth, and He was Light. We also fail to identify the ten revelations that the writer of the Gospel of John gave us.

The Revelation of the Life in Jesus

I was saved at a young age and preached a youth service for my Southern Baptist church at sixteen. I appeared to have this Christian thing down pat. It was a road and a journey that I had been well taught by my mother, whom I loved and respected greatly. She was a disciplinarian when necessary but generally loving and levelheaded. If I was under her watch, I could hold it together quite well. When I went off to college, however, that became another story. The surroundings and the activities of those I encountered were very different than the bubble in which I grew up. I just wanted to be one of the guys and fit into my new surroundings. I found myself participating in things that were not good for me but growing to enjoy the atmosphere.

  I began to spiral out of control. It continued until the relationship and comfort that I had found with God as a youth was not on the radar. I had given away the peace and control that I had found in Christ and the guidance of my mother for a life of immediate pleasure. Now, I do not desire to converse over doctrine. I can only tell you that for me, I felt alive only when I was interacting with the crowd after dark. My flesh was in total control of where I went and with whom I went. If this is the life of a saved creature of God, and one ready to meet the Master in the sky, then God is most lenient and forgiving of those who are not asking. Every man must determine the risk of his behaviors based upon the theology that he or she has been taught. I knew better! The enemy of my soul was in an all-out attempt to destroy my life before I could be developed into the person God had called me to be. I was in a backslidden condition, and when I would have time to think about what I was doing, right there in the middle of the pig pen, I knew it. I guess the risk and chance that one takes based upon his interpretation of God and how he perceives the Gospel must be a personal one. For me, I knew better!

During the summer of 1976, I had quite a time. I had learned to be quite a party animal, thanks to my dear friends. It was all fun and games. We drank, stayed up until all hours of the night, and generally called ourselves having a "good" time. After an all-night party, my friend and I did not report for work. We had spent that summer with the Bartlett Tree Company spraying right of ways with a chemical that killed basically everything in its path. The crew boss found us somewhat unresponsive when he came to our house to see why we did not show up for work. We were relieved of our jobs and were in no real condition to care.

This led me to the final week of the summer. Knowing that without a job and without a college to attend in December, I would have to be going home. My parents had moved to Ohio. Lord knows had they been in North Carolina, there would have been no such behavior. My mom is just under five feet tall and just over one hundred pounds. The most unusual thing about her is that before there was a stretch man who could reach you from anywhere, or a Spider Man who could catch you and hold you in his web, there was Erma Springston! My behavior, so I thought was executed with the greatest of stealth to not allow her to know. She loved us dearly. But she was not up for any mess! I grew to appreciate her as I got older. Not so much as a young fellow.

So a week of transitional behavior culminated in my packing up and heading for Ohio. I'm not exactly sure how I did it, but at some point, I wound up in Danville, Virginia. Nearly out of gas, I stopped at a roadside station. I had become a chain-smoker, as well as the other issues that accompany being a party person. I really enjoyed the smell of a cigarette.

I guess I had driven the 126 miles very unaware of my surroundings. But when I arrived at this gas station that was located on the banks of the Dan River, the foliage was so green and beautiful on either side of the river. It was really the first thing that had struck me with such intensity in a long time. I commented such to everyone that was around the pumps. After filling up, I got back in the car and moved forward with the trip to Belpre, Ohio. Within a few minutes, something happened that was the beginning of a journey that has brought me to writing this book.

As I rode down the highway with the window down and the breeze coming through the window, something miraculous happened. I was quiet and alone. I believe I had reached a state of normal conscientiousness when in front of my eyes, I stopped seeing the road. There appeared to me a ticker tape. It streamed across the window in front of me. This is what it said,

> For God so loved the world that he sent his only begotten Son that whosoever believeth in me shouldn't perish but have everlasting life. (John 3:16 KJV)

It startled me! I said, "What? That isn't true. If it were, I would not be in the condition I am, and I surely would not have done the things that you know I have done! I don't believe that!"

A second time I heard the ticker tape as it reappeared before my eyes. Here again is what it read:

> For God so loved the world that he sent his only begotten Son that whosoever believeth in me shouldn't perish but have everlasting life. (John 3:16 KJV)

Again, I began to argue and vehemently disagree with what I was seeing. "If You really loved me, the things that I have done, You would have not allowed me to do. How can You love me? I have hurt myself and others. Why would You love me?"

Then a most amazing thing happened. The ticker tape appeared again, but this time it had something included in it that let me know that God knew me. He knew where I was, and He knew precisely what I had been involved in. But He loved me more than I loved myself.

> For God so loved the world that he sent his only begotten Son that if Mike would believe in me shouldn't perish but have everlasting life.

There it was. I was personally included in John 3:16. I repented of my sin immediately! I repented of my disobedience, my unfaithfulness, and my rebelliousness. I wept tears that purged my soul and my flesh for the next four or more hours. I discarded my cigarettes and was delivered from the addictions that had overtaken my life.

My spirit had been quickened and come alive within me! Later in life, I found this scripture. In my mind's eye, it had my picture posted on it. Why? Because it was absolutely the story of where I was when the grace of God found me.

> And you hath he quickened, who were dead in trespasses and sins; wherein in time past ye walked according to the course of this world, according to the prince of the power of the air, the spirit that now worketh in the children of disobedience among whom also we all had our conversation in times past in the lusts of our flesh, fulfilling the desires of the flesh and of the mind; and were by nature the children of wrath, even as others. But God, who is rich in mercy, for his great love wherewith he loved us, even when we were dead in sins, hath quickened us together with Christ [by grace ye are saved]. (Ephesians 2:1–5 KJV)

I was alive, and Jesus knew my name. That, my friend, is great news!

Can anyone doubt the fact that there is life in Jesus Christ? Any man that has ever experienced the cleansing of their sin can attest to the new life that exists in Christ Jesus. This new life, which we identify as the new birth, is one that connects us to our Creator. It does so to such an extent that the eternal, personal Creator begins to transform us from the inside out. What an awesome revelation of Jesus. He cleanses us by the life that is in Him, and we begin to take on the nature of life. Love, joy, peace, longsuffering, gentleness, goodness, temperance, meekness, and faith become the model for living.

Further, there is no law that can supersede or overcome the truth that is present in this life. What a glorious position from which to live for every believer!

> In him was life. (John 1:4 KJV)

In the Word of God was the power and authority to speak, and for that Word to put the Holy Spirit into action. This action is the process that caused the world to be formed.

> And the earth was without form, and void; and darkness was upon the face of the deep. And the Spirit of God moved upon the face of the waters. And God said, let there be light: and there was light. (Genesis 1:2–3 KJV)

Here the procedural plan was explained. The Word of God spoke, and it was. This process extended throughout the creation for a six-day period until the following was established and in place:

1. The face of the deep was filled with light.
2. A division of light and darkness occurred.
3. The firmament was created.
4. Land was divided from the waters.
5. Vegetation was placed upon the land.
6. The division of day and night.
7. Life was placed in the waters.
8. Life in the air was created.
9. Life in the earth was created.
10. Life in the form of man was created, male and female.

11. Man was given dominion over all the life that was created, regardless of what form that life presented itself

So it is rather obvious that the Word of God had power within the grasp of His words to create. More importantly, the Holy Spirit had complete understanding of the structure in which life would be developed. He (the Holy Spirit) did not miss the mark on any of the created beings of which Jesus spoke. The Holy Spirit clearly saw and made the express image of the beings of which the Word of God spoke. So it is no surprise that when Paul described Jesus in Romans 8 that he described him as the Spirit of Life!

> For the law of the *Spirit of life in Christ Jesus* hath made me free from the law of sin and death. (Romans 8:2 KJV)

He is the one who quickens mankind and brings life into their spirit man. Jesus Christ, the spirit of life, has reconnected the spirit of man back to his original status. We are alive because of what He has done. He is the life-giver!

> Jesus saith unto him, I am the way, the truth, and the life: no man cometh unto the Father, but by me. (John 14:6 KJV)

It is only through his life-giving measure that a man can come to spiritual life. Paul said in Ephesians 2:1,

> And you who were once dead hath he quickened, who were dead in trespasses and sins; wherein in time past ye walked according to the course of this world, according to the prince of the power of the air, the spirit that now worketh in the children of disobedience. (Ephesians 2:1 KJV)

The word *quickened* in the Greek means "to make alive, give life, preserve, recover, and repair." This is what Jesus did for mankind in general, including you and me.

1. He made our spirit man alive through the acceptance of the blood and the body of His sacrifice.
2. He made us alive because of His resurrection from the dead.

Please notice this: We who were once dead in trespasses and sins walked after the course of the world. Do you see that? What was the course of the world? It was the direction that Adam caused our relationship with God to go after the fall in Genesis 3. Man was relegated to a world where his spirit was dead to God. Man was eternally separated from the God who had created him.

Think on this. God chose to reenter the arena of men through the children of Israel. Have you ever considered the personality of the Jews as a whole? Do they resemble the relationship that Adam had to God in the garden? The answer is unequivocally no! They were stiff-necked, hardheaded, and rebellious people. This was so, even though their Creator was attempting to help them and lead them into a land and place for their own well-being. Why was their behavior, opinions, and ideas so far removed from the behavior and work of Adam? The answer is clear. Their spirit man was dead! They lived their lives covered with sin and with trespass.

The purpose of God for dealing with the Jews was because of the prophecy delivered in Genesis chapter 3 to the serpent.

> And I will put enmity between thee and the woman, and between thy seed and her seed; it shall bruise thy head, and thou shalt bruise his heel. (Genesis 3:15–16 KJV)

Can you see that life is being produced in this scripture? The woman that was created by God, was from her own disobedience going to be used by God, to solve a problem which she had played a major role in creating. It would not be easy; it would not come without much pain; it would not come without her being placed under the leadership of a husband, and it would not happen without the seed of a man, but it would happen. When it did, it would conclude the reign of death and terror of which Satan had held men captive! The woman would produce from a seed the one that would bruise the head of the serpent. The serpent would be able to bruise his heel, which was the death of the cross.

Can I take this prophecy one step further? In Habakkuk chapter 3 verse 13, we read,

> Thou wentest forth for the salvation of thy people, even for salvation with thine anointed; thou woundedst the head out of the house of the wicked, by discovering the foundation unto the neck. Selah. (Habakkuk 3:13 KJV)

This refers to Jesus and is directly related to the prophecy in Genesis 3. The word *salvation* in the Hebrew is translated "Yeshua"! So this verse is directly related to Jesus and the work that He would accomplish concerning how He would deal with Satan. Jesus would do two indisputable acts to the head of the house of the wicked.

1. He would wound His head.
2. He would discover or uncover the root of every evil act, torment, and piece of the cause for the separation between God and man.
3. He would leave absolutely none of it to ever again lord over His people, from the foundation of the works of which He has done to mankind, through the neck of Him who had devised such atrocities upon man.

In Deuteronomy chapter 7 and verse 6, we read,

> For thou art an holy people unto the LORD thy God: the LORD thy God hath chosen thee to be a special people unto himself, above all people that

are upon the face of the earth. (Deuteronomy 7:6 KJV)

These words, of course, are being spoken by the Spirit from the Word of God. He defines the children of Israel as He sees them.

1. They are in His eyes a holy people because they are the ones He has chosen to be called holy.
2. They are holy unto the Lord. This declares how God saw them, not how their actions and deeds expressed their nature.
3. They were such because God had chosen them for His purpose.
4. They were considered as a special people unto Him because they would eventually serve the purpose of bringing in the Son and crucifying the Lamb.
5. Again, this is God's declaration of them as He viewed them. It did not and does not account for their human nature that was tainted by the fall, just as it had been for every people and every man. It strictly identified what God saw in them, what God saw come from them, and how God designed the eternal plan and purpose of God to happen due to them.

He would come through Israel. He would be a given life through a virgin from Israel. He would then give life to the world because of Israel's lack of understanding concerning who the Messiah was and how He would present Himself.

Now, let's look at how He describes Himself in John 14:6.

> Jesus saith unto him, I am the way, the truth, and the life: no man cometh unto the Father, but by me. (John 14:6 KJV)

Here He defines Himself as the way. The hearer would have recognized this statement as referring to the entrance into the outer court of the Tabernacle. The entrance was the Way, and it was the only way to approach God. He is also the Truth. Again, they would have recognized this as it refers to the opening in the tent that allowed them to enter the tent of blessing. In the Truth was the Holy Spirit, Jesus, and the worship of Jehovah God. Then He refers to Himself as life. Here they would have also recognized this expression, as they knew that inside the veil was the God that provides life for the blessing and satisfaction of Israel.

He was life to the people. He was the sweet smell of His presence to the people, and He was the power that was expressed by His people when they encountered any obstacle. Then He declares that no man can approach God unless they come by Him! He was the only method under heaven's economy whereby any man could ever again find his life. What does this mean? Man's spirit could never again flourish, except it be born again by the life-giver. Man could never again be able to spiritually approach God, unless His Spirit be translated by the Lamb of God. Man could never again be in any relationship, short term or otherwise, unless it began with a belief in the Alpha and Omega.

> The thief cometh not, but for to steal, and to kill, and to destroy: I am come that they might have life, and that they might have it more abundantly. (John 10:10 KJV)

In John 10:10, Jesus now identifies the depth of the reason He had to come to fulfill the prophecy of Genesis 3. He identifies the need for a life-giver. Now, notice life was ongoing, and He was speaking to real people when He makes this statement. So He is not referring to having more children through natural means.

He is here describing what the thief had done to the spirits of men. He had stolen the spiritual birthright of all men. The intention was to kill man for eternity and to destroy the work, plan, and design of God. Jesus here tells us precisely the reason for His coming. I Am has come that the people who are covered in darkness might not only see a light but be translated by that light into the kingdom of life!

The life which He offers is a life of abundance! It is abundance in the spiritual realm.

It is projecting the following from your spirit:

1. Love
2. Joy
3. Peace
4. Gentleness
5. Meekness
6. Kindness
7. Goodness
8. Temperance
9. Faith

Man would be transformed by being quickened or made alive into a new life, with a new attitude and new behaviors that are driven by a spirit that is in tune with the Word of God!

Man in the spirit world would be brought back to the relationship that Adam held in the garden. Along with this reinstated relationship would bring a reinstitution of the spiritual relationship of man to God. The authority, power, and dominion of the original work would be reestablished in the latter work!

> I am that bread of life. (John 6:48 KJV)

Now, how would man continue to operate in the blessing, dominion, and power that his new birth relationship has afforded him? Jesus tells us how in John 6:48. Continue to eat the bread of life. Continue to seek, meditate upon, and walk with the spirit of life that is in Christ Jesus! He is the food that will produce a spirit and a nature that is like His. Paul in Romans 8:29 states it this way:

> For whom he did foreknow, he also did predestinate to be conformed to the image of his Son, that he might be the firstborn among many brethren. (Romans 8:29 KJV)

So we are expected to conform to the image of Christ. We are expected to have His projection exuding from our being. The only method for us to accomplish such a dynamic life and lifestyle is to be brought to life by His Spirit in our inner man!

> For the bread of God is that which comes down out of heaven and gives life to the world. (John 6:33 KJV)

He is the means God has provided for our salvation. and our life. So when we see Him as the salvation of God, we see the following:

1. He has *saved* us, so He is our life-giver!
2. He has *preserved* us, so He is our salt and keeper!
3. He has made us *safe* in him, so He is our haven of rest!
4. He has *healed* us, so He has carried our infirmity!
5. He has delivered us, so He is our champion!

> I am the living bread that came down out of heaven; if anyone eats of this bread, he will live forever; and the bread also which I will give for the life of the world is my flesh. (John 6:51 KJV)

If any man eats, he will live forever! When does forever begin? When a man accepts Jesus? Does it begin when we finish our race here on earth and die? Does it begin when the trumpet sounds and we go to be with the Lord?

For every person that accepts Jesus Christ and who is translated and transformed in their spirit to know Jesus, their eternal quality of life begins immediately. Your eternity and the promises of the Salvation of God begin that moment. Why then do we struggle? Why then are there trials? Why then do I sometimes fail?

The answer to those questions could be any one of the following:

1. The Lord is developing you and working in you the great hope of glory.

2. You are being engaged in the process of going from childhood to adulthood through the education of trials and struggles.
3. The failures that you incur are opportunities for you to experience healing, forgiveness, and the love of God.
4. There is a need for growth in the Word so that you can experience a deeper knowledge of the Word of God so that in the future you can overcome temptation by His prescribed means of escape.
5. There is a chastisement that every child must go through to navigate life with a greater understanding about how to represent the truth and become the witness you were called to be.
6. There are many reasons that could be listed in this section. Here is a truth that we must reconcile ourselves to, and it comes from Paul's writings.

> Wherefore, my beloved, as ye have always obeyed, not as in my presence only, but now much more in my absence, work out your own salvation with fear and trembling. (Philippians 2:12 KJV)

We must spend time with our new life. We must make this life a priority. We must identify where, what, and how we need to grow and place full purpose and intention upon doing so. This salvation is designed for us to be relational, personal, purposeful, and intentional as we develop in the life-giving Word of God!

So every new Christian may be purposing his new life on a foundation that is unscriptural and prepares conditions for future failure. In most instances, the first thing he does is go back to the church to begin his Christian life. They offer themselves to do anything and everything needed. They are so excited with their new-found relationship that they desire the involvement with the saints and the work of the ministry. This is a trick of Satan, because instead of sitting at the feet of Jesus and learning His Word, His ways, and His desire for us, they find themselves busy ministering to and in

His house! In all this, they think they are doing something for God and being spiritual, when what Jesus wants is for us to be like Mary and sit at his feet and learn of Him. All in all, I can see how this happens, because the church has very little to offer in instruction to the new Christian, Bible studies, and preaching that will help him/her to learn how to be a spiritual success. Therefore, they think it is in their works. We elevate a "belong to believe" message that encourages the newborn to get busy in the church. The outcome is that their faith is built upon what they can do that represents their new life. This structure, no doubt, is the reason so many fall by the wayside! They have no legitimate foundation on which to develop the thing that God is pleased with—their faith.

We are aware of the physical ability to work. That is generally a position that is available to every man. We also know about those who place their relationship to God on such a shaky foundation that they do not grow and mature into strong Christians. Therefore, their lives are subject to the turmoil and troubles of life that often lead them away from the same relationship that they were once so excited about. We must grow our newborn under the same premise that Jesus did. Sit, listen, and learn the fundamentals of the truths of the Gospel. Develop your faith on the tenants of life. Then locate your ministry from a position of understanding. This will create longevity for the individual. This is not so because I said it was so; it is so because Jesus worked it that way.

The purpose of the life that is in Christ Jesus is to develop and sustain those who come to Him until their earthly life concludes. We cannot discount the personal makeup of people, meaning that we do not know who will be in the 25 percent Jesus referred to in the parable of the sower. There has not been enough time-lapse to develop a serious idea concerning the "belong to believe" theory. Of course, it is possible that this may sustain itself. The outcome solely rests with the individuals and their personal constitution to develop their relationship with Christ and the church.

What is known is that humans do not develop the skills necessary to function in their human life without intense and directed training. This is what the book of Proverbs is all about. We also know that we must be extremely cautious of anything that counterfeits the foundation of the Gospel. Therefore, to function as the Lord did, the ministry should, and must, be looking for ways and avenues to ensure that all new converts be taught at the feet of someone who is providing them with the words of life. That must be our initial and goal. The Gospel and the future of the church depends upon that commitment.

The Revelation of the Light in Jesus

The Word of God is just a story to a person who is listening, but it becomes real to the hearer, when the Word of God is quickened into the spirit of mankind. Then and only then does the man become pregnant with the light of which the Bible speaks.

> The spirit of man is the candle of the LORD, searching all the inward parts of the belly. (Proverbs 20:27 KJV)

This scripture declares the inward relevance of the Spirit of God. It is in one's spirit that the real issues of life are defined. Our spiritual life is the real us. It is here that the battles that we encounter in our outward life are won or lost.

In 1988, I had gone to the State of New Mexico to be a part of the ministry with the Church of God in that area. My job was to travel the state and preach revivals. The state was a desolate place where travel was concerned, but it was beautiful in its own way to look at. I traveled it in every direction conceivable to go to churches where there would be just a few people.

My first revival was to be in Farmington, New Mexico. There I was, walking into a church where the pastor was under pressure. I went for the express purpose of building a revival that would accomplish a few things. First, I was to vet the pastor and get to know him. Second, I was to attempt to build a fire that would last after I was gone. The word is that there is an alternate style of worship in Farmington, and that does not include the Navajo Indian religious practices. So when I went, I really did not know what to expect. The first Friday service there might have been twenty-five people in attendance. That was of no consequence to me.

I had been with the Lord during the four-hour drive to Farmington. I sensed an anointing in my spirit. It was as if I could relate to David's words concerning running through a troop and jumping over a wall. I was super charged on the inside. We had church that night in a big way. The anointing was rich and thick. I preached, and the Spirit of God moved. The next day I spent with the pastor, who was a nice guy. He told me of some experiences that he had been involved with, prior to coming to Christ, that were mind-boggling. His family was beautiful. I found him to be a good fit for the church. Although he could be critical of some things, I felt certain he was going to do a great job. On Saturday, I began to do something that I had not done before. As I would encounter people on the street, I would invite them to church. That Saturday evening, we had basically a full house. The anointing was present. The candle was lit, and the Holy Spirit was flowing in such a great way. People were moved, saved, and lives were changed.

As I went throughout New Mexico, the same experience seemed to follow. The anointing to preach and minister to the people was in every town and in every church. It was fun, and it was exciting. However, I was struggling a little with myself. It was difficult to maintain the pace that I had set and be so far away from everyone I knew and loved. But despite working a full-time job, preaching four services a weekend, and attending the university to complete my master's degree, I kept on going. This is the critical secret. Despite my personal struggles and my workload struggles, somehow my body maintained the strength and stamina to keep going. I now understand that I was sustained and quickened by the light of the Gospel for the work that was required of me to do.

On one occasion, I was asked to be the night speaker at our summer youth camp. It was an honor and a need that I could not turn down. The problem was that I was in summer school in Albuquerque, and the camp was in Alto, New Mexico. I would fly from Albuquerque to Roswell in the afternoon, drive seventy miles or so to the campground, preach the night service, get up at 4:00

AM, drive back to Roswell, get on a plane bound for Albuquerque, attend a 10:00 AM class, and start the cycle over again. Over a five-day period, I made seven plane rides to preach for these young people. The Holy Spirit moved in an awesome way.

I remember standing back and watching the Spirit of God, like a wave, flow over those kids. They worshipped, cried, prayed, and sang praises to the King of Glory. They were often slain in the Spirit by the power of God. It was a wonderfully anointed time for them and for me. Through it all, the light of the Gospel was shining on me. My body was not only sustained, but it was refreshed. Looking back at this time, I do not see how I was able to keep up with myself. Then it becomes very clear to me. When the light of Christ is burning, and the oil of anointing has been prepared meticulously, then the fire can burn continuously just as it had in the Temple.

Matthew 5:14–16 sheds a great light upon this subject if you will allow me to phrase it that way.

> Ye are the light of the world. A city that is set on a hill cannot be hid. Neither do men light a candle, and put it under a bushel, but on a candlestick; and it giveth light unto all that are in the house. Let your light so shine before men, that they may see your good works, and glorify your Father which is in heaven. (Matthew 5:14–16 KJV)

When the calling of God is upon a life, and that man yields himself to that call, the candle of the Lord will burn with an oil and a light that the work itself will not be able to extinguish. The light will shine in darkness, and the darkness will be driven backward. That darkness does not just include the darkness of sin. It includes the darkness that is included in any work associated with the fall of man. So when man lives under the light of Christ and allows it to shine in everything he does, then others will experience it and be brought into the good works of which the light produces. Then those brought in will glorify God with you and the blessings of God will flow. I found out through this revelation that when we think that we are insufficient in ourselves physically or mentally, we need to listen to what was told to Paul.

> For this thing I besought the Lord thrice, that it might depart from me. And he said unto me, my grace is sufficient for thee: for my strength is made perfect in weakness. Most gladly therefore will I rather glory in my infirmities, that the power of Christ may rest upon me. Therefore I take pleasure in infirmities, in reproaches, in necessities, in persecutions, in distresses for Christ's sake: for when I am weak, then am I strong. (2 Corinthians 12:8–10 KJV)

What a great revelation of the strength of the burning candle that lights our path.

Jesus is the Light of the world. He is the Light that exists that supersedes the sun and the moon.

His light is so strong that it can light the entire premises of the heavenly domain. It is also so penetrating that it can light the candle that is in man's spirit. It is so dynamic that it can knock a man from his own horse and blind him for three days. Then that same light can open those blinded eyes so that they can see a completely new path upon which to spend the rest of his life. His light truly is a light unto my path and a lamp unto my feet.

> And the life was the light of men. (John 1:4 KJV)

The most quoted and recognizable scripture concerning light is found in Psalms 119:105.

> Thy word is a lamp unto my feet, and a light unto my path. (Psalms 119:105 KJV)

Here David uses the term *word* as the "things that are spoken." He declares them to be both a lamp and a light. Let's look at the implications of this verse as it relates to how a person successfully navigates the world in which we live.

1. The spoken Word is the object of this verse. We know that the spoken words were under the office of the Word of God, Jesus Christ.
2. Then he begins to speak about what the Word does for him as he goes about living his life.
3. The Word is a lamp for his feet. The Word of God is designed to guard every step that a man takes. The Bible declares this, and we locate the scripture in Psalms 37:23.

> The steps of a good man are ordered by the LORD: and he delighted in his way. (Psalms 37:23 KJV)

Every step that man's feet take in a world that is filled with lawlessness and iniquity can be treacherous and potentially unstable. It is imperative that we understand, use the Word of God, Jesus Christ, and the words which He spoke, to help us to walk in and among an evil world, while being able to live free from a life encumbered by sin.

Paul alluded to what the Word of God would become to a man, who was seeking for help and direction, when he wrote these words in 1 Corinthians 10:13.

> There hath no temptation taken you, but such as is common to man: but God is faithful, who will not suffer you to be tempted above that ye are able; but will with the temptation also make a way to escape, that ye may be able to bear it. (1 Corinthians 10:13 KJV)

Man does not live without a light to brightly identify, not only the correct path to pursue, but also the problems and pitfalls that block the way. The common things, then, become the things Jesus described in John 10:10, concerning how the enemy operates to sidetrack and distract the person who is attempting to connect with God.

> The thief cometh not, but for to steal, and to kill, and to destroy: I am come that they might have life, and that they might have it more abundantly. (John 10:10 KJV)

The thief always comes. He does not leave any person who has a heart for God from being attacked by his devices. You can count on his prompt attention to defeat anyone who names the name of Jesus. So do not be caught off guard when the issues of life appear. Jesus said they would. He also described many who, when problems came, fell by the wayside and discontinued their pursuit of the Word. He is coming to block your spiritual life, by intervening in the area where man is vulnerable. What is that area? There are two of them in the tripart man that can fall under the scrutiny of the enemy. These two are the areas in man, where man is not only vulnerable, but due to his nature, bent to follow ideas and desires that seem to be satisfactory to his wants.

These two areas are the flesh and the soul. The flesh is identified here first, because it is here that man falters first. The soul then cosigns with the flesh. When these two team up, the spirit of man is overshadowed. This is precisely what occurred in the Garden of Eden when Eve used her flesh to make determinations concerning her future. I think we all are aware of the devastating results of her fleshly decisions. So be aware! Be ready and expect him to show up. You may not know when or how, but if you know He is coming, you can prepare yourself with the light, Jesus Christ. You can prepare yourself with the armor of God. When you do, Paul declares some awesome news for us in Ephesians 6:10–11.

> Finally, my brethren, be strong in the Lord, and in the power of his might. Put on the whole armor of God, that ye may be able to stand against the wiles of the devil. (Ephesians 6:10–11 KJV)

I can, by prior proper preparation, prevent poor performance! I can make myself strong in the Lord. I can make myself strong in His ability! I can stand and withstand the wiles or the inroads the devil may attempt to make into my mind and my flesh! My expectation of the attack determines my ability to remain alert. My prior preparation then established the confidence required to face the attack. Lastly, my recognition of the attack is my ability to know what to use to fearlessly defeat the attack and the attacker. There is no question that the way has been made. The light had been shed abroad in the heart of every man to be able to stand and withstand the attacks of the devil!

1. He comes to steal! What is he attempting to steal from the believer? Some would say that he is attempting to steal the Word that has been heard by you. That would be true, as it is the Word that brings faith, according to Paul's writing. This faith, when applied to grace, is how you got saved. So there is truth in this statement.

But it goes much deeper than this for the devil. His goal is to steal the spiritual connection that has been quickened on the inside of you. That is how this whole mess got started to begin with. Someone would inquire as to why trials and troubles seem to persist. Why do some seem to have more than others? Well, the answer is clear. Trouble persists due to the ultimate vision of the enemy for mankind. He desires to again cause man's death within his spirit. He wants man to eternally fail. So his plan is for constant and continued trouble for all men.

Then why do some seem to have more than others? The answer to that, I think, is found by examining the life of those in trouble. They probably have not come to the conclusion of what Jesus has given them. They remain encumbered by the flesh, and therefore, although they are saved, they struggle with the nature of sin. The enemy knows the words of God. He is also aware of those that do not possess the words of God within their spiritual makeup. Those people, who have a weakened defense structure, then become vulnerable to the consistent attack of the enemy. Jesus taught us concerning this in Matthew 13:3–9.

> And he spake many things unto them in parables, saying, behold, a sower went forth to sow; and when he sowed, some seeds fell by the way side, and the fowls came and devoured them up: some fell upon stony places, where they had not much earth: and forthwith they sprung up, because they had no deepness of earth: and when the sun was up, they were scorched; and because they had no root, they withered away. And some fell among thorns; and the thorns sprung up, and choked them: but other fell into good ground, and brought forth fruit, some an hundredfold, some sixtyfold, some thirtyfold. Who hath ears to hear, let him hear. (Matthew 13:3–9 KJV)

The seed was devoured by the one who was searching for the very thing that the broadcaster was sowing. This is the plan of the enemy. He is searching to steal away the thing sowed in a man's life. The fowl does it quickly and seamlessly, because that is what he is designed to do. Then the seed was fallen into places with no depth to receive it. This resulted in no possibility for growth. The seed died prior to having any hope of living. Why? There was nothing to grow in. There was no water, pressure, and temperature to cause the seed to germinate. Is this not precisely how the enemy functions? He will take a person out of the group that supports them, get them encountering shallow people, and then cut them off from the foundation from which they need to flourish.

This group saw the light, but the lack of depth caused them to be scorched. This tells me, when I relate this to people, that people choose not to hear the words of God and to allow the words of God to legitimately change their lives. The words of God scorched their lifestyles, and they decided there must be a more convenient way for them to live. Possibly, there is a way without standards, expectations of personal control, no necessity for assembly, and no need to study the Word of God and the words of God.

Then, the third group was the group that was in a place where they were so entangled with their environment that they had absolutely no chance to develop. Jesus said they were choked off by the thorns among which they had fallen. This says to me that they attempted to maintain the so-called friends and acquaintances they had been with, even after they were given the seed.

Can you see that the enemy knows where the seed is falling? He knows to whom the seed is being given. This represents the exact insight that he had in the garden. You know the story. The warning was given to Adam, not Eve. The warning concerning spiritual death was shared with Adam. Eve was a part of the equation and knew the command, but it was as a seed to her. The enemy crawled in and reared his head with a means to steal the seed. She entertained the conversation and included Adam in the conversation with respect to eating the fruit, and the seed was captured from them by an adversary, whose intention it was to steal their spirit man from them.

As we know, they did not physically die. But something very real occurred to them. They found themselves naked and hiding from the God, who earlier had been their friend and companion. Without the seed, they were not in relation to God. Without the seed, they found themselves totally undone. Without the seed, they were no longer fit to be under the protection of the Garden of Eden and God's care. Naked, exposed, and destitute of the internal mechanism to relate to God, they had to be removed from the protection of God. This removal then placed them under the watchful eye of an enemy, who meant them eternal harm and eternal damnation. As you can see, when Jesus identified Satan as a thief whose role it is to steal, He had firsthand knowledge from which to speak.

Of course, there is the fourth portion of the seed that fell on good ground. Let's look at what happened to that seed.

1. It became concealed in the ground so that the fowl of the air could not see it and get to it.
2. It fell into good soil so that it could receive the nourishment the soil provides. It could receive the gentle application of pressure. It could be maintained in a constant state

of temperature that made it comfortable. It received the correct amount of water so that its outer shell could not be broken down.

3. Then once it began to grow and come into itself, it received the light that was filled with the nutrients devised for the seed to become exactly what it was designed to be. What an awesome process.

This all identifies the process that God designed for man's spiritual growth.

A. Find a church and a church family that will give you a place to hear about Jesus and love you while you grow.
B. Get in there and learn the Word, learn how to be faithful to your church. Receive the nurturing of praise and worship and prayer from a people that are caring for you. Become an active worker in your church. Then learn how to crucify yourself and to bring your body under subjection to the cross.
C. Those that were to be referred to as falling on good ground bore tremendous fruit. Why? Because they chased the light! They were the ones who avoided the pitfalls that were present when they were planted. They dug in for the long haul, and when they came forth, what they were to accomplish was an awesome thing. Some a hundredfold, some sixtyfold, and some thirtyfold, but all of them were able to become what they were designed to be.

What a revelation for us! If we go to the correct place, for the correct reason, associate ourselves with the correct people, receive the correct instruction, and stay in there until it's time for us to break forth, the blessings for us will flow from us. Then everyone who partakes of what we produce will be blessed to over flowing! Not to mention the satisfaction that comes from knowing that we were able to do what we were designed by God to do!

4. The thief comes to kill. We have established that he comes to kill the spirit of man. But he also comes to bring man into eternal condemnation.

We often forget that this entire message of the cross is about the eternity that man will inevitably enter. Every man is an eternal being. Sometimes I think that this message is lost to those who refuse the message of the Gospel of Jesus Christ. Man will live eternally in the presence of God, or he will live eternally in the region of the damned. There is no doubt that the Bible teaches this fact. This is what the enemy of our soul is attempting to ensure, that the creation that God made is corrupted by the effects of the fall, and thereby, separated from God, when the time for eternal evaluation occurs.

Satan's anger at God for being cast down from heaven and his desire to be God have dictated his pursuit of the destruction of mankind. There is no other way that he can devise a kingdom for himself, except through the nature of fallen man.

5. And to destroy.

The thief's role is to eliminate all things that pertain to God, that is or could be present in a person's life.

Let's look at his declaration in Isaiah 14:13–22 to see the goal of Lucifer and his ultimate outcome in the economy of God.

> How art thou fallen from heaven, O Lucifer, Son of the morning! How art thou cut down to the ground, which didst weaken the nations!
>
> How did you do this despicable deed? Why would you have chosen to revolt against your creator? For what purpose would you have been unsatisfied with the position which you were created? Look at what your ambition has cost you. Look at where your personal desires have taken you. Your treasonous decision has caused harm to the nations, as you now will attempt to over-

throw the harmony of the universe. For thou hast said in thine heart, I will ascend into heaven, I will exalt my throne above the stars of God: I will sit also upon the mount of the congregation, in the sides of the north. (Isaiah 14:13–22 KJV)

The problem with Lucifer began in his spirit. It was a matter of his personal ambition that gripped his spirit and translated those desires into an action that were totally out of harmony and unity with his Creator. Due to his looks and his abilities that were provided to him by the nature of his creation, he deemed himself to be powerful, have leadership ability, and no doubt, he felt that his musical ability would soften the resistance of those who already were under his command. So exaltation of a higher dimension than heaven had been exposed to was devised in his spirit. His intention was the destruction of the heavenly economy as it had been designed by God.

The only way in which he could accomplish this destruction was by total mutiny within the ranks. His plan was to tear down the standard of righteousness that was the bastion of heavenly behavior, heavenly demeanor, and heavenly character. The elimination of the environment of righteousness meant the usurping of power from the hands of the Godhead. The destruction of righteousness then brought an exaltation of evil that exceeded the position of the current heavenly structure. He would be greater, bigger, and in total control when he reached the pinnacle beyond the stars of God!

I will ascend above the heights of the clouds; I will be like the most high… (KJV)

The concept continues as Lucifer declares his intentions to ascend above the location of the current place of God, to heights above his created space. Then Lucifer declares,

I will be like the most high. (KJV)

Here, we must stop and examine the language used to describe these comments that ultimately caused him to be expelled from heaven. "I will be like the Most High God." These words explain to me the real feelings that Lucifer must have possessed concerning God. First, he knew he was a created being with no creative power. Second, he knew that his ability only extended to his personal characteristics which God had designed in him. Third, he knew that even with the elevation of status, the best he could do is to be like God. He could never be God because he did not possess the creative requirements to hold that position.

So the concept was to elevate himself. He desired to sit in a position that was above the structure that God had made and make himself to hold the power over those who followed willingly and those who would do war against him. Then he would declare himself God by sitting upon the higher throne and exalting himself to a status like the Most High God. His ultimate ending was to destroy the structure of God, destroy the economy of God, destroy righteousness as the standard of heaven, and make the Creator subject to the created.

Paul addressed this very issue in Romans 1:24–25.

> Wherefore God also gave them up to uncleanness through the lusts of their own hearts, to dishonor their own bodies between themselves: who changed the truth of God into a lie and worshipped and served the creature more than the creator, who is blessed for ever. Amen. (Romans 1:24–25 KJV)

This well defines the purpose, plan, and goal of Lucifer as his spirit's intentions became known in the heavenly realm.

So Satan's plan was to be a thief and steal heaven. It was to kill and destroy everything that God stood for and to exalt himself to the position and place of God. God, knowing the thoughts and intentions that were in the spirit of every created being, dealt with him and did so swiftly. When looking into the writings of Isaiah concerning the history of this incident, we easily recognize the outcome of his rebellion. The following verses clearly describe the precision with which God dealt with him and his cohorts.

> But yet thou shalt be brought down to hell, to the sides of the pit. They that see thee shall narrowly look upon thee, and consider thee, saying, is this the man that made the earth to tremble, that did shake kingdoms; that made the world as a wilderness, and destroyed the cities thereof; that opened not the house of his prisoners? All the kings of the nations, even all of them, lie in glory, everyone in his own house. But thou art cast out of thy grave like an abominable branch, and as the raiment of those that are slain, thrust through with a sword, that go down to the stones of the pit; as a carcase trodden under feet. Thou shalt not be joined with them in burial, because thou hast destroyed thy land, and slain thy people: the seed of evildoers shall never be renowned. Prepare slaughter for his children for the iniquity of their fathers; that they do not rise, nor possess the land, nor fill the face of the world with cities. For I will rise up against them, saith the LORD of hosts, and cut off from Babylon the name, and remnant, and son, and nephew, saith the LORD. (Isaiah 14:15 KJV)

His plan of stealing, death, and destruction culminated in him being sentenced to an eternal position of death and destruction to himself and to everyone who followed him. That curse extends to everyone who continues to follow him after the cross! This left Satan with but one option. Being doomed eternally with no source of recourse, he began to look for a means to disturb God's creation of mankind. He found the weak link in Eve. Eve found another weak link in Adam, and the spirit life of man was, in fact, stolen.

Here is the good news, and it is the second half of John 10:10.

> I am come that they might have life, and that they might have it more abundantly. (John 10:10 KJV)

This statement, in and of itself, discloses the ultimate measures that God used to shut down the destroyer. Jesus—the I Am of heaven and the righteous Son of God—was come to become the Lamb so that we who believe could be redeemed and restored to a life of abundant connection with God. Jesus had revealed Himself to men as life, but He has shone forth as a great light that destroyed darkness. He destroyed the plans that darkness had for our utter destruction.

The revelation of Jesus as the light of the world brought us a restored view of the economy, righteousness, character, and behavior that was associated with heaven. This was nothing new to the heavenly structure, but it was very new to the earthly structure, as man had been disassociated with God from a spiritual perspective since the fall. However, with the advent of the life and the light came a new dawn for the hopes of mankind. There was to be the opportunity for man's spirit to thrive in love, righteousness, and peace. Paul put it very appropriately in Colossians 1:13 when he wrote,

> Who hath delivered us from the power of darkness, and hath translated us into the kingdom of his dear Son: how did he translate us out of the power and grasp of the prince of the power of the air? (Colossians 1:13 KJV)

Isaiah told us,

> The people walking in darkness have seen a great light; on those living in the land of deep darkness, a light has dawned. (Isaiah 9:2 KJV)

Matthew told us,

> The people living in darkness have seen a great light; on those living in the land of the shadow of death a light has dawned. (Matthew 4:16 KJV)

John told us,

> When Jesus spoke again to the people, he said, "I am the light of the world. Whoever follows me will never walk in darkness but will have the light of life." (John 8:12 KJV)

Matthew confirmed Isaiah, John confirmed Matthew, and the speaker in the Gospel is the Light Himself. Whoever follows Jesus will never have to live under the thief again! He will never have to concern himself with death or the destruction of the heavenly economy again. Why? Because the light, which regardless of how little of it appears, always disburses darkness. Where there is light, there will always be the possibility of life! Jesus Christ is the light of the world. He continues to offer a life that has the potential to grow to depths and go to places that only Adam has experienced. As long as there is light in this world, the possibility exists that man can and should be able to have his world in complete dominion as Adam did. The light of life is the avenue in which that can be experienced.

The Revelation of the Illumination in Jesus

Here is a truth that we all need to consider. God knows who you are, He knows where you are, and He knows exactly what you need. The question is not what He knows; it is in your position to receive from him what He is trying to get to you. Before you move forward, please read 2 Corinthians 2:9–10.

The illumination of the plan of God in Jesus resides there. During my lifetime and my ministry, there have been many times when the Lord has literally opened my eyes so that I can have clear insight into a situation that was pressing upon my life. This was never clearer than when I arrived at Eastern Kentucky University.

The reason we went to EKU was simple. We thought that this program had such a dynamic tradition that winning would not be that difficult. They had ruled the Ohio Valley Conference since the legendary Roy Kidd had been the head coach. Danny Hope had done a great job during his tenure following Coach Kidd at the school. I was confident that with Coach Hood's ability to coach defense and my ability to coach offense, winning would be happening regularly. What I did not know was that the team had lost twenty-seven seniors from the 2007 conference championship team. That number of players in college football is a lot of quality people to replace.

We won during our first year and went to the national playoffs. That was fun! We had done what I thought we could and would do. Fans were fickle and gave us little credit for what we had accomplished. We had lost a football team and a half and still found a way to win.

The reason I had come to Eastern Kentucky now became as much a curse as it was a help. They expected to win. They thought winning was in their DNA. And they were not schooled concerning the changing landscape of the college football recruiting scene with respect to the number of Division 1 football programs that had sprung up within the regions that had been extremely fertile recruiting areas for EKU. Recruiting got tougher because we had chosen to execute the Wake Forest model, which meant we looked for the character of kids first. This was before we determined his football ability. That meant that all too often, we were coaching players that were not really Division 1 athletes. This made winning more difficult, and it forced the coaches to outcoach our opponents. This was expected regardless of the caliber of athlete that they brought to the competition.

The development of great men is an essential part of coaching. I think that those of us who are old school recognize this. The rest of the world does not. They want to win first, then if you have a struggling athlete, you deal with it, rehabilitate as you can, and move on. Our goal was to build character, good fathers, and good teammates. We accomplished this on all fronts. Our kids played hard, worked hard, and cared deeply.

That was absolutely not enough against some of the teams that we competed against! We were, in many games, outmanned but never outcoached. This brings me to the game where there is no doubt in my mind that I received the illumination of the Holy Spirit.

It was November 6, 2010. We were playing a night game in Roy Kidd Stadium against the number 2 team in the nation. We were struggling at four wins and five losses. They were eight wins and one loss. The weather was frigid, one of the coldest games in my career.

As I said, we were playing Jacksonville State University of Alabama. This bunch was great—big, fast, strong, talented, and well coached. They rolled into Richmond as the number 2 team in the country at the IAA level. Did I mention that earlier in the year they had gone into Oxford, Mississippi, and beaten Old Miss? Yes, they were a specimen of a football team. During the week, while studying them on film, we thought we had located a flaw in their defense. We did everything we could do with our players to exploit what we saw. We got ahead by 10–7 in the first quarter. Then in the second quarter were behind 17–14. They were good, and we were trying to stay in the game. They consistently found ways to take advantage of their superior talent. They did not panic. They knew they were better.

The game came near the half, and we were behind by three points. That was an awesome effort by our players. We had the ball around our thirty-five-yard line. The half was about to end. We had traded scores to get it this close. We had run our plan almost to perfection. After a run play put us in second down, we called time-out. We ran another play and added a fake to our left slot back into the play. We now had third and seven. We called another time-out.

As I walked onto the field to meet the team, something hit me. In my career, I had never called this play in a game. I was never one to attempt "trick plays" as I always felt I could coach what I knew better than others could coach what you knew. If we executed what I coached, we would always be in the game. That confidence and comfort with my system had always worked. That mind-set would have to reign supreme at EKU! So as I approached the team, I heard myself say something that even I didn't expect.

Out of the blue, I turned to our most athletic player and said to him, "They did not cover you on the last play, did they?"

I will be honest with you when I make this statement, I had not seen him run uncovered. Obviously, my spirit man had. Naturally, being a guy who always wanted the ball, his answer was one quick and simple word, "No!"

I stepped in the huddle and said with extreme confidence, "Men we have them right where we want them. They are not going to be ready for our slotback pass."

I'm sure it caught our kids by surprise. We had practiced it just like we had other trick plays, but they knew that I did not and had not ever called a trick play in the game. That had been documented in the Richmond newspaper. But in this instance, I felt so deeply and so strongly that this was the call for the moment. It was my Rhema moment. I was about to be called to come out of the boat and walk on the water just like Peter had. I never considered that it might not work. I never considered that we might throw ourselves into a turn over that could change the game. No, sir! I felt a Rhema word from the spirit. The players ran back into the game as if they had this under control. The player called upon to throw the pass had been a high school option quarterback. This was predominately because he was not a great passer. At EKU he began as a defensive player, as virtually all our kids did. Early in this season, we were short of personnel at the receiver position, so he was moved to offense.

I called the play so that he could run to his right, which was his dominate hand. The ball-handling was done with flawless precision. Jet had the ball and was rolling just as we designed. He began to get some pressure from the JSU defensive players. He handled it perfectly as he made it look like he was going to keep the ball. Suddenly, he rose up and lofted a pass down the right-side line toward our best and fastest player. As the ball went airborne, things began to happen. I felt myself begin to chase the ball. In an instant, and with a great burst of speed, my receiver ran under the ball and completed the catch. Touchdown EKU! When I looked up, I was standing at the goal line. It was as if my feet had taken the wings of Elijah, and I had run with a fluidity that exhibited an ability that at fifty-three I did not possess. I showed up at the goal line beside an official. I distinctly remember the look on his face and the shake of his head. I quickly retreated to the safety of our coaches' box. EKU 21-JSU 17. We went on to not only beat the number 2 team in the country but have the ESPN play of the day. Final score EKU49-JSU 37. What a game!

The Spirit had illuminated my understanding with an answer that was required at the very second that it was needed. The revelation of Jesus that comes from the illumination of His Spirit to ours is an awesome thing. There is not only a hope of his glory, but there is a Rhema word that is available to speak specifically to our need. That word will allow us to walk on the glassy sea or on top of the white caps. Either way, it will come if we will listen. It will work if we will pursue the instruction of the illumination of the revelation of Jesus that is in us.

It has always amazed me how that a man's heart came to be changed. The power to do so was strictly in the power of the Word of God to illuminate the depravity that resides on the inside of man. Then to illuminate in such a way that man's spirit could grasp the power and presence of the Word of God and suddenly be translated into the kingdom of God's dear Son.

What a miracle occurs when the eternal personal Creator, who is Life, becomes Light and that illumination destroys all the work of the devil! *Awesome* is too small a word to describe the activity that occurs within the spirit of man that happens when the illumination enters the portals of darkness and man sees that light and is changed.

> And the light [Jesus Christ] shineth in darkness; and the darkness comprehended it not. (John 1:5 KJV)

We are aware of the scripture that begins the documentation of what the Word of God did in Genesis 1. Let's look at what He did to bring the illumination of light into the darkness that became the habitat of every creature.

> In the beginning God created the heaven and the earth. And the earth was without form, and void; and darkness was upon the face of the deep. And the spirit of God moved upon the face of the waters. And God said, let there be light: and there was light. (Genesis 1:1–3 KJV)

In the case of illumination, the Word of God's word was the directing factor that propelled the Holy Spirit into action. At His command, the world that had received the light that would define the structures one from another. And that went from without visible form and from the void of darkness to become full of the light that was the illumination of the Word of God. This illumination was not the light that would shine to separate day and night. It was the illumination of the presence of the Word of God. The light provided for that purpose would be created later. This we do know concerning the Son of God and the light which He projects. It is enough to illuminate all of heaven. It is enough light so that heaven requires no other method to be able to operate.

So it does not surprise us when we read that when He spoke light into existence during the designing of the new creation of the world, light was. The initial formation of light came from His presence and His existence. What was the initial experience in the new creation was the influence of His presence upon what would become the structure we now call earth! This is quite a revealing understanding as the Word of God's impact upon the earth's formation was the input of Himself. This was the second area within the three worlds that He would have ultimate impact upon. We will soon see how this illumination of the light of His presence would change the course of man's opportunities for their eternal existence.

So we conclude that the illuminating power of the Word of God is identified in heaven as the light that lights the city of God. We further conclude that the illumination of the Word of God also is the illumination light that brought about the creation of earth as the structure in which we live. Now, there is one more world and one more place that the illumination of the light of the Word of God must invade for Him to be the Lord of Lords and the King of Kings in all three worlds and in one most important place. Let's look now into the last place the Word of God had to appear with His illuminating presence for the benefit of His own creation.

Paul provides us with great insight into this concept in Colossians 1:12–13.

> Giving thanks unto the Father, which hath made us meet to be partakers of the inheritance of the saints in light: who hath delivered us from the power of darkness, and hath translated us into the kingdom of his dear Son. (Colossians 1:12–13 KJV)

Because He is the Light and because we have accepted the life-changing power that is in the Light, we are now made into the righteousness of God. I want to stop for just a few words on the word *made*. In scripture, the word *made* refers to the force which it took to cause something to become. Let's look at how Paul described the use of force in Ephesians 1:19–20.

> And what is the exceeding greatness of his power to us-ward who believe, according to the working of his mighty power, which he wrought in Christ, when he raised him from the dead, and set him at his own right hand in the heavenly places. (Ephesians 1:19–20 KJV)

In the Greek, we recognize that power is force. Paul here describes the process under which Jesus went for raising Him from the dead. God applied a force that Paul defines as a mighty show of strength. Why did He have to use such a flow of power for this cause? Well, we find that in 2 Corinthians 5:21.

> For he hath made him to be sin for us, who knew no sin; that we might be made the righteousness of God in him. (2 Corinthians 5:21 KJV)

Jesus was engulfed in the depths of sin. These depths were absolute and complete. No other infilling would serve to accomplish the required result. He was by force, made, hammered, and had sin put upon him. His ingredients became the makeup of sin.

The word *make*, or *made* means "to be formed in a particular process." So He was formed. This implication implies that a force was applied to cause Him to become what he was. That is true for any object that is formed from its initial form into a finished product that does not resemble what it was initially.

Jesus was no different. When the sin of mankind began to form in Him and He took upon Himself all the sin nature of every man, there was a power and a force that had to grip Him for Him to become what it was that was necessary for the sacrifice, not only to be legal, but to be all-encompassing. He laid Himself open to all the forces of hell. Now, let's consider the position that Jesus was in. First, Satan knew who He was. They had met and had discussion concerning the Lord's intentions in the wilderness. Secondly, Satan did not personally ever approach Him himself again after the original encounter. Thirdly, Paul tells us in 1 Corinthians 2:7–8,

> But we speak the wisdom of God in a mystery, even the hidden wisdom, which God ordained before the world unto our glory: which none of the princes of this world knew: for had they known it, they would not have crucified the Lord of glory. (1 Corinthians 2:7–8 KJV)

They thought that the cross was the place where He would have no choice but to bow to the original tempter. So the fury of hell came upon Him. He was made by all the forces of hell to become all the sin that was possible for Him to hold. How much was that? It was the equivalent of all the sin that would be necessary to satisfy the need for man to be redeemed once and for all! God stood back and watched the darling of heaven transformed into the very sin that had caused Lucifer to be cast out of heaven. The power of this event was total and complete as it related to the person of Jesus Christ. However, He did not die a sinner; He became what sin is. With that in mind, we then can see how sin, formed in Jesus, redefined Him. By the force applied by the power of hell, Jesus was made to become something that He was not originally. The product that He became made Him prepared to enter hell and be accepted as one of theirs.

Can you imagine the atmosphere in hell when He arrived? They had to have heard Lucifer say, "I told you so! We now have the one who was the activator of all that is. We now have the one who God thought was going to be the one to deliver his creative plan out of our hands. We have now accomplished what we set out to do. With the cross, His death, and His coming to me, we have succeeded in truly sitting on a throne that is higher than God."

Although this did not last long, it had to be seen as a victory for those who stood in opposition to God. What they had been promised by following Lucifer had, in fact, come to fruition. They possessed the body of the Son of God!

Paul puts it beautifully when he said, "Had they known!" They could not see the power that was about to be transferred from the region of the damned into the hand of the Redeemer/Savior. There is no doubt that the scene was one of euphoria. There is also no doubt that He was totally engulfed in the presence of the enemy. But the enemy who always mishandles the Word of God has been successful doing it again. He has forgotten the words that David spoke in Psalms 16:10 concerning His sojourn in to this region.

> For thou wilt not leave my soul in hell; neither wilt thou suffer thine Holy one to see corruption.
> (Psalms 16:10 KJV)

God had no intentions of relinquishing the power of the control of Jesus's Spirit. He would relinquish His body because a body was required to execute a sacrifice according to Hebrews 10:5–7.

> Wherefore when he cometh into the world, he saith, sacrifice and offering thou wouldest not, but a body hast thou prepared me: in burnt offerings and sacrifices for sin thou hast had no pleasure. Then said I, lo, I come [in the volume of the book it is written of me] to do thy will, O God.
> (Hebrews 10:5–7 KJV)

God prepared a body to go to hell. He had no intention for the Spirit that possessed that body to remain there. There was something that heaven required to retrieve from there. The will of God was to come forth from that domain. Let's see how He did it. Paul has already shared with us that He exerted a power that was greater than the power present in hell to extract Jesus from the grasp of his enemy. Look again at these words of Paul.

> And what is the exceeding greatness of his power to us-ward who believe, according to the working of his mighty power, which he wrought in

> Christ, when he raised him from the dead, and set him at his own right hand in the heavenly places. (Ephesians 1:19–20 KJV)

What God did was done with an ability that surpasses any other acts of greatness that He has done. This is how the Greek defines the word *exceeding*. When we put the two words together, we see a surpassing magnitude of the body of work which it took to deliver Jesus as David had prophesied in Psalms 16. The word *magnitude* describes "the size or the extent of something." So the change completed was of seismic proportions and could only have been done by the God of the entire universe. Then Paul uses the word *power*. This word means "force"! He sent the Holy Spirit into the presence of all the resistance of hell to extract the spirit of the Word of God. Jesus who was the Redeemer and Savior of all mankind was removed by the power of God purposefully and with direct intention. How do we know that? Let's look further.

Paul writes in the latter part of Ephesians 1 verse 19 and concludes in verse 20 by saying this:

> According to the working of his mighty power, which he wrought in Christ, when he raised him from the dead, and set him at his own right hand in the heavenly places. (Ephesians 1:19 KJV)

His dominion and might extended into this region. His power was evident when the Holy Spirit arrived. The Holy Spirit's extraction of Jesus was brought about effectively and efficiently. There was a mighty show of force that occurred when Jesus was removed. This is how the word *wrought* is described in the Greek. Verse 20 describes the result of this force. God raised Jesus from the region of the damned where He was deemed as dead. This identification with death satisfied the legal requirements of the sacrifice for sin. His place of death outside the city also served to legitimize His sacrifice as this location was the location of the sin sacrifice in the Old Testament. What was left for Him to do during the three days in which He was held in the grasp of the enemy? He was to destroy the works of the devil, lead captivity captive, and take the keys of death, hell, and the grave. In so doing hell's gates would forever be locked for all mankind. Any man who goes to hell will not have access through the gate. That person will be cast down and over the walls into everlasting punishment from which there is no means to be released. Why? Because the gate is locked, and Jesus possesses the key!

Now, notice that the act in and of itself took the mighty power of God to act by force upon the region in which He was held. But the removal was only a part of the story of how Jesus was to illuminate the world with the light of His works. The Bible tells us that during the extraction of Jesus that hell had to stand by while the very thing that gave them strength and hope for the fulfilling of Satan's desire was stripped from them. Hell must have been paralyzed by the presence of the Holy Spirit. They must have gone from a state of euphoria to a state of complete devastation when Jesus completed His last few minutes with them.

What did He do? Revelation 1:17–18 describes a scene that John the revelator shares with us that will fill in the blanks.

> And when I saw him, I fell at his feet as dead. And he laid his right hand upon me, saying unto me, fear not; I am the first and the last: I am he that liveth, and was dead; and, behold, I am alive for evermore, amen; and have the keys of hell and of death. (Revelation 1:17–18 KJV)

Here it is the words of Jesus to John. The revelation to John is this:

> I am the first to go to hell and come out of that place to live again. I am the first to be a living sacrifice. I am the first to take upon himself the sin of all the world. I am the first man to die as a sacrifice for the sin of all men. I am the first dead man to be raised from hell by the force of God. I am the first dead man from hell to be

> seen of men. I am the first dead man from hell to ascend into heaven. I am the first dead man to be the high priest of my own sacrifice. I am the first dead man to be seated at the right hand of My Father. I am the first dead man to execute the sending of the promise of God into the spirits of men. I am the first mediator, intercessor, and advocate for mankind. I am the first commander of the Holy Spirit.

Yes, there is a man up there! With all that said, He then shares a critical word.

> I am also the last! There will never be a need for another! I have done it all. Whatever man needed, I have completely supplied.

How does He let us know that what He is telling John is so? This next verse identifies Jesus's "last act as he was removed from hell." It lets me know that hell and its workers had to be paralyzed by the appearance of the Holy Spirit. Jesus tells John the following:

> I am he that liveth, and was dead; and, behold, I am alive for evermore [amen] and have the keys of hell and of death. (Revelation 1:18 KJV)

He brought the strength and power of hell from hell with Him when He left. Death no longer held men captive and in bondage. Hell no longer would be the destiny of men. Why? Because the one with the promise of God had destroyed death, hell, and the grave once and for all that will believe. In the regions of the damned, there was an illumination of light that sprang forth out of darkness, and it accomplished an overpowering and overwhelming work.

> For God, who commanded the light to shine out of darkness, hath shined in our hearts, to give the

> light of the knowledge of the glory of God in the face of Jesus Christ. (2 Corinthians 4:6 KJV)

Do you see that? The light shone out of darkness. Hell, for the duration of this extraction, was illuminated with the light of the Son of God. This light caused the underworld to be shaken to such an extent that Paul described what Jesus did this way.

> Wherefore he saith, when he ascended up on high, he led captivity captive, and gave gifts unto men [now that he ascended, what is it but that he also descended first into the lower parts of the earth]? (Ephesians 4:8–9 KJV)

It is always the infusion of light that illuminates any region held in the bondage of darkness. The only means whereby anyone who is in the dark can comfortably navigate is to add light. Without light there is uncertainty. There is the infliction of possible pain. But more importantly, there is no clear-cut direction for the person to travel. They are consistently dealing with road blocks, pitfalls, and problems that leave them groping for ways and means to move forward. Often it leaves them trying to find a means of survival. Sometimes they do not survive. When this occurs, hell enlarges its borders. Those without the light that illuminates a distinct path then are doomed to see the corruption of the flesh unfold before their eyes for eternity. What a sad ending to a promising beginning!

He led the Old Testament saints out of their captivity and presented them to God upon His ascension to His right hand. This total picture, when put together, caused John to say that He destroyed the works of the devil!

> He that committed sin is of the devil, for the devil sinneth from the beginning. For this purpose, the Son of God was manifested, that he might destroy the works of the devil. (1 John 3:8 KJV)

Those held saw the light of his glory. They received it right in the midst of darkness. They were translated out of paradise and placed into the kingdom of His dear Son. This was a divine act of God on all accounts. The extraction, the inclusion of those being held captive due to there being no legal means for their release, the resurrection, the ascension, the seating, and the sending of the same Spirit that accomplished all that preceded His inclusion in the life of believers. He went to paradise, preached to them, and Jude tells us they believed him.

The illumination of man by the light that came into darkness is the still transpiring today. Man's heart absent from this light is as dark as the region in which Jesus went and was held for the short period of three days. It is unfortunate that, although men may have developed a character that allows them to do some good things and to be a benefit to their society, they without the illumination of the light in their hearts are still serving an evil master.

We have now qualified how Jesus is the Lord of all three domains wherein the spiritual forces exist. There is, however, one more place that the illumination of the light of the Word of God must express itself for the grand design of God to effectively defeat the plan of Satan. That place is to illuminate the spirit of mankind. The process of illumination is to shine within the inner man the light that is the light of the world. Jesus speaks about the illumination and infusion of light into the lives of men and the dynamic effect that this has upon men.

> Then spake Jesus again unto them, saying, I am the light of the world: he that followeth me shall not walk in darkness, but shall have the light of life. (John 8:12 KJV)

Upon the receipt of Jesus into the life of man, He no longer is under the bondage of darkness. It is the light of life in which He is encompassed. This is great news to every man who comes to Christ. The degenerative darkness and the paralyzing fear of the loss of direction that darkness causes are eliminated for man by the light of life who we know as the Word of God. Jesus came to do the same thing for men that He did in heaven, earth, and hell. Although the revelation of the illumination of light in hell was brief, there is little doubt that the outcome that occurred had to have been preceded by the illumination of the region because two-thirds of the Godhead were present at the event.

> To give light to them that sit in darkness and in the shadow of death, to guide our feet into the way of peace. (Luke 1:79 KJV)

What a beautiful scripture and a beautiful truth. Let's investigate these words. First, to give light to them that sit in darkness. Jesus has come to include men in the presence and impact of Himself. Who is He? He is the light that illuminates darkness. All men who sit therein have been given a means to remove themselves from the bondage and fear associated with darkness. Not only were they sitting under the cover of darkness, but they were sitting under the shroud of death and in the shadow of death. What an awful position to be in. Man is surrounded by death absent from Jesus, and they are unaware of their eternal outcome. Jesus here identifies for them where they are and in what condition they remain when they choose to remain in the darkness of the deception of the devil. I refer to this as deception due to the words that conclude the verse. Jesus states,

> To guide our feet into the way of peace. (KJV)

There is a way out for all men. It is not only a way out, but it is a guided way. In other words, it is a way where an assigned person shows you the means to arrive at a place where you will be safe! Most importantly, it is a path of peace. This tells me that the illuminated way is a path where we can see the pitfalls and we have a hope to avoid the danger along the way. Again, David said it so well when he said,

> Thy word is a lamp unto my feet and a light unto my path. (KJV)

How? The Word becomes my guide. It becomes my spiritual road map. It interacts with my spirit man and gives me a personal hand up to know what to do and how to follow the commands of Christ. This then encompasses me with peace because it allows my soul to remain focused upon Him. Peace becomes my companion. It belongs to me when the mountains seem to crumble around me. It belongs to me when people reject me. How do I know it works? Because the one who said I would have it also told me these awesome words.

> These things I have spoken unto you, that in me ye might have peace. In the world ye shall have tribulation: but be of good cheer; I have overcome the world. (John 16:33)

We can be of good cheer! Our guide and our leader has spoken the peace that He used to overcome the world. Since He has accomplished this, we see and know that it can be done. We who live a life illuminated in our spirit by Christ living in us can live a life filled with the glory of God. We also can experience the peace that passes all understanding simply because we have experienced the place that needed to be illuminated. Our spirit man is filled with the light of the Son of God. Then Jesus again speaks of Himself with reference to the illumination of the light.

> I am come a light into the world, that whosoever believeth on me should not abide in darkness. And if any man hear my words, and believe not, I judge him not: for I came not to judge the world, but to save the world. (John 12:46–47 KJV)

Here is the dynamic relationship that exists between light and darkness. Only when a man's spirit is illuminated can that man be delivered from the darkness in which he abides. This means that no matter where he is or in what condition of emotion he exudes, a man without Christ abides and lives in darkness. Here is the dynamic that the lost fail to understand. Their condition is fatal, and it is eternal! The illumination of the Word of God was for man's eternal salvation; however, those men who reject the opportunity and the conviction of the Holy Spirit and choose not to believe will ultimately be judged by the same Savior that offered them a means by which to be saved. It is a true statement that man will either face Jesus as a Lamb upon the cross or a Lion upon the throne!

The last few words on this issue come from Paul's writing in the book of Hebrews chapter 4 and verses 12 and 13.

> For the Word of God is quick, and powerful, and sharper than any two-edged sword, piercing even to the dividing asunder of soul and spirit, and of the joints and marrow, and is a discerner of the thoughts and intents of the heart. Neither is there any creature that is not manifest in his sight: but all things are naked and opened unto the eyes of him with whom we have to do. (Hebrews 4:12 KJV)

Do you see the term *the Word of God*? The Greek refers to this as "the divine expression which is Jesus Christ." It is His Word, thought, and presence that is described with the next few words concerning Him. He is quick, powerful, and sharper than a two-edged sword. His words are filled with the expression of his authority. He alone is the expression of all the authority heaven offers within His office. His office is to be the Word of God. The Word of God is light, and the Word of God illuminates all areas in which it is released.

Now let's consider the word *piercing*. This word in Greek means "to penetrate or reach through." When the Word of God speaks into any of the three worlds or into the place which is the heart of man, it speaks with such authority that it pierces through the armor and covering that the fall has placed between the Word and those held captive. It is only the Word of God that has any chance to illuminate the inner parts of hell, the earth, and the inner man. The operation that is associated with his office as Word of God has complete dominion in the areas in which God knew that darkness ruled. In this scripture, the writer is referring to the place where illumination occurs in man. That place is in the inner man. The soul is the portion of man that contains his mind, will, and emotions. When the Word of God powerfully and quickly strikes the soul of man, it illuminates a truth to that soul that has been hidden.

The illumination of truth which comes from the light of the Word of God then begins to cut across the current condition in which the Word found the soul. The condition of sin is uncovered and the necessity of choosing a new direction for the individual's life is revealed. Now know this: this does not insinuate that every time the Word strikes the soul of men, they choose the correct new life. However, they do choose a new life! That new life may be the life of a new creation in Christ Jesus, or it may be a new life of sin and darkness. But a choice is made every time the Holy Spirit exposes the soul of man.

The Word divides the soul and the spirit. Both parts of the tripart man are exposed to the Word of God. The spirit naturally yearns for its rebirth. The convicting power of the Holy Spirit is a presence that man's spirit recognizes. Due to this, man has an innate desire to reconnect with the God of his creation. Man has a deep desire for the supernatural relationship for which he was designed. But the soul is another entity in and of itself. It has attachments to the flesh. Unfortunately, that is the area that agreed with Eve's personal interpretation of the words of the Word of God when she determined the value of the fruit. Her soul was feeding her fleshly desires as she ate of the very thing that would kill the connection to the Word of God.

Eve used her soul, which again was her mind, will, and emotions, to make the decision to destroy the creation and sever the relationship between God and man. She was on fire with the possibilities of who she may become and what she may be able to do. God saw this in the same way, and that was why He had to remove them from the Tree of Life. So when the writer expresses the dividing of soul from the spirit, there is a reason. The soul and the spirit must be divided in order that the spirit may take control! Where there is no spirit control, you will always find a man that is out of control. The flesh becomes the driver, and darkness becomes the atmosphere in which he drives, operates, and lives. Only when the illuminating power of the Word of God, which is the divine expression, Jesus Christ, flows into the spirit of man, does man begin to function in a new way and follow a different path. Notice that the Word of God does not stop with the soul and spirit. It is thorough and complete. It divides the very existence of man. His joints, meaning "how he moves," and his marrow, meaning "how he lives."

The thoughts, meaning "how he devises his course of action, intents, and deeds," are all illuminated and inspected. Man's intentions are of vital importance because they expose what is on the inside. It is not what you do that always defines who you are. It is what you would do without the filter of the salvation that God has given you that must be searched out by the Word of God. This is of vital importance as it opens the door for man to safeguard the work that has been accomplished in the life of a new creature in Christ Jesus.

Then the Word of God makes manifest the deficits that the individual produces. We are all blessed to have this wonderful opportunity for the illumination that will serve to sanctify our spiritual life. David said in Psalms 139:23–24,

> Search me, O God, and know my heart: try me, and know my thoughts: and see if there be any wicked way in me and lead me in the way everlasting. (Psalms 139:23–24 KJV)

This is the most amazing part of the illumination of man. He divides, He searches, and He manifests in man the things that man needs to know concerning himself. Jesus through the Holy Spirit executes the following in man:

1. Man needs to know the sin for which He must repent. So Jesus, through the Holy Spirit, divides the soul from the spirit and convicts man of his personal sin.
2. The Holy Spirit then searches the places that man goes and the way that he lives. So that man can know the way to

avoid paths that lead to destruction and darkness and know the influence of the Holy Spirit to judge his ways.
3. The Holy Spirit sees the thoughts and intents of the heart and discerns the desire of man. This is so that man can convince himself to meditate upon the Word of God and His goodness and choose always the paths of righteousness.
4. Then Jesus accomplishes Acts 1:2,

> Until the day in which he was taken up, after that he through the Holy Ghost had given commandments unto the apostles whom he had chosen. (Acts 1:2 KJV)

For the people who have been manifest before him. He manifests Himself to men who follow his commands. Jesus said He would in John 14:21.

> He that hath my commandments and keepeth them, he it is that loveth me; and he that loveth me shall be loved by my father, and I will love him and will manifest myself to him. (John 14:21 KJV)

Thank God He is finding in and among us those that are obedient to him. When He searches and exposes sin, wrong actions, wrong living, wrong thinking, and wrong intentions, He is using the illumination of His Word to help us find the means of escape He promised in 1 Corinthians 10:13!

> There hath no temptation taken you, but such as is common to man: but God is faithful, who will not suffer you to be tempted above that ye are able; but will with the temptation also make a way to escape, that ye may be able to bear it. (1 Corinthians 10:13 KJV)

So now that I have had the light illuminated in my spirit and turned on in my soul, I can understand what Paul meant when he wrote in 2 Corinthians 5:17–24,

> Therefore, if any man be in Christ, he is a new creature: old things are passed away; behold, all things are become new. And all things are of God, who hath reconciled us to himself by Jesus Christ, and hath given to us the ministry of reconciliation; to wit, that God was in Christ, reconciling the world unto himself, not imputing their trespasses unto them; and hath committed unto us the word of reconciliation. Now then we are ambassadors for Christ, as though God did beseech you by us: we pray you in Christ's stead, be ye reconciled to God. For he hath made him to be sin for us, who knew no sin; that we might be made the righteousness of God in him. (2 Corinthians 5:17–24 KJV)

I am a new creature because the light of life was illuminated in my spirit. That illumination captures my soul. The divine order that was arranged in Genesis 1:26–27 has been reestablished within me. I have been changed! I have been translated into the kingdom of His dear Son! I have mutually agreed with God to accept what He offered in Christ. I have exchanged darkness for light, death for life, and the divine favor of God has been restored to me! What an awesome exchange! I am no longer in captivity and the bondage of the fall of man. I am free to commune with God from this moment forward! I am totally restored to the divine favor in which Adam lived in the garden! Now, friends, that's high living!

Due to the illumination of the truth in my life, I have become a representative of Jesus Christ. Now we can see why the Word of God is so extensive in its search of man, as we are to so live in such a way as to represent the nature and character of God. Representatives are compelled to do what Jesus commanded in John 14:21 to ensure that the message is not tainted by the acts and works of the flesh. How do we accomplish such a large task? Paul told us in 2 Corinthians 5:21,

> For he hath made him to be sin for us, who knew no sin; that we might be made the righteousness of God in him. (2 Corinthians 5:21 KJV)

Our sin is under the blood. The search light is ongoing within the world to detect the things that can so easily distract us, these distractions have been carried away and defeated by Jesus. With the defeat and destruction of sin, we are placed, by faith, into a new dimension for living. We are made by the force of what Jesus did in the nine works associated with the cross, the righteousness of God in Him!

The standard established by God by which He determined what righteousness would be, were defined by the actions of the Word of God. Those actions have been transferred to us because we believed and received the accomplished work of the cross. Therefore, the Word of God shining abroad in my heart has made me something that I could never have been absent from the Word of God. I have been made a righteous representative with a heavenly mission! Saved, sanctified, and filled with the Holy Spirit and living in the eternal blessings that are released to me as He continues to illuminate Himself to me. I think I'll stop and just shout awhile! Glory to God!

In closing, just a note of caution—if you ignore the Word of God, you do so at your own peril.

The Revelation of the Salvation in Jesus

Life is a difficult task to navigate. There is the reality of trouble, pain, and hurt that life has a way of inflicting into the life of people. Life casts its shadow of fear and uncertainty upon people. This results in distinct physical and medical issues such as depression, oppression, stress, and many other medical disorders.

The truth is that life happens to everyone. None of us are exempt from the potential troubles that life imposes. We do not have the ability to dictate our personal constitution nor do we have the opportunity to choose our DNA. What is left for us is the simple living of the life that we have been given. Although there are no guarantees in this life as to what may become of or what may befall us in our human state, there are guarantees that are provided for our spiritual welfare. It is that guarantee that becomes the ultimate pursuit for all of mankind.

When we look at the concept of salvation, we are forced to identify that there is a way God does things. Salvation is the divine plan of God that is provided for man so that man be able to know god. This also becomes the way man experiences God. These experiences are recognized in the six parts of the plan that are distinguished for man as the acts of God toward the people. The parts are identified as preservation, deliverance, healing, soundness, wholeness, and being saved. These six parts make up the divine plan of salvation.

These can be identified in the Seder meal that the children of Israel took prior to leaving Egypt. It is important to remember that Israel knew God's acts. Only Moses knew His ways. The true description of God would not be disclosed to the world until Jesus came. The Gospel then declared who He was to the world. We know He was Son of Man, Son of God, our Savior, Substitute, and King. Only John defined Him by means of a comprehensive revelation in John chapter 1.

My brother Bob was a wonderful person. He loved the Lord and was an excellent husband and father. His wife was of Jewish decent and was devout in her religion. I often went to visit my brother and his family. Whether I was recruiting or headed to our parents, Bob's place outside of Atlanta, Georgia, was a convenient stop—not to mention that I adored Bob and he adored me. We were two brothers that had spent our lives enjoying each other and our personal accomplishments. We had also shared our failures. Regardless of what came into our lives, we always had each other.

One spring, as I was on my way home on spring break, I called Bob and told him I was going to stop by for the night. He was extremely excited to have me, as he always was. He shared with me something of which I was completely unaware. He said that he and his family were having friends over on the Saturday evening that I was to be there to celebrate the Seder meal. Both of us were reared as Protestants, and this celebration was something about which I knew nothing. But if Bob was going to be involved, that was good enough for me. The company arrived, and I realized quickly this was a rather large occasion for the Jewish community. There was a meal prepared that included *matzah* bread, *matzo* soup, gefilte fish, there was a lamb shank, a saltwater dip with parsley, an applesauce mix, and four cups for a nonalcoholic kosher wine. There was a prayer provided for each step of the meal. It was spoken in Hebrew. I just watched and ate as I saw them eating. There were songs also sung with the meal.

Although the food was not appealing to me, I could tell that the celebration of which I was a part was of the utmost importance to those with whom I shared the occasion. The process took awhile, but it was interesting to be a part of a religious exercise of remembrance. My unfamiliarity was unimportant. So I watched and followed along as they prayed, sang, and ate food in small portions. Little did I know the significance of the event. Even less did I realize how this event would become included in this book under this part of the revelations of Jesus Christ. So as the years have gone by, I have taken the time to study the Tabernacle and to investigate the Passover meal. This activity has great meaning as we relate it to the salvation of God.

The process that I saw in this celebration defines the acts of God toward the children of Israel. We will be able to see how God disclosed His intentions by the completion of acts that would define the future for Israel. As I looked more deeply into the food that had been set before me on that occasion and I reflected upon it, I saw some very interesting information that I want to attempt to share. This meal involved the story of Israel's departure from the slavery of Egypt. That is a known biblical story. The meal included *matzah*, which is the unleavened bread; *karpas*, which is a parsley that is dipped in salt water; *maror/chazeret*, which is a mix of bitter herbs; *charoset*, which is a mixture of fruit, nuts, and honey; a shank bone of a lamb; and an egg.

The matzah identifies that Israel went from slavery to freedom, and the event happened so quickly that there was no time to wait for the bread to rise. It also identifies the separation and purity that was required for the people to live among the nations that would encompass their God-given lands. The lesson for us in this food is this: First, God does what He says He will do concerning the speed of His actions. That was relayed to us in Jeremiah 1;12. Secondly, the New Testament relationship is established here for all who believe on Jesus. They can immediately be changed and processed into the kingdom of His dear Son according to Colossians 1:13. The act of eating the unleavened bread identified the piece of salvation we know as being saved.

The *karpas* and salt water identified the bitter tears that were shed due to the hardships associated with the life that the Egyptians imposed upon the children of Israel. The people were in tears due to the physical and mental hardships that living under the slavery of the day caused. This identifies with the life of man in that it shows us the pain and suffering of sin. When we eat of the bitterness of sin and its behaviors, we take into ourselves the sorrow that comes with our actions. Again, this identifies the need for the piece of salvation that we know as healing. What man has ingested into his life through rebellion and fear requires the salvation of God to be made free from the entanglement of sin and its hardships.

The *maror,* or *chazeret,* which is a mix of bitter herbs, again identifies the hardships of the life of slavery. But it also identifies the transition that occurred for the people as they went from the problems of slavery to the exodus from the ones who caused them pain. This represents the deliverance that occurred as a piece of the salvation of God.

Then there was the roasted shank bone of a lamb. This was just a bone, and it represented the vision of the sacrificed lamb. When they looked upon this bone, they knew that they were ready to exit the land. As we also know, the blood of this lamb had been placed upon the doorpost. This placement represented the future as it was placed at the top and on each side of the doorframe. This represented the coming of the cross. In terms of salvation, this represents the preservation and safety that is in the plan of salvation for Israel. There was coming a lamb that would serve to shed blood that would keep the people safe from the destruction of sin.

Then there was the egg. The egg symbolized the new beginning that Israel would encounter as they left Egypt and began the journey toward the promised land. There would be a rebirth of the nation that would come into a land that flowed with milk and honey. This food shows us the soundness that salvation brings to the person. The good food that was in the land to come would make them physically and mentally complete to live and to be prosperous in the new life that lay ahead.

Then there were the four different wines that all speak of the redemption that God has provided for Israel. As they drank the wine, they knew that He would bring them out, He would deliver them, He would redeem them, and He would take care of his people. This represented the wholeness that is a part of the divine plan of salvation. They could rest in what had been done and the covering upon their nation. They would be whole, strong, and an independent people, and God would be the Jehovah that would meet every need. Here is the difference of the Passover meal we refer to as the Seder as it relates to the exodus of Israel and the infusion of Jesus. All these wonderful symbols pointed toward something. They were a type and representation of something that was coming. When Jesus came on the scene, Simeon said that his eyes had seen the salvation of the Lord. In other words, he had seen the way God was going to do a new thing in the earth. His name was Jesus.

I had experienced the traditional foretaste of what the Jewish people still practice today. It was a great experience. I had seen the acts of God as it was related to Israel. But thank God, I was exposed to the way God was to operate in the earth when I met Jesus Christ as the complete representation of all the symbols that Israel celebrates. I know Him, His ways, and His acts. They are all exposed in the Book we refer to as the Holy Bible. The salvation of God is clearly defined and understood in one person, Jesus Christ. Jesus was God's revealed Savior to mankind; of that there is no doubt. But from the foundation of the world, He was the revelation of God's salvation. In my opinion, the Savior is an expression of the plan of salvation that God designed for man.

When the names of Jesus are described—such as, Wonderful, Counselor, Prince of Peace, Mighty God, and Everlasting Father—He precedes those names with a comment that must have some clarification in the divine plan. "The government shall be upon His shoulders" is the phrase that catches my attention. What does this mean? The Hebrew refers to this as the empire. Well, what is the divine empire of God as it relates to mankind?

> For unto us a child is born, unto us a Son is given: and the government shall be upon his shoulder: and his name shall be called Wonderful, Counsellor, the Mighty God, the Everlasting Father, the Prince of Peace. (KJV)

That divine plan for the divine empire of God is wrapped up in the plan of salvation. Jesus possesses all the characteristics of the names ascribed to Him. But within those names is one overarching theme. He is the divine design which is manifested in the plan of salvation for all mankind.

When you see the names that relate to the character and nature of Jesus, what you are seeing is the relationship of those names to one central theme…salvation! Luke 1:69 gives us some insight into this matter.

> And hath raised up a horn of salvation for us in the house of his servant David; here we identify the horn of salvation, or the power of salvation that would come from the house of David. (Luke 1:69 KJV)

A mighty man full of the Seven Spirits of God would be born into the world. One of his objectives would be to become the Savior of the world.

Before we go much further with this, let's see if we can develop a thesis statement that will provide us a foundation for our look into this revelation.

> Blessed be the God and Father of our Lord Jesus Christ, who hath blessed us with all spiritual blessings in heavenly places in Christ: according as he hath chosen us in him before the foundation of the world, that we should be holy and without blame before him in love: having predestinated us unto the adoption of children by Jesus Christ to himself, according to the good pleasure of his will, to the praise of the glory of his grace, wherein he hath made us accepted in the beloved. In whom we have redemption through his blood, the forgiveness of sins, according to the riches of his grace. (Ephesians 1:3–7 KJV)

Here we recognize the plan of God as designed by the three persons in the Godhead for redemption of mankind from the fall. Jesus was a spiritual blessing to men. He, through his name, provided us with every spiritual blessing. His name is salvation, and Jesus is the all-encompassing person that gives us all and every spiritual blessing in heavenly places. Notice that these blessings are in Christ Jesus. They are in his name. Salvation is His name, and the spiritual blessings that man receives are derived from that name. Being saved is an appropriation of that name. It is not the total package of which that name exists.

Peter, speaking in Acts 3, shares this reality with us concerning the name of Jesus.

> And his name, through faith in his name, has made this man strong whom ye see and know: yea, the faith which is by him has given him this perfect soundness in the presence of you all. (Acts 3:16)

Peter defines the process and plan of salvation. It comes through the name. It is received by faith. It serves to make a man strong. It results in the perfection of soundness.

The key word in this text is *soundness*. Salvation is the plan that makes any man, who by faith receives Jesus, sound in spirit, soul, and body. Salvation is a divine plan which expresses itself in many forms. In whatever form a man requires, when he comes to Jesus, he can rest assured that his answer resides in one all-encompassing word, which is *salvation*. It is His name. His character, nature, and relation to man are all outward manifestations as signs of who He is. His signs, wonders, and miracles are descriptors of that name.

> But as many as received him, to them gave he power to become the Sons of God, even to them that believe on his name. (John 1:12 KJV)

We now enter the seventh new revelation of John's gospel concerning Jesus Christ. He is the salvation of God. We can reference this in the Old Testament and locate the prophetical scripture that develops this revelation. Salvation is generally considered as the process whereby man is saved, delivered, healed, safe and sound. This is true, as Jesus has accomplished these works for every man who believes in His name.

When John says that He gave them power to become the Sons of God, he is referring to the fact that the six parts of salvation translate man from one spiritual condition into a completely different condition. When man receives Him, sonship is conferred upon him. Salvation then operates in him to execute the five areas that will serve to keep him. It is through his name that salvation exists. Paul said that at that name every knee would bow and every tongue would confess that Jesus Christ is Lord of Lords!

So let's look at the salvation that is in the name. The name *Jesus* is mentioned over one hundred times in the Old Testament, and anytime you read a reference to the term *salvation*, you are reading about the name Jesus. In Hebrew the word *salvation* means "Yeshua." In Jewish custom, your name had a meaning, and it depicted who you were or what you were to become. Consider the following:

1. *Noah* meant "comfort."
2. *Abraham* meant "the father of many nations."
3. *Sarah* meant "princess." This associated her with Abraham as she would bear children to be heirs and leaders of many nations.
4. *Isaac* meant "he will rejoice."
5. *Jacob* meant "holder of the heel," but his name would later be changed to *Israel*, which means "God contended," and this name was due to Jacob's wrestling with the angel of God.
6. *Moses* meant "to be drawn forth." This correlates with the fact that he was taken out of the water by Pharaoh's daughter.

So in the Hebrew custom, names were associated with the person's content, character, or demeanor. It should not surprise us that the name of Jesus appears in the Old Testament as well as in the New Testament. An article called "The Name of Jesus in the Tanakh" by

Arthur Glass is a most revealing and interesting read. He defines the places in the Old Testament where the name of Jesus is identified by the word *salvation*!

Some of the references that appear in this section are related to his article. His references to such scriptures as Psalms 91:14–16, Habakkuk 3:13, and Isaiah 12:2–3. They are Old Testament testimonies of Jesus Christ, or Yeshua, as the salvation of God for Israel.

Look at Psalms 91:14–16.

> Because he hath set his love upon me, therefore will I deliver him: I will set him on high, because he hath known my name. He shall call upon me, and I will answer him: I will be with him in trouble; I will deliver him, and honour him. With long life will I satisfy him and shew him my salvation. (Psalms 91:14–16 KJV)

This scripture identifies the life of the Word of God. It is the Word of God that will be delivered and set Him on high because He has known the name of the highest God. When He calls, God answers. There is no question that this is so. As He completed the miracles of His earthly ministry, countless times He called upon his Father, and His Father answered Him speedily. He satisfied Him and showed His salvation in Him to the world. This salvation is Jesus.

Look at Isaiah's reference to salvation.

> Behold, God is my salvation; I will trust, and not be afraid: for the LORD JEHOVAH is my strength and my song; he also is become my salvation. Therefore with joy shall ye draw water out of the wells of salvation. I will drink of the wells of Salvation. (Isaiah 12:2–3 KJV)

I will drink of the accomplishments of the one who is salvation.

Who is the one who accomplished salvation? He is no other than Jesus Christ! All men would look upon Him. This would be done visibly by the people of his day, or it will be done through the foolishness of preaching, but all men will behold God's salvation.

Here it is important to identify a piece of this scripture that we have discussed before. Notice the office that the Word of God was asked to perform. He, the Word of God, is become my salvation. In other words, the Word of God has become Yeshua, Jesus Christ, which means "salvation." It is of Him that we drink of the righteousness of God. Our salvation, who is our Savior, was made sin even though He knew no sin, that we might become the righteousness of God by that same salvation!

Now let's look at Habakkuk's writing concerning the salvation of God, who is the Word of God in the office which God designated as His distinct role in the redemption of man.

> Thou wentest forth for the salvation of thy people, even for salvation with thine anointed; thou woundedst the head out of the house of the wicked, by discovering the foundation unto the neck. Selah. (Habakkuk 3:13 KJV)

Jesus went forth himself for the people.

He was, according to Luke 4:18, anointed for this role. It was His office and His role in the plan of God.

Then Habakkuk describes what He accomplished. He wounded the head of the house of the wicked. This is precisely what He did to Satan. More importantly, it confirmed the prophecy of Genesis 3:15.

> And I will put enmity between thee and the woman, and between thy seed and her seed; it shall bruise thy head, and thou shalt bruise his heel. (Genesis 3:15 KJV)

Jesus put a crushing wound upon the empire of hell and death. He did so with thorough efficiency. As Habakkuk declares, He did it from the foundation to the neck. There are no overcoming components left for the devil to use to ever defeat the work that salvation has done.

He has been defeated in every possible corner within the spiritual world. The flesh of all men has not yet come to that conclusion. But salvation, with the anointing, has come into the atmosphere of the earth and earthly people for that express purpose. Salvation in Himself, Jesus, has accomplished the work of saving any man, woman, boy or girl who would believe upon the name of the Word of God!

This is the person that the Lamb referred to in Revelation 22:3.

In Salvation is Yeshua, the Lord, who is the lamb.

He has been in the Old Testament by name all along. We may have failed to recognize Him, but he has been there nonetheless!

> Therefore the lord himself shall give you a sign; behold, a virgin shall conceive, and bear a son, and shall call his name Immanuel. (Isaiah 7:14 KJV)

The name *Immanuel* means "God with us." When the virgin birthed the Savior, then literally God infused the earthly atmosphere with Himself. First, let's look at Isaiah's identification of *salvation*. In Isaiah 62:11–12, Isaiah identifies Yeshua as the Savior.

> The LORD has made proclamation to the ends of the earth: "Say to daughter Zion, 'see, your Savior comes! See, his reward is with him, and his recompense accompanies him.'" They will be called the holy people, the redeemed of the LORD; and you will be called sought after, the city no longer deserted. (Isaiah 62:11–12 KJV)

The salvation of the Lord comes. It is Jesus who is being revealed in these scriptures. The recompense that accompanies Him is the salvation that is Him! The people that come to believe and receive Him will be called a holy people. They will be referred to as the redeemed of the Lord. Why is this? Because they have believed and received the salvation of God, who is the Word of God made flesh. The revelation of the salvation of God by John is directly related to the revelation of Yeshua in the Old Testament. For it is He, Habakkuk declares, who will wound the head of the wicked and discover the foundation unto the neck.

> Thou wentest forth for the salvation of thy people, even for salvation with thine anointed; thou woundedst the head out of the house of the wicked, by discovering the foundation unto the neck. Selah. (Habakkuk 3:13 KJV)

Romans 10:10 gives us some insight into the method of salvation.

> For with the heart man believeth unto righteousness; and with the mouth confession *is made unto salvation.* (Romans 10:10 KJV)

This word is a dynamic condition when it relates to the spiritual condition of man. When man's spirit is convicted and convinced of the judgment that awaits him when he is absent of the righteousness of God, the man's mouth then has the ability to literally speak life into his spirit. He can confess the Lordship of Jesus Christ into his life. Paul says that we can lose all the condemnation of the past and receive the spirt of life that is in Christ Jesus.

In Romans 8:1–2, he tells us that there is a great exchange; we exchange death for life! This occurs for man through the revelation of rescue, deliverance, safety, and spiritual health that the term *salvation* demands. How do we know that it is demanded in this word? Because Paul describes this event by using the word *made*. This word means that anything that it describes has had force applied to it so that it can become something that it was not prior to the applied force.

There is a force applied with salvation! Consider this.

1. There is a force in the blood that translates a man from darkness into light.
2. There is a force for transfer that transfers the Spirit of life in Christ Jesus into the newborn spirit of man.
3. There is a force of righteousness that is established in the newborn that is provided by salvation Himself, Yeshua.
4. There is a force in the words that make the confession.

Allow me to address this thought for a minute. Words that are spoken that agree with the righteousness of the Word of God and the blood which was shed have a dynamic affect. They become words of creation. Second Corinthians 5:17 attest to this statement.

> Therefore, if any man be in Christ, he is a new creature: old things are passed away; behold, all things are become new.

When we confess the Lordship of Jesus Christ from a spirit that is convicted and convinced of the judgment that was required to provide us with the salvation of Jesus Christ, our words take on the same creative power that Adam had in the garden. Our own words carry the dominion over the spiritual world that shuts off the effects of the fall and the curse! How else could our confession couple with our belief and produce the effects of salvation? We have, through the power of our tongue under the correct spiritual conditions, the ability to do the following:

1. Speak a new creature into our spirit.
2. Dispel the condemnation of the past.
3. Bring on a brand-new beginning that exists in Christ Jesus!

That, my friend, is a most powerful and creative individual who has the power through his own words to master his own spiritual life!

This should not surprise us, as Solomon declared the same in Proverbs 18:21.

> Death and life are in the power of the tongue:
> and they that love it shall eat the fruit thereof.
> (Proverbs 18:21 KJV)

My lips will produce the dynamic power of the fruit of righteousness. They will produce the dynamic change of the fruit of the Spirit. They will produce the results of the fruit that will be after the kind of words spoken. My lips will yield the fruit of God's purpose in my life.

Jesus is the revelation of salvation to all men. He is the righteousness of God to all men. He is to be received, by grace, through the confession of the mouth unto the complete package that is in Him.

> Whom having not seen, ye love; in whom, though now ye see him not, yet believing, ye rejoice with joy unspeakable and full of glory: receiving the end of your faith, even the salvation of your souls. Here is the end of salvation for man. We have not seen this man called Salvation, yet we know him, and we love him. Why? Because we recognize the undeniable truth concerning the vast change that has occurred since we encountered him. (1 Peter 1:8–9 KJV)

We cannot but sing the words to the song "Amazing Grace," how sweet the sound that saved a wretch like me! Yes, our story is one of being lost and undone without God or his Son, when He reached down His hand for me. We are changed! We experience peace and joy that makes the world angry, because they are so focused on their pursuit of things that do not satisfy. Often, we have none of the things which they pursue, but we have Jesus, and somehow, He makes what we have more than enough. We are not rich, but salvation has brought us to a position of having no lack. We do not have a large bank account, but because we love Him, we have a full supply.

Why are these things available and present in those who believe? Because the man, Salvation, who is the Word of God, is upholding us with the right hand of His righteousness. This allows us to rejoice in the provisions that accompany salvation. We are full of glory! As a matter of fact, Paul tells us that we are changed into, and even fashioned after, His glorious body. Look at Philippians 3:21.

> Who shall change our vile body, that it may be fashioned like unto his glorious body, according to the working whereby he is able even to subdue all things unto himself. (Philippians 3:21 KJV)

He is subduing all things that pertain to us unto Himself. Where are all those things accounted for? In the person of salvation, which is Jesus Christ. My safety, my healing, my deliverance, my soundness, and my preservation are all subdued by Him for me because I confessed what I believed concerning Him, because I received the words that I spoke as life's effect upon my spirit. Because those words, coupled with the life in Him, so changed me that my body is now fashioned like His. Then He proceeds through His righteous condition to make by force, the ingredients and elements that I need to be more than enough for me! Glory to God and the revelation of salvation, which is His Son!

> Which were born, not of blood, nor of the will of the flesh, nor of the will of man, but of God. (John 1:13 KJV)

The plan of salvation through Jesus Christ is the plan of God. The plan that is known as salvation, then, is really the revelation of Jesus Christ to mankind. It is really the result of Jesus being placed in position to complete the prophecy of Habakkuk with respect to His defeat of Satan.

Man then experiences a subsequent birth in the spirit. Man, having come through the canal of sin, must be exposed to a birth that will supernaturally supersede the condemnation that came due to the treason that occurred in the garden of Eden. If man could have had the ability to rectify his spiritual situation, God would have found a way for man through that means. But due to the complete depravity and death under which man fell when his spirit died, there was no means available within any flesh. Nothing less than the grand design of God for the revelation that is Jesus Christ would suffice. The operation of salvation and the characteristics that accompany this plan is the only means for man to be reconnected to God. The only place whereby man could be reconnected was in his spirit. The flesh would forever express its own nature. Sin would always be a present enemy for all men to be forced to deal with. But the plan of God would overcome the death of man's spirit through Jesus Christ.

Paul fills us in on this connection in Romans 8:1–6.

> There is therefore now no condemnation to them which are in Christ Jesus, who walk not after the flesh, but after the spirit. For the law of the spirit of life in Christ Jesus hath made me free from the law of sin and death. For what the law could not do, in that it was weak through the flesh, God sending his own Son in the likeness of sinful flesh, and for sin, condemned sin in the flesh: that the righteousness of the law might be fulfilled in us, who walk not after the flesh, but after the spirit. For they that are after the flesh do mind the things of the flesh; but they that are after the spirit the things of the spirit. For to be carnally minded is death; but to be spiritually minded is life and peace. (Romans 8:1–6 KJV)

There is no condemnation in the plan of God for any man who believes and receives, by grace through faith, the Word of God, because we are not any longer birthed in the robe of flesh. This is great news for us, since we no longer are left to be in bondage to the acts of treason that occurred in the garden. There is now a law associated with the plan and design of God. Since this is a law, it supersedes any law or agreement that came before it. What law came before the law of the spirit of life in Christ Jesus? It was the law of sin and death! That law existed and held men in its grip until Jesus took the keys of death and hell. He left the presence of the rulers of darkness just prior to His earthly resurrection.

That law had to have a legal remedy for new law to have a superseding effect. Now watch this. The old law is not void, and it is not eliminated. It is still in effect. The law of sin and death is as real today in the lives of men as it was when Eve filled her belly with death! Men, who are ignorant of the better law, are still filling their lives with the ingredients of the works of the flesh that exposes them to their ultimate enemy. It is most unfortunate for man that many of them continue to live a life they think is free of consequences, because they do not see the immediate effects of their lifestyle. But the result will be that they will inherit the law of sin and death. What a pity!

But the person who listens and seeks the truth will find a better law! We will find a law that supersedes the old law. We will find the means to come into a spirit of life that is only found in the person of salvation. This new way will not be absent of the old nature, but it will be a way that is paved by the blood of a righteous and legal sacrifice, who is raised from the dead and ever lives to make intercession for His people. This spirit of life is a better covenant. It is a better way. It exceeds any of the animal sacrifices because of the person who became the sacrifice. For what the law could not do, notice this, Jesus was born under the law, lived under the law, and died under the law, but the law and its means of sacrificial offerings were not enough to reconnect men's spirits with God. It could only serve as a type of what was to come.

Why was it just a type? Because men could not find a way to work the flesh from themselves. Therefore, the offerings in the Tabernacle continued daily. Men would bring an animal that represented their sin to be slain, and God would accept that offering for their sin resolution. But man himself was not changed! Why? Because man came through the birth canal of sin. Notice this also: All the other people that inhabited the earth had no relationship with God. Only Israel was given the law. The world was lost, so a part of God's creation was outside the possibility of a covering from God.

This covering was incomplete since man and his flesh could not stop the interaction of sin within himself. They could activate the five offerings and go through the rituals associated with the offerings, but they still had to deal with the nature of their natural birth. But when Jesus, the salvation of God, appeared, He appeared in the same form as man. He took on the sins of the natural birth canal just as all men before Him. The difference was that He, as the form of man, did not execute the deeds of the flesh. He lived a sinless and perfect life before God. He was obedient, when the rest of mankind had followed their own soulish ways. Through faithfulness and obedience, He was the one who was able to destroy the sin of the flesh. He was able to deny Himself and pick up the cross and follow the plan of God.

Again, watch this, because here Paul is referring to the new law that he described in verse 1: that the righteousness of the new law might be fulfilled in us. How was that to be? Because the new law quickened our spirit man and made us alive in Christ! The new law connected our spirit to the spirit of life that is in the risen Savior. The new law connected us to the measures involved in salvation. The new law redirected our path, until we began to walk after the spirit. Is this familiar? Of course, it is! It is the reenactment of the plan for Adam in the garden. Adam walked with God in the cool of the day and communed with Him. We, by law, are now given the same opportunity!

We are thinking higher thoughts than we were before we came to receive the revelation of salvation. We are walking under a new authority. Isn't it amazing that when Adam walked with God, he had a thought pattern that even God was in a position of wonderment?

> And brought them unto Adam to see what he would call them: and whatsoever Adam called

every living creature, that was the name thereof.
(Genesis 2:19 KJV)

Man is connected to God; he operates in a deeper dimension than he did before. Adam was the poster child for such depth of thinking.

This is exactly why Paul penned these words:

Let this mind be in you that was in Christ Jesus.
(Philippians 2:5 KJV)

Jesus was a man who walked with God in a higher dimension. Due to the Spirit of life that is in Him, we can as well. Salvation is always a walk of life to the believer. Any life that is not under the covering of this covenant and law is destined to the death that the law under which they live provide.

Here is the beautiful part of the spirit of life that is provided by the revelation of the Word of God, who is our salvation. He has brought us not only life but peace. Both are eternal, and both begin at the moment of confession. We become subject to a higher and more efficient law. Why would anyone choose to live under a law that ultimately condemned them to death when there was an alternative that guaranteed them life, abundance, and peace for eternity? That is the age-old question. The age-old answer is that God made us to function by free will. Man is choosing death.

We can only assume that the needs of the flesh are so alluring that man can only see the desperate need for immediate gratification. Surely, it is not the dissemination of the Word as we see and hear that everywhere. The law that they are living under, then, is a law that they have accepted as their guide. Again, what a pity.

The Revelation of the Glory in Jesus

The glory of God is an awesome position for any person to locate. There is no doubt that when David identified the position of the secret place of the Most High in Psalms 91 that he was describing the glory of God. As I consider the personal application of the glory of God, it occurs to me that there have been entirely too many instances where the glory of God has been exposed to me to put in a book. Let me explain. When I preach or teach the Gospel, there is an anointing present that I really do not have an answer for. There have been many times when the preparation of the people for the Word of God has been nonexistent. But when I stepped to the microphone, the power of God came upon me. I preached under a deep anointing and revelation of the power of God.

I remember my first revival in New Mexico. The power of the anointing was so rich that as I preached, the people were stirred to stand and praise God. The power of God would come in waves that would set my feet to running! It was the glorious power of the glory of God. The glory through the anointing that comes in the power of God upon my mind is something that I have often attempted to explain. Here is the best description that I can give. The glory of God seems to speak into one side of my brain while I am talking with the other side of my brain. I am listening and speaking at the same time.

This is not an unusual occurrence. There is scientific evidence that when men use the heavenly language of tongues that they are speaking from a completely different side of their brain than the side that was created for human speech. So when the ministry of the Word is being preached through me, there is a revelation of the glory of God. It is there in the power of the Word. I hear it, and I speak. By the way, this is precisely how Jesus defined His own work when He made the statements concerning what He saw and what He heard that became His actions in John 12:49–50 and John 5:19 and 30. It is clear that He received instruction from the Father what to do and what to say at the moment that this information was required. Along with this, Jesus informed us that this would be a part of the mission of the Holy Spirit when He came. He would give us what to say at the moment that we needed to give a response. He further substantiated this in Acts 1:2 when He said that He gave commands to the Holy Spirit for the apostles. The glory of God requires this sort of communication between the Father, Son, the Holy Spirit, and the believer. This is the prescription for turning the world upside down.

The power of the anointing is also the missing link that exists in the pulpits of our day. Liturgical emphasis and education have taught our pastors and speakers to program the anointing of revelation from the Word, out of our ministry. We regulate our services to such a degree that it becomes a brief motivational speech and our preaching is relegated to driving the mind toward positive thinking. In their place, these may have value. In the ministry of the Word, they have none. It is the power of the glory of God through the anointing that did the work in the New Testament. It still will today.

In Jal, New Mexico, I preached a revival in a wonderful church. On Sunday morning, the Lord spoke to me while I was preaching.

He said, "Get that little boy and take him to one side of the church. When you get there, tell his mother to stand up. Then whisper to the child to run to his mother."

I was preaching along at the time, and I did not think that this action had much to do with the sermon, but I did as instructed. When the child took off running to his mother, she knelt and extended her arms to him. She cradled him, and the Holy Spirit ministered to her. Tears began to flow. I was stunned with what happened next. A large man who worked the gas fields in that area stood to his feet. I was still preaching. He began to move down the aisle. Tears were flowing as he fell upon the altar. Naturally, I went to be with him for a second. He looked up at me through tears and said, "Brother, I love my children, and I have not been the father that they needed. When I saw that child run to his momma and her response, I knew that was what I needed to do to become what I need to be. I had to run to Jesus."

The altar was filled, and lives were changed. The glory of God in power was present. But also, the glory of God in his purpose was being shown to his people. A little child running to the open arms of his mother was the visual that the Holy Spirit used to minister to the people.

There is a beauty that the glory of God shadows over the people of God who are prepared for its appearance. It is a shadow of hope, joy, and peace that the people function under. Their needs are met, their lives are full, and they know that the means that has supplied their need will continue to do so, if they continue to abide under the shadow of the wings of the Almighty.

Prior to every game at West Virginia Tech, we would have a voluntary team chapel service. Most of the time, I spoke at those services. The atmosphere was always electrified as we were just a few hours from playing a game. The responses were always excellent, and our kids would involve themselves in the services.

During my second year, our Fellowship of Christian Athletes coordinator asked to bring a guest speaker on a Wednesday evening. I consented and assembled the team. Again, the room was electric. The speaker had been a world champion kickboxer. He had won the championship at nearly fifty years old. His testimony was excellent! As I watched and listened, I knew that there was something special happening. When he gave the call for anyone who would like to be saved, twenty-seven men stood to their feet and went forward to accept Jesus. The glory of the Lord filled the room. Big men, small men, and older men prayed the prayer of faith. This was the most awesome experience! The beauty of God appeared within our program. We began to accomplish things that the school, community, and football world in general could not believe. Tech became a bona fide winner! The beauty of the glory of God had come into our midst. Our coaches and players were operating in the secret place of the Most High. The shadow of His wings hovered over us as we represented the cross of Christ and its power, purpose, and beauty to change, transform, and transfer His blessings to men. Our lives were forever altered by the glory of God.

John begins his gospel with these words: "In the beginning." This lets us know that there will be support for Jesus being with God as a part the revelations of which He is about to unfold. From the beginning, the Word of God shared glory with the Father. He was the dynamic second person of the Godhead then. This glory has been restored to Him in His current position. He is called the Word of God from the beginning. We intend to define the glorious position that He held then, held during his ministry, and holds now. This is a significant revelation concerning Jesus that must be shared prior to our looking into the glory of God as it is expressed in Jesus. In Matthew 1:23, the angel tells the world something that is important to understand when we speak concerning this section.

> Behold, a virgin shall be with child, and shall bring forth a Son, *and they shall call his name Emmanuel, which being interpreted is, God with us.* (Matthew 1:23 KJV)

Here the angel identifies for us the nature of the child that was to be born. He would be God with us. So it does not surprise me when I study the revelation of the glory that was in Jesus, I locate the glory of the Father.

As you read on, you will see exactly what I mean.

> And the word was made flesh, and dwelt among us [and we beheld his glory, the glory as of the only begotten of the Father] full of grace and truth. (John 1:14 KJV)

Jesus lived in glory in three distinctly different domains. He lived in the glory of God in the domain we know as heaven. He lived in the glory of God while He was the Word of God made flesh and operated in the earth. But He also lived in glory for a brief time in the underworld while facing the torment of hell, after the crucifixion. We will attempt to divide the three during this chapter.

We will begin this by looking into the glory that He had with the Father as we look at John 17:5.

> And now, O Father, glorify thou me with thine own self with the glory which I had with thee before the world was. (KJV)

Jesus was in a position as the Word of God to share the glory of the Father. The question is, "What did that glory look like?" We must look at Moses's encounter with God to determine what it was that God revealed about Himself to Moses that answered Moses question concerning God's glory.

> And he said, I beseech thee, shew me thy glory. And he said, I will make all my goodness pass before thee, and I will proclaim the name of the LORD before thee; and will be gracious to whom I will be gracious and will shew mercy on whom I will shew mercy. And he said, thou canst not see my face: for there shall no man see me, and live. Moses makes a request of God to show him his glory. (Exodus 33:18–20 KJV)

Here is how God refers to His glory.

1. "I will make all My goodness pass before thee." So the goodness of God is His glory. The Bible is full of scripture that describes the goodness of God. Why? Because it defines Him and His personal glory. God is good! This goodness reflects who He is.

This goodness, according to the Greek, is a part of His beauty. It includes welfare and joy that His presence expresses.

So when Moses saw Him from behind, the first thing that God showed him about Himself was His goodness. This is a serious message to us concerning the glory of God. His ability to offer goodness from Himself is the side of Him that he presents to everyone, not just Moses! This represents the general personality and character of the Godhead.

> 2. "I will proclaim the name of the Lord before thee." So His name is His glory! Elyon, the God of creation, is the name of the Lord. Who does this directly refer to? The Word of God who we know as Jesus Christ. He is El Elyon; He is the God Most High. He is Adonai; He is the Ruler and Master. He is El Shaddai; He is the God of heaven who is more than enough. When He proclaimed his names to Moses, He exposed the glory that was in His name. As we described concerning Jesus in the chapter on salvation, in Hebrew, a name meant everything about the individual.

He further referred to Himself when he reflected upon His glory by naming Himself Jehovah. They saw Jehovah in eight different ways. He was Jehovah T'Sidkenu, the God of Righteousness. He was Jehovah N'Kaddesh, the Sanctifier. He is Jehovah Rophe, the God that Heals. He is Jehovah Rohi, "my Shepherd." He is Jehovah Nissi, "my Banner." He is Jehovah Jirah, "my Provider." He is Jehovah Shalom, "my Peace." He is Jehovah Shammah, meaning "He is There."

When God showed His glory to Moses and subsequently to all mankind, He identified the glory that man would locate in Him. What a blessed revelation of the presence of God in the activities of man. It becomes very difficult to locate a part of the life of man that God has not placed His glory upon. His revelation to Moses was done in such a fashion as to let Moses know that His service to God had no place where He would not show up with glory! These names represent the character of the Father as He relates Himself to mankind. It is his personality that men recognized when the children of Israel received the revelations of Jehovah.

3. His glory is next identified in His graciousness. In this case, the God of heaven exposed His glory by stooping down or bending down in kindness to an inferior. He favored man with His desire to come near Him.

God is gracious to His people as He favors them with Himself. He granted Moses and man in general with the glory of his ability to be favorable to them. Here we begin to see the Word of God identified specifically in the personality of the Godhead. He is known and is identified as grace by John.

4. His mercy or compassion to man is also expressed in His showing His glory to man. He reveals His compassion to us as a part of His personal glory.

This is a part of the character and personality of the entire Godhead. In Exodus 33, Moses showed us a piece of His glory. Then in Exodus 34, He continued the revelation of the glory of God.

> And the LORD descended in the cloud, and stood with him there, and proclaimed the name of the LORD. And the LORD passed by before him, and proclaimed, *the LORD*, the LORD God, *merciful* and *gracious*, *longsuffering*, and *abundant in goodness and truth*, keeping mercy for thousands, *forgiving iniquity and transgression and sin*, and that will by no means clear the guilty; visiting the iniquity of the fathers upon the children, and upon the children's children, unto the third and to the fourth generation. (Exodus 34:5–7 KJV)

The Lord appears in the cloud that we know shrouds His glory, and there his Shekinah Glory is in the smoke. Here He appears to Moses in more depth in the following ways:

1. God again identifies the glory that is in His name as He is the Lord, who is the self-existent and eternal one.

The personality of the Godhead is here recognized.

2. Then He describes Himself as the Lord (eternal) God who is Almighty God of might and power. Again, He expresses himself and His glory by the names that He communicates to Moses and, in the future, to His people.

The qualities that are eternal are shared by the entire Godhead.

3. To this list of glory, He adds that He is longsuffering and that He is patient and slow to anger. This feature of His glory is especially significant to Israel as they consistently acted rebelliously and irresponsibly toward God.

It is no less essential to us as we identify the glory of God. Thank God, His glory expresses His patience. Thank God, He is slow to anger and willing through patience to develop His people. This quality extends to the entire Godhead.

4. Truth is another element of the glory of God that is revealed from this encounter with Moses. God is the Truth, and in him is no lie. He revealed this side of his glory to Moses so that when Moses spoke of God's glory, he would tell the people that His character is that of complete truth.

Truth showed up when His glory came down. This truth was His stability. He was the same through and through with no variable parts that would cause Him to have to change. Truth identified that we can completely trust Him, we can completely depend upon Him, and we can completely be assured that whatever He instructs is sure. There is no doubt about who He is or how He operates. His glory declares Himself, and it is pure truth. This is active in the Godhead, but the Holy Spirit and the Word of God are identified to share this content of personality and subsequent scripture.

> 5. Found in His glory is forgiveness. His nature is to forgive. What is His glory forgiving? His glory is on display through forgiveness of sin, evil, and lawlessness.

It now becomes apparent how God disassembled the fallen kingdom of Satan. He did it through his natural nature to forgive from evil. He would not forgive Satan because Satan had espoused his own direction and chosen to create insurrection against the kingdom of God. The evil perpetrated in the heavenly environment could not be tolerated. So Satan had to be removed and ultimately defeated.

Look at how God handled man. In Genesis chapter 3, God knew the progression of man should they remain in the garden. So expulsion was the only answer. What God did next shows us the glory of God in His goodness.

> Unto Adam also and to his wife did the LORD God make coats of skins and clothed them. (Genesis 3:21 KJV)

Do you see the glory of God revealed to Adam and Eve? Because He loved them so much, He sacrificed one of His own creation. He first sacrificed an animal, and the first blood shed was made to provide clothing for Adam and Eve. Later, God would institute the sacrifices in the outer court of the Tabernacle to serve as offering for men's relationship to Him.

He would also institute the sacrifice for sin that was done outside the camp so that man's sin directly against God could have a means of atonement. This sacrifice first happened outside of Eden, and it happened for Adam and Eve. Outside of Eden, an animal that Adam had named had to be slain. Blood had to be shed for the protective clothing to be made for their journey. God had walked with them and talked with them in the cool of the day. God had shown them His glory and designed them in His image. Again, He shows His glory to them through the process of forgiveness.

For them, there was an atonement. But for their seed, there would exist the stain of evil that cast a shadow of sin upon mankind that would only be eradicated through another sacrifice. His glory places the works of iniquity, transgression, rebellion, and sin, which becomes the habit and habits of lawlessness and rebellion, in a position that a sacrifice can eradicate the actions of unrighteousness. What a great and mighty God who sits on the circle of the earth in His glory!

God's glory of forgiveness is so much Him that even in what appears to man to be the greatest rebellious act that is conceivable, His response could not deny who He is! Glory to God! That is great news for you and me! With this information, we can then begin to track the plan of God as it relates to the process of atonement for man. The first animal sacrifice was provided for Adam and Eve. Their rebellion in the garden was atoned for due to the glory of the Father that was shared in forgiveness of sin.

This process transferred to the children of Israel in the book of Exodus. God had introduced the sacrificial lamb process just outside the garden of Eden, for those for whom He had created it for forgiveness. We know this process worked because Adam and Eve carried forward with this process, and they taught it to their boys. There is no doubt, since Abel was accepted by God through the process of appropriate sacrifice that their parents identified the act of God prior to their expulsion as a sacred act of atoning for their sin. They were under the protective clothing of the glory of God.

When Abel sacrificed as he did, he had learned the process of atonement. He was the person who God saw as doing the sacrificial system correctly. He did not wake up one day and think of this. Just as his parents had been taught concerning a blood sacrifice for their protective clothing, Abel had learned and followed their instruction.

Cain, on the other hand, had the same opportunity. He was in the same family that functioned under the atonement process. Here was the difference. Abel was operating under a system that God, the Creator of his parents, had designed. Cain was operating under a system that his maker had designed. What do I mean? Cain was the prodigy of those created by God, but he had gone the way of his maker. He was under the influence of the deceiver, the destroyer and the enemy of God.

Let me show you something. Man has a Creator, and he has a maker. They are not the same! God is the Creator. As I have described devising the roles of the Godhead, God designed and created through this means the world and all that we know. He also created man as tripart spirit, soul, and body. Then there is the second side of man, and that is the side that is derived from his maker. The real man is always the spirit of man. The soul of man and the spirit live on, but the body will be the part that eventually fails and returns to dust. Since the spirit is the real you, it is obvious that in the garden, neither the soul nor the body died. The part of man that died was his spirit. The stolen portion or part of man that Satan required was man's spirit. This is for obvious reasons: God is a Spirit.

Now when man fell, his spirit died, and Satan went on the loose in the inner man for every man from that day until this. Man had a new maker. Until the day you meet Jesus Christ, if you ever do, your maker is the one whom your spirit serves. In Cain's case, knowing how his parents had taught him to live, he was content to serve his maker, the devil.

Look at Genesis 4:2–10.

> And she again bare his brother Abel. And Abel was a keeper of sheep, but Cain was a tiller of the ground. And in process of time it came to pass, that Cain brought of the fruit of the ground an offering unto the LORD. And Abel, he also brought of the firstlings of his flock and of the fat thereof. And the LORD had respect unto Abel and to his offering: but unto Cain and to his offering he had not respect. And Cain was very wroth, and his countenance fell. And the LORD said unto

Cain, why art thou wroth? And why is thy countenance fallen? If thou doest well, shalt thou not be accepted? And if thou doest not well, sin lieth at the door. And unto thee shall be his desire, and thou shalt rule over him. and Cain talked with Abel his brother: and it came to pass, when they were in the field, that Cain rose up against Abel his brother, and slew him. And the LORD said unto Cain, where is Abel thy brother? And he said, I know not: am I my brother's keeper? And he said, what hast thou done? The voice of thy brother's blood crieth unto me from the ground. (Genesis 4:2–10 KJV)

It was identified by God precisely who Cain's maker was by the offering that he attempted to produce. Look at the response of God to Cain. And the LORD said unto Cain,

Why art thou wroth? And why is thy countenance fallen?
If thou doest well, shalt thou not be accepted? And if thou doest not well, sin lieth at the door. And unto thee shall be his desire, and thou shalt rule over him. (Genesis 4:7 KJV)

In other words, if you do as you're instructed, then what you do will be accepted. If you do not do as you are instructed, then your maker's seed lay at your feet. You will fulfill the desire of your flesh and the desire of your maker. Your maker will cause you to desire to be the ruler. Do you see that? Therefore, Cain could not be accepted nor forgiven when his maker caused him to commit murder. Because the sin maker had complete rulership over his inner man. God said so!

This led Cain to speak with Abel, and subsequently a murdering spirit emerged from the spirit of his maker, and Abel was dead! God, who was in the same position He was in the garden questioned

Abel's whereabouts and received an answer that rivaled Cain's father's. "Am I my brother's keeper?" No, but your maker did make you your brother's murderer! Now let's contrast the difference between the sin maker and the righteous maker. Paul said in 2 Corinthians 5:21 these words concerning our spiritual maker and what he had made us.

> For he hath made him to be sin for us, who knew no sin; that we might be made the righteousness of God in him. (2 Corinthians 5:21 KJV)

Can you see the contrast in our makers? We have been made the righteousness of God by the actions of our Maker! Jesus was made to be sin so that we could be made the righteousness of God. Our Maker gave us a born-again spirit of perfect righteousness. Our Maker reconnected us to God. Our Maker made us what He is! We are accepted in the beloved and welcomed into the throne room of God because our Maker made us in His own image! What an awesome relationship God has designed for us through the perfectly righteous Word of God, Jesus, who expressed the glory of God to us. We, through grace by faith, experience the glory of God's forgiveness from our iniquity and our transgressions. This glory translates us into the kingdom of our Maker.

Abel had been defined by the Creator, God, and the process that atoned for his sin. His Maker was then covering his sin. Cain's maker was the maker of sin. He dominated Cain so much so that Cain's nature of sin arose in him, and God's man from whom he had received his atoning sacrifice was slain. The two sides of man that were on display by their maker were visible for us to behold. God knew that in Abel, and his sacrifice was the process that God required until the prophecy of Genesis 3 could reach fruition and the child could come forth.

Israel would be next to experience the sacrificial process. The glory of God would become present for the people through the five sacrificial offerings that God had directed. They would come to know God precisely as He described Himself to Moses. Moses saw all these ten elements of the glory of God in Exodus 34:5–7. What a sight it had to be. The most outstanding thought of it all is that he only saw these pieces of his glory from God's back. This revelation of God's glory is more than sufficient to captivate our attention with respect to the glory of God. We can know and understand how the glory of God is operating as it relates to man.

God then showed Moses seven things about His glory. As we know, 7 is the number of completion in the scripture.

1. He showed him the glory of His goodness.
2. He showed him the glory of His name.
3. He showed him the glory of His mercy.
4. He showed him the glory of His longsuffering.
5. He showed him the glory of His forgiveness.
6. He showed him the glory of His graciousness.
7. He showed him the glory of His truth.

The complete glory of God was exposed to Moses so that man could see it, hear of it, and know it. The reality of its impact upon the spirit of man defines how man responds to a maker. When God still shows His glory to mankind, we can see His glory in operation in many ways in the Old Testament in relation to his dealings with Israel. His glory is obvious in his relationship to the Tabernacle. We can also point toward his glory in relation to how he dealt with the great men of the Bible.

But what I wanted to know was how that glory related to how He functioned before all that glory was exposed to Moses and subsequently to all those to whom Moses would describe the encounter. My answer became clear when Moses requested to see His glory. Why? Because although God could not have Moses see His face, He was ready to reveal His personality and character to Him. In other words, this was not anything that had not been in operation in the character of the Godhead. It actually is who He was prior to it being who he is! Before His revelation to Moses, the makeup of the Godhead and the heavenly economy had always operated under the system that was now being exposed and expressed to Moses. It is simply who He is and how He does business.

He never functioned in eternity past any differently than He did when He put Moses in the cleft of the rock and passed by. The great news is, He still functions through the same modalities of glory in this moment that He did when Moses saw Him! There is still one remaining question that must be answered concerning the glory of God to forgive. Why did God not forgive Lucifer for his rebellion? Here is my answer to this question: For the same reason He did not forgive Cain!

> If thou doest well, shalt thou not be accepted?
> And if thou doest not well, sin lieth at the door.
> And unto thee shall be his desire, and thou shalt rule over him. (Genesis 4:7 KJV)

Sin was in the heart of the rebellion of Lucifer and those who followed him. He had held a great position in the heavenly operation and arena. But that was not enough. His desire was to over throw the kingdom of God. War ensued, and Lucifer was cast down. But here is the reason Lucifer's desire was to rule over God and everything of which heaven consisted. God could not forgive the actions of Lucifer as he was a created being for the express purpose of serving God.

There was no place for Lucifer's will to be in command of his position. He was a created. But the view from just off the throne was too vivid for him to maintain his role. He desired more. The creation of God rebelled, and this caused God to extricate him from access to heaven and place him in the earth. This did not stop his interest in overthrowing heaven, but it did create space between the throne of God and the insurrection of the rebellious. God, in His glory with all its attributes, could not accept these misguided desires. So the battle in the spiritual realm began. Although Jesus has paid the price for this battle to cease, Satan has continued to maintain control over the fallen spirits of mankind. This has kept man in slavery to him and brought many to meet their personal maker.

So once more let's look at Exodus 34:5–7. These revelations consisted of all the glory Moses required to live in a new vision for a new task. All the glory Moses would need to fulfill the design and call of God for His ministry to Israel was defined in the eleven descriptive words that express the composition of God.

> And the LORD descended in the cloud, and stood with him there, and proclaimed the name of the lord. And the lord passed by before him, and proclaimed, *the LORD, the LORD GOD, merciful* and *gracious, longsuffering,* and *abundant in goodness and truth,* keeping *mercy for thousands, forgiving iniquity* and *transgression* and *sin,* and that will by no means clear the guilty; visiting the iniquity of the fathers upon the children, and upon the children's children, unto the third and to the fourth generation. (Exodus 34:5–7 KJV)

This glory was enough for Moses, Israel, and it is enough for mankind. When the glory of God is further exposed in the person of Jesus Christ, man has the opportunity to experience each of these traits as they are enacted for man and toward man. This is the reason this Gospel must be preached and shared through every available means as man's future depends upon his acceptance of this message.

The Glory of God Manifested in Jesus as Righteousness and Sanctifier

Our family had lost a son and a brother. The call was devastating. I was unaware that he was having a minor surgery. I had been trying to reach him since Friday, but there was no answer. Sharon and I lay down on this Sunday afternoon for a brief nap after church. As we napped, I heard the phone ring. The call identification showed it was Bob. I answered the call by saying, "Hey, Brother Bob, where have you been?"

The voice on the other end was that of Bob's wife. She was in shock no doubt as she abruptly said, "Mike, Bob is dead!"

I lost total control of my arms. I sat up in the bed to remove the glasses that I was wearing when I fell asleep. I saw them flying across the room. Naturally, she told me what had happened. All I knew for sure was that my protector, my best friend, my confidant, and my dear brother was gone.

We were all devastated and spent a good while working through the recovery process. There were many tears and pure sadness that we were no longer going to share Bob's laugh, talent, and acts of love. As time went on, the story that was related to me by my mother concerning my brother and his new home helped me to see the righteousness that our Heavenly Father shows to us by His divine plan for mankind. He has separated us and sanctified us to a blessed hope that death cannot supersede. The glory of God's righteous separation is always a blessing to us in the end.

Here is the story as told me by my mother.

*****

Early one Sunday morning in August of 2006, I was awakened to the sound of a song. I could hear the song clearly in my ear. It was a song that I had sung several times in church. The title of the song was, "I'm Moving on Up Someday." I had a very strange feeling that I was hearing this song for a reason. I could understand this because my son-in-law was in the hospital in Orange Park, Florida, and my daughter and I were going to see him that day. The day moved on, and I didn't say anything about the experience, but I fully expected to find a problem when we got to the hospital. We had about 125 miles to drive to complete the trip, and when we walked into his room, everything was pretty well under control, for which I was glad but surprised.

We left early in the afternoon to return home to Jesup, Georgia. I really don't know why we left as early as we did, but when we got home, everything seemed to be all right, and the strange feeling that had come upon me seemed to be gone or at least lessened. We were not home very long when my daughter, Ellen, Ron's wife, came across the yard just wailing. I could hear her crying, and immediately I thought that she had received bad news about Ron. I met Ellen at the door, and she handed me the phone, and the voice on the phone was that of my daughter-in-law telling me that my son had passed away. I was stopped in my tracks. I couldn't believe what I was hearing. It made no sense.

I knew that Bob Jr. had gone into the hospital in Atlanta, Georgia, where they lived, but it was only for minor surgery and he would be out on that Sunday afterward. His death was sudden and unexpected. It was unreal. I sat motionless as she filled in the details. When she hung up, I was numb. I couldn't cry and I could hardly speak. Bob Jr. was so full of life, and he was only fifty-five years old. Besides, he was the third member of my family wiped out in eighteen years. Then, too, Bob had just been down for the Fourth of July, and by August, he was gone. He was so happy that weekend, and we enjoyed his being with us so much. Gone so soon, and it was a bridge too far. I had always been able to overcome the cards that life dealt, but this loss had set me back. I found myself unable to pray and unable to communicate how I felt. I just could not get beyond the shock of his death. I felt like a zombie, and I wasn't sure that I'd ever be able to go to church again.

Bob was a very different child. He was easy to deal with, and as he grew up, he noticed things that other children would pay no attention to. We lived in Parkersburg, West Virginia, when he was young. We would sometimes take rides with the children down to Charleston, West Virginia, and drive past the capital building. The capital building with its beautiful gold dome fascinated Bob every time he saw it. He said to his sister, Ellen, on one occasion when he passed it, "Sissy, every time I pass by the capital, my heart swells with pride." He was only ten or eleven at the time.

It was all over, and the funeral was coming. Bob had married into a Jewish family, and they do things quite differently. Let me say right here that I could find no peace and no way to deal with the blow of his death at this point. The funeral was no exception. There were no flowers, no music, no real ministry, and even the casket was so plain. So in it all, I felt no comfort for myself, no peace of mind. I felt faint at the funeral and found myself staggering as I walked. In fact, I wasn't sure I'd live over it all. I was devastated in a way that was unrecognizable to me. I had nothing to compensate for the loss I felt.

Then one night I went to bed just trying to find some rest from what I had been through. I did not go to sleep right away, but as I lay there, I saw a vision. I saw crystal towers beautiful beyond description. The light glistened upon them, and it was a scene I will never forget. Bob was standing, arms folded, in awe of the sight as he looked upon those crystal towers. I saw where he was and felt the pride and the glory he felt. The grief left, and the sorrow was over, and I could live again. Then I understood the song in my ear the Sunday morning of his death. Bob had truly moved up and was living in peace and tranquility. God always comes through. He may not come when we want Him to, but He'll come right on time.

*****

Join me now, and let's look at the glory of God in the New Testament as it appears in the Word of God. In John's gospel chapter

11 and verse 40, Jesus is speaking to Martha concerning the resurrection of Lazarus. Here is what He says about the condition of Lazarus as He lay in the grave:

> Jesus saith unto her, Said I not unto thee, that, if thou wouldest believe, *thou shouldest see the glory of God?*
> Philip saith unto him, Lord, show us the Father, and it sufficeth us. Jesus saith unto him, have I been so long time with you, and yet hast thou not known me, Philip? He that hath seen me hath seen the Father; and how sayest thou then, show us the Father? (John 14:8–9 KJV)

These two verses of scripture are extremely telling regarding the glory of the Father as it refers to Jesus. The key to this scripture is obviously not in the question that Philip asked but in the answer that Jesus gave.

> I have been with you so long and you don't know Me? If you know who I am, then you know who the Father is. Is it necessary for you to inquire more deeply? Have the works that I have done in your sight and for the people not spoken to the works of the Father who I have come to show you? How and why should you ask Me for more signs?

The Glory Manifested in the Names of Jehovah

Jehovah T'Sidkenu

Here is what He meant:

> First, if you know the revelation to Moses, then you can identify the Father in Me. Every name

by which you recognized Jehovah is present and operating in Me. If He was Jehovah T'Sidkenu your righteousness, then I am the embodiment of that revelation.

The term *righteousness* represents the quality of character represented in God and created by God's standards. In John 14:7 (KJV), Jesus expresses this quality in His own words:

> If ye had known me, ye should have known my Father also: and from henceforth ye know him and have seen him.

The righteous Jehovah has manifested Himself and the glory of this revelation in the person Jesus Christ. Jesus would go further and say that His relationship to the glory of God was such that He did not do one thing that was out of the character of His Father.

He was the righteousness of God revealed to man. He was of equal character, equal nature, and equal power. So when they saw Jesus, He was the glory of God revealed among mankind. The people did not have the ability to see it or understand the glory of God that was ministering through Him to their poor, captive, blind, and enslaved. But those to whom He ministered saw the glory of God manifested to them through the righteous Jesus Christ. Paul taught and wrote on this extensively in His epistles. In 2 Corinthians 5:21, Paul identifies our righteousness with the righteousness that was made for us by Jesus.

> For he hath made him *to be* sin for us, who knew no sin; that we might be made the righteousness of God in him. (2 Corinthians 5:21 KJV)

So when you see Jesus, you see the glory of God that was represented by the name of Jehovah T'Sidkenu in the Old Testament. In Jesus, we saw the manifestation of righteousness. Then the writer of Hebrews shares further insight into this revelation of glory as it relates to Jesus.

> And he is the radiance of his glory and the exact representation of his nature and upholds all things by the word of his power when he had made purification of sins, he sat down at the right hand of the majesty on high, the righteous standard of God is who Jesus was. (Hebrews 1:3 KJV)

We see and read about Him as the exact representation of His nature. He is exact and equal to the Father in terms of his spiritual makeup.

Allow me to stop here and say that when we refer to the righteousness of Jesus, we are referring to the content of Him spiritually. His inner man was in such a state of fine-tuning that He showed the world the Father that functioned on the inside of Him. Righteousness is not an activity that one does. Nor is it a designed plan of personal actions that people do that clearly define, by what they do, that they are righteous. No, righteousness is a spiritual activity that is provided for man internally only by the acceptance of the sacrifice of Jesus and received only through the cross.

Righteousness is the status that man's spirit receives upon the new birth. It will manifest itself outwardly through the flesh as the flesh begins to understand what the spirit is teaching. The fruit of the spirit becomes evident in the life of men. Righteousness becomes, then, an outward lifestyle. This outliving will never occur until righteousness becomes the foundation of man in his spirit.

What makes me say that? Because when Jesus was made to be sin for us and He died to destroy the works of the devil, He did so knowing that man would, by faith, receive the spiritual revelation of righteousness. God, then, by grace through the faith of men because of what Jesus had accomplished on the cross, transferred righteousness into man. This was done by the obedient work of a righteous man for us so that we could be reconnected with God. When we believed, the connection was immediately made with the righteous one, Jesus, and we became the righteousness of God in our spirit. This is a spiritual work. It will, and it must, eventually manifest itself in the flesh. If there is no manifestation in the flesh, then there can be no righteousness in the spirit. How do we know this? We look at Jesus.

> Then answered Jesus and said unto them, Verily, verily, I say unto you, the Son can do nothing of himself, but what he seeth the Father do: for what things soever he doeth, these also doeth the Son likewise. For the Father loveth the Son, and sheweth him all things that himself doeth: and he will shew him greater works than these, that ye may marvel. (John 5:19–20 KJV)

> I speak that which I have seen with my Father: and ye do that which ye have seen with your father. (John 8:38 KJV)

When He says the Father shows Him all things, again He is referencing the operation of the Spirit working within His Spirit. When Jesus refers to the things that He can do and the place from which He locates them to do, He is referring to the spiritual work that is coming from His Spirit. So His righteousness manifested itself in the works which He was able to do for the people. These works of the glory of God through righteousness addressed the needs that were represented by the people.

If our life expresses no fruit of righteousness and bears no resemblance to the life and works of Christ, then we must begin to seek for answers as to why. If the glory of God in righteousness exists, then it exists in abundance. If it exists in abundance, then our lives must reflect the works of the righteousness that exists within us. We need to check our righteous meter, friends, and determine who we really are!

It is possible that this concept is new, and you have not considered how righteousness should affect your daily living principles. It is also possible that you do know how the righteous should live and choose to live a life content with the concept of waiting upon the hope of your eternal life. Being saved is one of the greatest events in one's life. Living in the benefits of that salvation is the greater event that every believer must be compelled to pursue. The eternity now benefit belongs to the righteous!

If you are among the latter, then please take another look at yourself and the Word of God. You are missing the benefits of the Gospel. You are missing the depth of the relationship which the glory of God in righteousness offers. You are also missing the righteous standard that sets the promises of God in action for you today so that you can experience the benefits of eternity now!

The Glory in Jesus as Shown in Jehovah M'Kiddesh

Jehovah M'Kiddesh is the term by which Israel knew God. It means "Jehovah my sanctifier."

Did the Gospels describe Jesus in that way? Yes, He again was the manifestation of the sanctified God. He is the one who separated people for the work of the ministry. He is the one who called the disciples and prepared them for the work that God had established for them. The glory of God in sanctification separated those called to an eternal purpose.

> Now ye are clean through the word which I have spoken unto you. Abide in me, and I in you. As the branch cannot bear fruit of itself, except it abide in the vine; no more can ye, except ye abide in me. I am the vine, ye are the branches: he that abideth in me, and I in him, the same bringeth forth much fruit: for without me ye can do nothing. (John 15:3–5 KJV)

Jesus speaking here identifies how the disciples were clean. It was through the Word that He had spoken. So by His words men are cleansed, purified, and sanctified. Those hearing this could relate to it as this had reference to the laver in the Tabernacle in the dessert. They knew that the only means to be prepared for entrance into the Tabernacle was for the reflection in the water to be pure. Jesus shares with them the way to remain sanctified, which is to abide in Him. If you do, you will bear fruit.

> Sanctify them through thy truth: thy word is truth. (John 17:17 KJV)

Again, Jesus has referred to the Word of God that will accomplish the work of separating people from one distinct style of living toward another. The word *sanctify* means simply "to consecrate and make holy." This is what Jehovah did for the priests in the Tabernacle. It was the only method whereby they could serve God in the Tabernacle and live.

Jesus is exposing the glory of God to the people through the terms of sanctification, and those who were Jews could relate to the concept. Without the process of purification, which came only through the Word of God that washed and cleansed, there would be no means to proceed further into the depths of spiritual relationship. The glory of God in sanctification was of ultra importance to the Levitical priesthood. Without the purification process occurring prior to their entrance into the holy place, they could not live beyond the tent's door. Jesus, by manifesting this part of the name God shown to Moses, was showing the people the depth of relationship that man must have in order not only to approach God, but to live for him in the future.

What leads me to that conclusion? It is all in what Jesus said and then what became of those to whom He said it.

> I have manifested thy name unto the men which thou gavest me out of the world: thine they were, and thou gavest them me; and they have kept thy word. Now they have known that all things whatsoever thou hast given me are of thee. For I have given unto them the words which thou

> gavest me; and they have received them and have known surely that I came out from thee, and they have believed that thou didst send me. I pray for them: I pray not for the world, but for them which thou hast given me; for they are thine. And all mine are thine, and thine are mine; and I am glorified in them. (John 17:6–10 KJV)

Jesus said,

> I have manifested Thy name.

What name would that have been? Read on.

> The ones you gave Me have kept Thy Word. So what do we know that the Word accomplished in them? It cleansed, purified, and sanctified them. They had been exposed to the sanctifying glory of the Father that is in the name Jehovah M'Kiddesh! The words that you gave Me, Father, they have been both known and received. They have been faithful to the Word that I have spoken to them.

Now watch what he says:

> I am glorified in them. (KJV)

What part of Him was glorified in them? The portion of the name that represented the Father as the sanctifier. The words matched with the understanding of the name made certain that they knew who it was that was manifesting within their personal spirit. This spiritual activity created relationship of glory within those to whom it was expressed. Then we look past these statements to the lives that were lived after the ascension of Jesus. There we find people who are turning the world upside down. They were separated by the Word for service.

Luke wrote in Acts 4:20,

> For we cannot but speak the things which we have seen and heard. (Acts 4:20 KJV)

How could they do anything but tell of the work that had been accomplished in them? Then in 1 John 1:3, John wrote,

> That which we have seen and heard declare we unto you, that ye also may have fellowship with us: and truly our fellowship is with the Father, and with his Son, Jesus Christ. (1 John 1:3 KJV)

The fellowship to which he refers is the fellowship with the name of the Father and the name of the Son.

> That which was from the beginning, which we have heard, which we have seen with our eyes, which we have looked upon, and our hands have handled, of the word of life [for the life was manifested, and we have seen it, and bear witness, and shew unto you that eternal life, which was with the Father, and was manifested unto us]. (1 John 1:1–2 KJV)

This identifies where the relationship came from, and it identifies that he was handled. Now notice! John refers to hearing. He took something inward. He heard the Word and the Word of God did something for him on the inside. Jesus said it sanctified them. Then he said he saw. Again, he took something inward. What he saw painted an indelible imprint upon him on the inside. This meant that it impacted his spirit to such a degree that it caused a transformation. Why? Because faith cometh by hearing.

Then he says after that, "We handled. We touched the Word of life." They literally reached their hands and placed them upon Him. The life was manifested. "We saw, heard, and touched the Word of life." Now what Word was he speaking to them that allowed them to be so spiritually transformed? He was speaking the Word of the glory of God that is in the name of the sanctifier. That sanctifying name transferred them into the life that was in the truth concerning the name. Jesus related the glory of God to men through the Word of truth, and men were separated for service. Men were changed into a blessed fellowship with the Father and the Son because of this separation.

Today we do not consider this portion of the scripture as essential in most churches. But it is apparent how important it is to God. He revealed this to Moses and expressed it again in Jesus. Paul goes on in 1 Thessalonians 4 to spend the first part of that chapter addressing the importance of a sanctified lifestyle while living the Christian life. The effects of a life separated to God are readily and easily seen in the book of Acts. The question is, "Are any of these effects appearing in your life? If not, why not?" The effects of the Word of God upon the life of men has never changed. He is still speaking, directing, and separating those who are seeking Him. A newer and deeper relationship can exist. It is found in the glory of God represented in sanctification. It is one of those things that Paul refers to in 1 Corinthians 2:9–10.

> But as it is written, eye hath not seen, nor ear heard, neither have entered the heart of man, the things which God hath prepared for them that love him. But God hath revealed them unto us by his Spirit: for the Spirit searcheth all things, yea, the deep things of God. This depth is prepared for you by God. It is in his glory and it is in his name. But it will only be revealed to you by his Spirit. (1 Corinthians 2:9–10 KJV)

The Glory of God Manifested in Jesus as Shepherd and Healer

The Glory in Jesus as Shown in Jehovah Rohi

I was lying in bed and pretty well asleep when the phone rang. I looked through blurry eyes to identify the caller. I recognized the name on the caller identification. It was a close friend of mine from my days in the football profession. I had expected a call from him. Earlier in the day, I had received another call from a coaching friend who had informed me to pray as something had happened to one of his children. He was unaware of the details, but he did know that the family was at the hospital.

This family has four awesome children. When they send out a Christmas card with the family picture, it is always a highlight for our mantle. These kids are attractive, intelligent, centered on Christ, and extremely well behaved. They are tremendous students, and as you can imagine, they are the apple of their parents' eyes. Although this is a coaching family, the parents have made special provision to be there for their kids. When I had cancer and was in ICU, it was this great friend who came from Ohio to be with me for a while. However, he had to leave to get back to Kentucky to be able to attend his son's baseball game. They were and are awesome parents. On this day, however, something had occurred that was serious. I did not know the particulars, but it was a bad situation. My friend has always been tight-lipped concerning any situation that had arisen with the kids' health, so I did not see this as unusual.

I answered the phone by saying, "Hey, man, what in the world is going on? I've gotten phone calls. What has happened?"

The serious voice of a concerned mother answered me with a calm and clear response. She said, "Mike, I can't tell you about it right now because we are on speaker phone. We need you to pray for our son. He is in severe pain, and we need him to go to sleep. They gave him something awhile ago, and it has not worked. Can you pray please pray for him?"

"Of course," I replied, "I would."

I was not aware of the circumstances that surrounded the situation. I did not know what had happened. All I knew was that there was what appeared to be a desperate need, and I was asked to call on the God who provided the Lamb for our healing.

I prayed an anointed prayer for comfort, encouragement, and healing for the child and the entire family in general. The anointing to pray has been one that has weighed heavily upon me for quite a while. The Holy Spirit seems to rise within me as I call upon the name of the Lord. I have found the name of Jesus to be sufficient in each situation for which I have called upon His name. He is fully aware of the price He paid for our ability to use His name for the benefits that I was requesting. After a couple of minutes of prayer, I pronounced the final say upon the matter, amen! In my mind, it was the "so be it" that amen determines. I was convinced that heaven had heard, the earth would respond, and that the boy would be ministered to in the very fashion that I had asked.

This awesome mother said a quick, "Thank you and we will call you later to fill you in."

I promptly lay down and went directly back to sleep. In my spirit, I knew that I had touched God on this families' behalf. As I prepared for sleep, I remember distinctly wondering just how long it would take for this thing to materialize for them to actually receive and see the problem subside. I closed my eyes with the thought that I would know the details of the events the next day. Within ten minutes, I received a text from my dear friend. It shared with me the expediency of heaven's response to the needs of his children. It shared with me that our prayer had brought almost-immediate relief, and their son had fallen asleep and was resting well. It concluded with praise to God for his glorious blessing. We all know how difficult it to watch a child be in agony. In this case, the pain went from agony to comfort in a matter of ten minutes. The God of the universe listened to a fervent prayer of righteous people and dispatched angels from around the throne to swaddle a child in need.

He is the Jesus who is our Healer. He is the Jesus that is always our Shepherd. It is a fact that He will heal us during the time of our physical needs. He will search for us and shepherd us until we are nurtured back to becoming a person that is vibrant. He will train us and instruct us as we grow within the family where He has placed us. He has done this more times than I can count. He has revealed his glory to me and that to whom I have ministered in real and tangible ways. Thank God for the Lamb who was slain and provided the prosperity of healing to my life and the knowledge that when I call on Him, he is ever searching to take His best care of me and the needs that I present to Him. By the way, both child and family are doing wonderfully. He is a thriving young man with a bright future. He will never forget the God who saw and delivered him during his time of need. Neither will his family. This motivates me to pray even more deeply as I come across the needs of God's people. How could we ever be the same when we encounter the need meeting God who hears and answers our prayer?

So in this brief story, Jesus revealed the name of the Father when he revealed Himself as the Shepherd. This name of Jehovah was Rohi. It represented the nature of God to be intimate, tender, and caring. Jesus certainly identified with the glory of God in this regard. Look at the scripture where He identifies with this part of his divine call and His divine nature.

> I am the good shepherd: the good shepherd giveth his life for the sheep. (John 10:11 KJV)

Here he refers to Himself as a Shepherd. Do you think that He would refer to Himself using these terms unless He is attempting to relate Himself to something or someone? No, it is evident to me that He is making a personal connection between Himself and His Father.

God had shown Israel that He would be intimate with them and that He would care for them. He also exhibited a tender relationship with them. Jesus is saying to those who are listening that He would be as His Father has been. In reality, He would exceed the acts of Jehovah by not only shepherding but dyeing for His people. This life would be one that was gladly given for the people. On the inside of God's glory is the nature of giving. The Bible shows us this when John again states in John 3:16,

> For God so loved that he gave his one and only
> Son. (KJV)

The spiritual makeup of the pastor shepherd is to be a giver. Jesus exemplified this character in His dealings with the people. I see Him as a Shepherd in Luke 7 when He begins the journey to the centurion's house to minister to His servant. I see Him as a Shepherd when He healed Jairus's daughter and when He healed the young man with a demon spirit. Jesus was a teacher, a preacher, and a servant. Without question, the Gospels turn us to the glory that is in the name Jehovah Rohi when we follow the life of Jesus. The shepherd plays many roles in the life of the sheep. Jesus identifies possible the most important role in John chapter 10 and verse 27 and 28.

> My sheep hear my voice, and I know them, and
> they follow me: and I give unto them eternal life;
> and they shall never perish, neither shall any man
> pluck them out of my hand. (John 10:27–28 KJV)

The most important role of the shepherd is that his voice is ingrained in the ears of those that follow him. They not only hear him, but they know his voice and will not answer to a counterfeit. The voice of the shepherd is one of protection from the harm that they may not or cannot see. But due to his diligent leadership and his distinct voice, the sheep need not worry about their welfare.

Then the shepherd makes another very clear distinction of his relationship to the sheep. He knows them. He knows their strengths, weaknesses, and when they require extra attention. This must be a comfort to an animal that has very little personal ability to defend or protect against animals that are determined to make dinner out of it! Why is this part of the glory of God that is shared by Jesus important to you and me? For the same reason it is important to the sheep. That's why Jesus used the correlation between us and sheep.

The enemy of our souls and our lives is a trained assassin. His role is to steal, kill, and destroy anything that resembles the God whom he is attempting to overthrow. With that in mind, we as humans who have had our spirits hijacked by him in Eden are vulnerable to the part of our tripart self called the flesh. The sheep has qualities that cause him to have potential problems without the support of a watchman. He is subject to wonder off, he is subject to getting into things that he physically cannot get out of, and he has little or no defense mechanisms. Without the shepherd, he is vulnerable in more ways than one.

The language can change, but the message will be the same. Separated from the Shepherd, we are vulnerable to ourselves. This vulnerability will cause us to fall into what Paul described in Ephesians 6 as the wiles of the devil. The word *wiles* means "inroads of the devil." We will wander, we will get ourselves into things or places that we cannot get ourselves out of, and without our defense mechanism setting at the ready, we stumble as drunk men until we, like the prodigal son, look up one day and realize the pigsty in which we are living.

The voices that we have followed that brought us to this point have faded, and we are left with the guilt of the foolishness that has stolen our joy and would have killed us had we not come to our senses. Thank God for the good Shepherd that will lead us in a clear and clean path if we are smart enough and have depth enough in our spirit to follow His direction. Jesus was the Jehovah Rohi manifesting the glory of God to His people. The name of the Father was active and evident as Jesus ministered to the needs of all those who came to Him. They were able to experience the glory of God for themselves.

The Glory in Jesus as Shown in Jehovah Rapha

Jesus shared with us the glory of God in the manifestation of himself as Jehovah Rapha. The New Testament is full of stories that describe Jesus as healer. He healed the lame, the deaf, and the demon-possessed. He raised the dead, and healing was even in His clothing. Everywhere He went they followed Him and received from Him the power of health. The healings that most impress me must be the ones that involved some sort of regeneration, for instance, the healing of the lepers. Why? Because He was so powerful in this area of God's glory that diseases that men considered to be as deadly as a flesh-eating disease did not faze Jesus.

Then there was the story of the regeneration of sight to a blind man. That is quite interesting due to the methods Jesus used to complete the task. Jesus was passing by and saw a man that could not see. John says that he was blind from his birth. Look with me at John 9:1.

> And as Jesus passed by, he saw a man which was blind from his birth.

The question was asked of Jesus concerning who had sinned that this man was born blind. Jesus knew that the sin or a sin of a man was not the root cause of what had happened to this man.

He did, however, know what the root cause of the matter was, and He knew how this man could be made whole. The root cause was the fall of man and the origin of sin itself. Due to that, He began to work the works for which He was sent—that being the eradication of the original sin of mankind. Obviously, something had been out of place within the birth process as this man did not possess the ability to see as other men do. How do you know this should be your next question? They asked if sin was the cause. Jesus told them sin was not the reason, so something had gone wrong in the development process.

Again, how do you know that? Well, Jesus identified who would be the one to fix the problem.

> I must work the works of Him that sent Me, while it is day: the night cometh, when no man can work.

So the Creator of heaven and earth who made man from the dust of the earth identified that He was sent to fix the problem that the birthing process had left undeveloped. We often desire to judge people as if God is in the "get you, got you" business. He is not. Men have a DNA that sometimes is flawed. Jesus is about to take care of a faulty DNA system for this man. Watch what He does to do it.

First, He declares in their hearing the fact that He is the light of the world. What? We know that from a salvation perspective He is the light of the world, but He is dealing with a man who was blind from his birth. How would that correlate?

> As long as I am in the world, I am the light of the world. (John 9:5 KJV)

He then begins to do a creative act. He spits on the ground, which means He places his DNA into the dirt. Bear in mind this is the same DNA that created man from the dust in Genesis 2. So there is some serious creative juices flowing in this dirt! Clay was formed from the spit. This is familiar. He then completes a creative act. He anoints the eyes of the blind man with the dirt and the DNA. This is not just any man's DNA; it was the one who knew this process all too well as He had executed this before on a fellow named Adam.

The dirt was the conduit of the DNA. It was the piece that Jesus molded into the orbit of this man's eyes. As that dirt and DNA met with the flesh of the blind man, the physical attributes we know as eyes began to be formed.

> When he had thus spoken, he spat on the ground, and made clay of the spittle, and he anointed the eyes of the blind man with the clay. (John 9:6 KJV)

Now I want you to see something that is most beautiful about the glory of God and Jesus. When God made man, He breathed into Adam's nostrils, and he became a living soul. It has been explained through research that a person's breath has the same qualities of identification as a person's fingerprint. Therefore, breath can transfer information that defines and describes the person.

When God breathed into Adam the breath of life, He really was transferring the important information concerning himself into His creation. He was transferring his spirit and soul (mind, will, and emotions) and designing a flesh man to encompass these vital elements. As long as the spirit and the soul remained in the proper place and functioned appropriately, man would not have to deal with the flesh for more than a covering. Man, having the divine design and the divine fingerprint implanted on the inside, would be well able to complete all the tasks associated with life in the Garden of Eden. Man was given abilities that were essential to fulfill his calling and position. Things such as capabilities, understanding, knowledge, creativity, identification, and communication of information were parts of man that came from the breath of life.

This fingerprint did not simply start man's lungs to begin to inhale and exhale. The purpose was that man's inside could be designed into the image of God as related in Genesis 1:26–27. The outer flesh covering would then be the shell in which the fingerprint of God lived. Man would be considered a little lower than the angels due to the covering of flesh. But man's inner parts expressed the image of his Creator. What an awesome picture, and what an awesome product! More importantly, what an awesome opportunity for every man!

Humankind has come through the channel of life that God prophesied in Genesis 3. Therefore, we have been birthed by a process that was told to Eve. Within that process is the infilling of the breath and fingerprint of God. He is present within every child born because He was the progenitor of original life. In that breath, man became a living soul with all the internal attributes of God. Beautiful!

Now how does this relate to the man who Jesus saw that was blind? Here it is! The beautiful revelation in this scripture is that Jesus here identifies with His two sides. He identifies with His mother and with His Father. On His Father's side, He has the internal fingerprint of life. He is filled with the DNA of His Father. He has within Him all the attributes of the Godhead. Paul said that He is the completeness of the Godhead. Jesus, being the Son of God, had His Father's image imprinted on the inside. This is no revelation since we know that every living creature carries the imprint of his kind within his DNA. Therefore, animals become particular to their species; it is so throughout the spectrum of life.

But Jesus here identifies with His mother as well. He was man. He was flesh and blood. He was human. Humans regenerate through their DNA. He did not breathe upon the blind man. That would have been a total makeover. Adam was totally brought into a living being by the breath of his Creator. No, this man required a regeneration. Jesus used His mother's side for that. He spat and molded and spread the molded clay upon the eyes of the blind. The dirt and DNA began to do its work.

Why? Because the DNA was from His Father's side. It was the part of man that God designed to create the differences in man. Jesus used His Father's side to mix with the clay. But in His humanity on His mother's side, He had to rely upon what He knew was on the inside of Him. So He put His inside with the outside, and the man miraculously received his sight. The glory of God in the name Jehovah Rapha had been expressed in the regeneration of this man's sight.

Jesus had said that he was the light of the world. This again deals with His Father's side. In this miracle, Jesus had allowed a man who was blind from birth to see through a divine means. When men have their eyes opened by the divine illumination of the Son of God, they can clearly see the path that they need to follow. Jesus has identified for this man a path for him to follow. When we realize the DNA that is in us, we must change our pursuits, goals, desires, and paths. We must recognize the reality of who abides within us. We must get firm control of our flesh and begin to follow the light and the life that is in Jesus Christ.

The message of Jesus Christ is clear.

> I am not only the light, but I am the fingerprint of the Father. If you follow Me, even though you were born into sin that caused you to be blind concerning your spiritual connection to God, you can be miraculously, spiritually healed. This healing will allow you to see the paths of righteousness clearly and to follow Me!

The glory of God experienced by the people meant both physical and spiritual healing. Those that found Him as light and who were spiritually changed experienced the benefits of the fingerprint of God upon their life.

The Glory of God Manifested in Jesus as Banner and Provider

The Glory in Jesus as Shown in Jehovah Nissi

This chapter's lead story is shared with me by my mother, but I do want to share a personal insight into the story. This story is going to share with the reader the homecoming of my father. He passed away on the Friday of one our biggest rival games. We were playing Thornton High School, which was absolutely the most talented high school football team that I had ever seen. Three players from this team would become stars in the national football league. I had lain down to nap for thirty minutes prior to going to the stadium to get ready for the game. My sister, Ellen, called me to inform me of the news. Here was the difficult part. I had a game, kids, coaches, and fans that were waiting for this event to unfold. After trying to absorb the news, I made my way to the game.

On the first play of the game, we scored. I will never forget looking up to the sky and telling my father, "Thank you." You see, my dad was a coach Springston fan. He followed my teams whenever he could. I remember distinctly the Sunday afternoon when he walked by me and suddenly stopped. He turned and put his hand upon my head. Then he said, "Under my hand is more football knowledge than anyone in the country." As you can imagine, I felt ten feet tall. So that touchdown against such great competition meant a great deal to me. Eventually, the night ended in a hard-fought defeat. Our team played well, but the better team won in the end.

Afterward, Sharon and I were off to South Georgia to preach my father's funeral. My mother has always been a rock. We were all feeling the sadness and pain over the loss of our hero. During this process, I am sure that as much as we tried, none of us were really in tune with how all of this affected our mother. So the remainder of this story will be her reflections on how God showed Himself to her and provided the necessary comfort and encouragement that she needed.

****

My husband and I had retired and decided to move from North Carolina back to our home state of West Virginia. We had lived and worked in North Carolina for twenty-four years. Our relatives lived in West Virginia, and we would no longer have to drive five hundred miles to visit with them.

We sold our property and moved. Our first couple of winters were not bad, but after that the weather became very difficult to live with. The cold weather caused both of us to be ill. My problem involved sinus issues, but Robert's was much worse as he had pneumonia. Eventually, we decided that the climate in West Virginia was not conducive to our good health.

We found a place in Georgia not far from the coast and moved in 1995. No more snow, not really that much cold weather, and we were set. But not for long. I came home from church one night to find Robert lying on the couch hardly able to breathe. I called 911, and the ambulance came to take him to the hospital. It was there that he was diagnosed with congestive heart failure. It was all downhill from there. Not long after, he was diagnosed with cancer. An operation followed. The doctors thought that he would recover, but while he was in the hospital, I fell in the hallway and broke my hip. So he was in one room and I was in another two doors down from him. He was released to go home, but I remained in the hospital.

When I was able to leave the hospital, we were both trying to recover. Robert loved to work in the yard, so after he felt better, he decided to cut down a tree in the backyard. He cut the tree to a height of about five feet from the ground with a chain saw and then went back to take off another couple of feet down to the stump. I was still on a walker from the broken hip. Since I didn't hear him working, I went to check on him. He had picked up the log that he had cut from the tree and lifted it into the wheelbarrow. This lift had been more than his heart could take. So he put the equipment away and walked up on the back porch to sit down in a rocker. When I went looking for him, I found him sitting in the chair. When I spoke to him, he did not respond. As I moved out onto the porch, I could see that Robert was gone.

My heart dropped. I was astounded. I spoke to him again, but there was no response. I prayed for him, but nothing happened. In just a few short months, I would find myself in a similar situation at the church standing over another man who had been struck with the same fate. On that occasion, when I lay hands on the stricken man, God revived the him, and he is alive today. But not on this day was my prayer answered. Robert was gone forever. Again, I called 911, and they came and tried to revive him, without success. I called my daughter, who lived a few miles away. She came and took over for me. She helped inform the family, which I did not have the heart to do. She also was a tremendous help in planning the funeral. I remained in a fog and still on a walker.

He was buried in a beautiful fashion. Everything that could be done was carefully taken care of. There was no way to bring him back and nothing more we could do. Robert had passed beyond the reach of human hands, a helpless feeling indeed. With the funeral behind me, there was the business of settling things pertaining to ownership. The first time I put the key in the door to let myself in the house, I realized that it was all my responsibility. But the loneliness was hard to deal with. Yes, he had bought a new car ten days before he died; yes, I had a house; and I had his insurance, but I was alone.

Robert was a gardener. He could fix a yard with flowers and take care of it professionally. He was so good at it that people would stop and take pictures. Far from me. I never mowed a yard in my life, and at seventy-two, I had no intention of starting. So the yard would never be the same again. True, I may have looked at things a bit differently after Robert was gone had I not been dealing with the broken hip. Because of it, I was very immobile.

One day, as I sat alone on the couch, something happened to me. I suddenly went out. I don't know how long it lasted, but during the time, I saw Robert, where he was, and what he was doing. He was in the most beautiful place, standing in front of the most beautiful mansion, looking at the flowers he was tending to. The pride and exuberance in his smile was glorious to behold. Everything looked so new and fresh. The grass was so green and flowers so brilliant.

When I woke up and came to, I realized he was, indeed, in Beulah Land and would say, "No, thanks!" to coming back here. I felt like my loneliness was healed, and I could and would go on alone. God knows where I am, and I am never alone.

*****

My mother would later share with me that as she sat at my father's funeral, she began to look around. She saw me with my wife, Sharon, Bob with his wife, Ellen with her husband, Ron and her brothers with their wives. She told me that under her breath, she said, "Lord, everyone has someone but me. What do I do?"

Quickly the Lord replied to her, "You are not alone, I am with you, and the Holy Spirit will guide you."

My mother lived alone in South Georgia for nearly twenty more years. We eventually had to force her to come and live near us. During her twenty years "alone," she had a television show, taught Bible study, appeared on other broadcasters' television shows, and generally became well-known as a foremost Bible teacher in her area. Yes, Jehovah is both our Banner and our Provider. My mother is ninety-six years old and going strong. During a recent service, the Holy Spirit spoke through her a message to our church in a powerful way. He has been more than a Shield and more than a Provider, and I have had a ringside seat to watch how God has intervened in the hurts, pain, and travails of life to make this mother more than an overcomer. My friend, God does what He promises He will do. You can count on it!

Jesus was the manifestation of the glory of the Lord with respect to the name Moses gave for God in Exodus 17:15. Moses said, "The Lord is my Banner." As we know, Israel was directed where to place their tribes in reference to the Tabernacle. When a tribe would identify any potential trouble or need for help from the rest of the tribes, they would raise their banner, and the children of Israel would come and be prepared to help.

Jesus was the manifestation of the Banner of the Lord. John 12:32 declares,

> And I, if I am lifted up from the earth, will draw all men to myself. (John 12:32 KJV)

Jesus was the Banner that God raised from the earth to make it clear in all three worlds that help was coming. He was the Banner of heaven. He was the one who had been sent with the divine design of God to serve as heaven's answer to the sin problem and heaven's answer to the requirements of a legal sacrifice. He was perfect in all His ways. He was obedient, and He was sinless. He was the spotless banner that could be raised to legally be held accountable for the sin of mankind.

He was the Banner for all men who dwelt in the earth. When He in his humanity was elevated to the cross, he was raised as the sacrifice for all men. The sin of all mankind was placed upon Him, and sin engulfed His person. Then He was the banner for the underworld. There He would be the banner for sin, fully engrossed with all the sin that mankind had to offer.

Isaiah put it this way:

> Surely, he has borne our griefs and carried our sorrows. (KJV)

There was no part of Him that was not covered in sin. Those that saw Him considered Him smitten and stricken by God. His appearance was such that He had been battered beyond recognition. The underworld had within their grasp the Banner of sin. He was what we would call the poster child for the depravity of mankind. But in the middle of that scene, something dynamic occurred. The Banner who was lifted to be the sacrifice for sin became the Banner that was the champion over death, hell, and the grave! He would be the one who would draw men out of captivity and lead them to the victory land.

The Spirit of God came to retrieve the champion from the confines of hell. Here Isaiah says it so well:

> So shall they fear the name of the LORD from the west, and his glory from the rising of the sun. When the enemy shall come in like a flood, the Spirit of the LORD shall lift up a standard against him. (Isaiah 59:19 KJV)

Like a flood, righteousness filled the borders and region of the damned. The power and presence of the Spirit of the Lord was on awesome display. He had come to complete a work that had been in the divine design from the beginning.

Paul would declare in 1 Corinthians 2:7–8,

> But we speak the wisdom of God in a mystery, even the hidden wisdom, which God ordained before the world unto our glory: which none of the princes of this world knew: for had they known it, they would not have crucified the Lord of glory. (1 Corinthians 2:7–8 KJV)

Had they known what was to become of their kingdom, they would have never allowed the Banner to be raised. They would have never put the divine plan of God in motion beyond the birth of Jesus. But they did not know! Because the wisdom of God concealed it. Therefore, when the Banner was raised, like dominoes on a board the process was released. The prospects initially looked dim for those who were not privileged to the inside information, but as long as the clues were in place, the outcome was certain.

Hell had to be in utter shock as the Spirit of the Lord made a way of escape for Him. Isaiah calls it a standard. The Holy Spirit put to flight the powers of hell while Jesus spoiled the goods of his enemy. The power of death, the entrance to hell, and the fear of the grave was dissolved when the Banner that was lifted finished His work in the utter most parts of the earth. Jesus is the Banner that men see when they see Him seated at the right hand of the Father. This is obvious when we read Revelation 1:18.

> I am he that liveth, and was dead; and, behold, I am alive for evermore, amen; and have the keys of hell and of death. (Revelation 1:18 KJV)

Jesus is the Jehovah Nissi manifested to be seen in all three worlds!

The Glory in Jesus as Shown in Jehovah Jirah

When God revealed His glory through Jesus as the Provider to the people, the multitude was fed. Jehovah Jirah, the Provider for the children of Israel, was manifesting Himself through His Son to the people who were following Jesus. Matthew chapter 14 describes the situation for us as the provision of God is given to the people. The multitude has followed Him, and He has done healings and miracles for them. They had remained with Him for that purpose.

As the day wanes, the disciples encourage Jesus to allow the multitude to go and find food. Jesus, hearing their concern, makes a statement that defines the glory of God in relation to the needs of the people. "They need not depart. You give them something to eat." The disciples are dismayed with this comment. Their response investigates the things of which they possess that can be used to meet this need. After taking stock of their own food, they found very little and certainly not enough to feed five thousand people, not including women and children. The glory of God is manifest in His compassion for the people. When they follow the instructions of Jesus and when He presents the offering and the need to the Father, the glory of Jehovah Jirah manifests itself through Jesus to the food.

The disciples who did not see with their natural eyes how what they had could be enough to feed themselves than begin to watch the glory of God, Jehovah Jirah, fill the hunger need for the entire multitude. The disciples did exactly what Jesus had told them to do. They took the food that they had, they brought it to Jesus, and He presented it to His Father, the Father. Due to His offering, manifested His glory of provision, the disciples gave them food to eat, and the people were filled. At no time did Jesus put one morsel in the lap of any of the people. The disciples did the work. Jesus manifested the glory of God in the sight of the people.

When we investigate how God manifested His care of Israel in the wilderness, God provided the manna, and the children of Israel were responsible for picking it up, using it appropriately, and gathering only what they needed. In this case the same thing happened. Had Jesus been feeding them by His hand, the people would not have had to correlate the miracle to the name of God that was manifesting through Jesus. Therefore, the concept that Jesus was driving home to the people concerning His relationship to the Father would have been lost. The people would have had no biblical story to relate to the incident, and the message of Christ would have been misconstrued by the people. Remember, the reason for the displays of the glory of God through Jesus was to disclose to the people who Jesus was in relation to the God that the Jews had known throughout their history. If there was a misunderstanding or a miscommunication, it would not be because the divine plan was mishandled. We could locate many stories to describe the glory of God as Jehovah Jirah in Jesus. They would all be as mesmerizing as the one found in Matthew's gospel. But I feel led of the Spirit to conclude this part of the glory of God by sharing how God showed His ultimate provision for mankind.

Yes, we must go to the most memorized verse in the entire Bible. John 3:16 expresses the glory of God in the provision of his Son.

> For God so loved the world, that he gave his only begotten Son, that whosoever believeth in him should not perish, but have everlasting life. (John 3:16 KJV)

This verse is the foundation of the Gospel. It set the stage for everything that occurs between God and man. It identifies clearly the character and nature of God. It identifies clearly who He is going to provide for, the purpose of man's opportunity, which is to have everlasting life. Then it provides the clue for why man must receive this provision—so that he does not perish.

What a scripture indeed! God is a giver! I have often said that you will never be more like God than when you are giving. How true that is. God chose a provision for mankind that left no loose ends in his walk, talk, obedience, or life. When Jesus revealed Himself in this way, He was, in fact, revealing the glorious work of the divine design. God, Jehovah Jirah, would provide a Lamb without spot or blemish who would serve as the sacrifice that would redeem man from the bondage of sin. The glory of God's provision resided upon Jesus. Luke said He grew in wisdom, in stature, in favor with man, and in favor with God. He was the one that, when God looked at mankind who had been created as his crown jewel, was set to pay the price for man's reconnection to God. God had given many things to men throughout the time from genesis to Matthew, but men had continually squandered his goodness. Now there was one provided who would be in perfect unity with being the provision.

Now, I showed you one instance where the glory of God appeared, as through Jesus came provision for the people. Now I am going to show you how through Jesus came provision for all people. The cross was a tragic place. Jesus was mutilated for all intents and purposes. The sin that was unleashed upon Him was done so in devastating proportions. He bled from seven different places, but that far from describes the picture of His person.

God knew what the cross would look like. Now, I want you to see this: crucifixions were nothing new to men, so they were nothing new to God. But the purpose of this crucifixion was what made it different. The devastation of sin was what made this event so different! Paul said, and I want this to sink in as you read it,

For he hath mad him who knew no sin.

Let's stop there for a second. The reason this provision was different was because God looked down upon a guiltless man—one that He had designed and heaven's angels had declared His birth. The man that had faithfully executed a life that told the known world about a Father of love. The man who had spoken the words,

> For God so loved the world that he gave his only begotten Son!

God, because of His love for man, put upon Jesus the extreme amount of the rebellion of sin. The glory of God, the provision, Jesus Christ, hung on a tree and cried in thirst. He gasped for air, and they mocked him with no mercy. Then the loud words came through the crowd Matthew 27:40, saying,

> Thou that destroyest the temple, and buildest it in three days, save thyself. If thou be the Son of God, come down from the cross. (Matthew 27:40 KJV)

Then in verse 43, we read a statement that had to have torn at the very heart of God.

> He trusted in God; let him deliver him now, if he will have him: for he said, I am the Son of God. (Matthew 27:43 KJV)

Jehovah Jirah, the Provider, was manifesting His glory in and through the giving of his Son. If it were not enough for sin to have taken its effect upon the gift, now the people have spoken against the God who has made the provision! But through it all, the glory of God found in the person of Jesus Christ resolutely remained upon the tree. The giver had provided the gift, and the gift manifested the glory of God. It was a difficult visual for the Father as darkness fell upon the glory of God. Sin's overwhelming result had taken effect upon the sacrifice.

My God, My God, why have You forsaken Me?

There was no option. The effect of sin upon the sacrifice had to be total and complete. It was! The provision has died. The sacrifice has been accomplished. Once and for all, the glory of God that was required for man to have the clutches of sin removed is done. The veil in the temple is torn from top to bottom as man has no more need to use the methods of the law or the Old Testament sacrifices to approach the God who has provided a way of escape. Jesus was the glory of God as through Him the provision of God has been given. He manifested the Jehovah Jjireh glory of God to the people as He ministered to them healings, deliverances, food, and many benefits. But He also is the provision of God and the glory of God as He is God's gift as God's sacrificial Lamb.

In ministry, the provision that He gave lasted for a brief time. A man's hunger or a man's health would need to be addressed again and again for man to survive. But as the provision for the spiritual life of man, there is no further need for another sacrifice. God loved man so deeply that He gave Jesus. God loved Jesus so deeply that when He endured the cross, His tour in the uttermost parts of the world, His resurrection, His walk among men, His ascension and His seating at the right hand of the Father God ensured that this event would never be required again.

> But this man, after he had offered one sacrifice for sins for ever, sat down on the right hand of God; from henceforth expecting till his enemies be made his footstool. for by one offering he hath perfected for ever them that are sanctified. (Hebrews 10:12–14 KJV)

What a wonderful scripture of the perfection of the sacrifice. This provision of God was able to once and for all reconnect man to God. After He had completed the work of being the sacrifice, He was accepted and seated at the right hand of the Father. This seating signified the conclusion of the sacrificial process. It also placed Him in the position of excellence that allowed Jesus to know that from that day forward every knee would bow to His exalted position. The only thing between the principalities, rulers, demons, and humans being called into account for their rebellion was time.

For the believer, His position of Provider and His location as being seated at the right hand of God serves to perfect the believer. How? With Himself and His righteousness. This righteousness then serves to sanctify or separate the people who believe from the people who have used their will to deny the cross and the work thereof. For these believers, time is the only separator. Isn't that beautiful! Both the believer and the unbeliever operate in Jesus, under the same condition. Both await a change. The believer is to be fashioned into the image of the Son of God according to Philippians 3. The unbeliever is to be fashioned into the damnation of his father, the devil, according to John 3.

In both cases eternity is now! What do I mean? For the child of God, the provision of the glory of God is provided for them to experience the benefits of the cross now. Their eternal and everlasting life works in them a greater hope of glory. For the unbeliever, who is serving a master that is leading them into the desires and works of the flesh, their eternity is now also. They live for today, and today is exactly what they will receive. The lost have the hope of a world that is full of evil. They must look forward to a life of fear, hurt, and devastation. This is only the beginning of the devastation that will come their way. Why do we struggle today with the world as it is? This is a microcosm of what is to come in the underworld for the unbeliever.

Jesus readily ministered to them, and they all were healed. Some of their healing may not have lasted due to their irreverence, but they were healed. Why? Because He was operating in the glory of the Father. He was involved with man from heaven's perspective. Men through Him could receive the glory of God. Now, they did not realize that what He was dispensing was the glory of God, but they were privileged to receive it nonetheless.

Some of those on the peripheral wanted to equate the power of God that manifested in healing to be demonic. Jesus quickly dispelled such foolish speaking. Only a fool would suggest that the enemy, who was the reason for the physical decline of mankind, would counteract his own work by acts of kindness toward a humanity that he despised. Nonetheless, to demean Jesus in the eyes of the people, this is what they did. Jesus went on to heal many more during His earthly ministry. There were no circumstances under which the glory of Jehovah Rapha manifested in Jesus Christ could not deliver healing to His people.

The Glory of God Manifested in Jesus as Peace and He Is There

My sister related these two stories to me concerning the glory of God that she found in Jesus on the occasions of our oldest sister and her husband's departure from this life. God is most faithful to be present with peace and the sense that in all the circumstances of life he is there. I am sure as you read you can relate to these two wonderful experiences of comfort from our Lord.

****

The Sunday after Christmas 1986, my family and I were preparing to go to Ohio to visit my husband's family. My packing was interrupted by the ringing of the telephone. On the other end of the line was my mother with news that my sister had had surgery on Friday. What was to have been a simple lumpectomy turned out to require major surgery for a malignant tumor. As a result, they had removed her entire left breast, along with several lymph nodes. The doctors assured her family they were able to remove all the cancer, and with chemotherapy to kill any stray cells, there should not be any other problems.

Thanksgiving 1987, we went to North Carolina to be with my parents for the holiday. My sister and her family came from Winston-Salem, North Carolina, for the day also. My sister showed me markings on her left side where the breast had been removed. These markings were to start treatment on the area, due to the return of cancer.

Cancer had come out through the skin, and within a period, it began to appear in various parts of her body.

During 1988, she became more and more ill, lost weight, and was totally emaciated by this terrible disease. In the middle of this crisis, her husband was moved with his job to Birmingham, Alabama. I lived in Chicago and was unable to be with her, but I called her often to let her know of my concern and my love for her. Those calls were always amazing to me, because she seemed to have such peace during pain, sickness, disease, and uncertainty.

Philippians 4:7 reads,

> And the peace of God, which passeth all understanding, shall keep your hearts and minds through Christ Jesus.

I don't think I had ever fully understood this scripture until I saw it in action in her life. I never heard her complain, no matter how bad things were. Not only did she not complain, but she did not feel sorry for herself or ever blame God or feel that he had failed her. Truly, the Lord had given her great peace and was comforting her.

On September 30, 1988, Wilda went home to be with Jesus… the giver of peace. At her funeral the song was sung, "To God Be the Glory." This was her favorite song, and so well expressed the love and thanksgiving she felt for our gracious Heavenly Father. During times of crisis and difficult times, I would think of the great peace that enveloped her. Truly, there is peace that passeth understanding!

On Tuesday, November 15, my husband became very ill. He had dementia and was being serviced by hospice. When the hospice nurse came for her daily visit, she saw that he was very ill and called transport to come and take him to the emergency room. After testing, the ER doctor came and told us he had a severely infected gall bladder, which would need to be removed immediately. He was admitted into a room, and surgery was scheduled for Thursday afternoon.

All went well with the surgery, but the next morning, they told me he would need to be transferred to Savannah for further surgery to have stones removed from the bile duct. That was to be done

I SURRENDER

on Saturday. Ron was seventy-seven years old and already in poor health, so I was a bit leery of two surgeries in two days, but nonetheless, the doctors said it had to be done.

Within a few days after the surgery, he was released to come home. I picked him up and made the two-hour trip home. He was unable to walk, so the hospice nurse met me and helped me get him in the house. From there on, he became totally immobile and was never able to walk again. He lost his appetite, lost down to one hundred pounds, and was very lethargic. Eventually, they ordered a hospital bed, and it was a waiting period, as they could see things were not going to improve and he was in a steady decline.

I spent my days in and out of his room, nursing him and caring for him like I would a child. What little he ate was spoon-fed. He wore diapers, had to be bathed and shaved, and whatever his needs, they had to be done by me or an hour-a-day hospice visitor.

On January 19, I went into his room early to check on him, and he seemed to be sleeping peacefully. I kept going in and out all morning during my prayer and reading time, and every time he was sleeping. When he hadn't awakened by around 11:00 AM, I was beginning to get quite concerned. About that time, I made a trip back into his room and found that he had vomited the little bit of food he had eaten the evening before. I realized he was really having a problem and called hospice and asked them to send his nurse over. I was combing my hair and getting ready for her to show up when I heard him vomit loudly. I went in to check, and it was pure red blood. I made another call to hospice and asked them to get the nurse here immediately because I thought he was not going to live long. She arrived around 11:20 AM and, after checking his vitals, said it wouldn't be long. At 11:54 AM, he slipped out of this world and into the arms of our loving Savior!

For him, I know it was a wonderful experience. He was a retired minister and had preached and sang about heaven for many years. I knew where he was, and he was more "okay" than he had ever been. That knowledge brings such peace to those left behind.

The hospice nurse had also called in the hospice chaplain to be with me. She left after filling out paperwork and taking care of whatever duties she had. The chaplain was kind enough to stay with me till the funeral home personnel arrived. That was around 3:00 PM in the afternoon. They took Ron's body, the chaplain left, and I was alone... Alone!

We lived in South Georgia and had no family in the area. In fact, the closest family was nearly four hundred miles away. Our son and his family lived in Chicago; my mother and brother lived in Winston-Salem, North Carolina, and all of Ron's family were in Ohio and other distant places. It was winter, and weather up North was terrible with ice and snow. It was impossible for my son to get to me. My brother was in Chicago, also officiating at the wedding of their son. My mother in Winston-Salem was ninety-five years old and had no way to come, so I was totally alone!

At 4:00 PM, they came from the medical equipment company and took all the equipment out of Ron's room, and it was empty. I was left in a house that felt like a tomb. I went in and sat down in the den alone, thinking, "What does my future hold, what will I do, how will I be financially?" A million questions and ifs and hows and whens crossed my mind.

Typically, every evening I shut the TV off around 5:30 PM or 6:00 PM and begin to read the Word and have prayer, then listen to YouTube on my computer of ministers from the past who seem to be deeper in the things of God than most ministries of today. However, I felt drained and not very spiritual, so I thought I just wouldn't do it. No reading, not praying, no listening tonight. I also felt like the circumstances of his death, not being near family and knowing I had tried to sell the house for quite some time to get closer to family, so when or if something like this happened, I would not be alone, all added up to some resentment for having been let down by God—or at least that was how I perceived it at the time.

Instead, I did just the opposite of what I felt. I went to the recliner, picked up my Word, and began to read and pray. I can't explain what happened next, but the Spirit of the living God enveloped me like a cocoon. I could literally feel the presence of God. I didn't feel alone; I knew someone was with me and would continue to be with me. The sadness was gone, and I felt hope. I knew whatever needs I had would be met. I knew he would be everything I would need when I needed it! The Word says He is an ever-present help in time of need, and He was being just that to me!

At the end of the period is a little addendum. God sent a Realtor to my house and sold a house that I had been trying to sell for several years in two months. Six months to the day of Ron's death, I moved into my new home in West Virginia. I had been gone fifty-one years from my childhood area, but God allowed me to return home where I have friends and family. He is faithful, and He does do all things well! In the days ahead, though being alone, they may be a little uncertain at times, I'll keep "looking unto Jesus, the Author and Finisher of my faith!"

The Glory of God in Jesus as the Jehovah Shalom

This representation of the glory of God is that God is my peace. There is no doubt that Jesus was to be identified with this part of the glory of the Father as Gabriel describes Him in Luke 1.

> To give light to them that sit in darkness and in the shadow of death, to guide our feet into the way of peace. (Luke 1:79 KJV)

An awesome truth is spoken by Gabriel as he concludes his explanation of the events that would become the birth of John the forerunner and Jesus the Son of God. Jesus would guide our feet into the paths of peace! This peace would come as the result of the five promises that Gabriel spoke concerning Jesus. These promises would be consistent with his name. We now know that His name was the reflection of the glory of God. So when Gabriel said to Mary that he shall be great and shall be called the Son of the Highest, the Lord God shall give unto Him the throne of His father David, He shall reign over the house of Jacob forever, and of His kingdom there shall be no end, the outcome of these promises was to be the paths of peace. Jesus, being the glory of God, would be identified as the presence of peace as His name became great. We know that it did!

He was peace to the hurting and the hungry. He was peace to the sick and the lame. He was peace to the dying and the mourning. He was peace in the day and the night. He was peace on the sea and in the storm. He was peace when attacked, and He was peace when at ease. Jesus reflected peace because that was in His DNA. He simply conferred and conveyed to mankind the glory of the great name of His Father. He was the Son of the peacemaker. He was the Son of the one who cut the covenant of peace with Abraham. He was the one who walked through the blood with His Father to ratify the covenant.

He knew the peace that comes from total agreement between two willing participants, and He shared that with everyone He encountered. He exhibited the peace of knowing His designed outcome. When the glory of God as Jehovah Shalom resides within you, there is a sense of comfort and confidence that allows one to face the trials and tests of life with little concern for the outcome. Jesus was not left out of the grand divine design for His earthly mission. As a matter of fact, the Bible declares that He was formed from the foundation of the world for the purpose of being the sacrifice.

No. He was aware of the torment that He would endure at the hands of man. How could He not be? The reason for the need of a Savior to begin with was due to man's sheer rebellion and disdain for a relationship with the Father. This fact was in full view of the Father's exposure of Himself to His people through His own glory. But man was so encompassed in the bondage and degradation of sin that they became oblivious to the God that was extending Himself to them. The glory of God had to be revealed within the life of a man who had a human side for the paths of peace to become available for the world. Once the path was provided (Jehovah Jirah in Jesus), the way of peace would be offered to men for their personal decision.

Many have rejected this path. Many will continue to do so. However, those who located this path will find the glory of God by the only means of which it is to be located, Jesus Christ. When the glory of God, which is Jehovah Shalom, enters the heart of man a most dynamic event happens. First, love becomes the method of operation by which the person begins to view others. Why? Because the peace of God is expressed through the love that has caused the new birth experience. When Jesus prayed for the disciples in John chapter 17, He prays for them through the expression of His love for them.

> And the glory which thou gavest me I have given them; that they may be one, even as we are one: I in them, and thou in me, that they may be made perfect in one; and that the world may know that thou hast sent me, and hast loved them, as thou hast loved me. Father, I will that they also, whom thou hast given me, be with me where I am; that they may behold my glory, which thou hast given me: for thou lovedst me before the foundation of the world. O righteous father, the world hath not known thee: but I have known thee, and these have known that thou hast sent me. And I have declared unto them thy name and will declare it: that the love wherewith thou hast loved me may be in them, and I in them. (John 17:22–26 KJV)

So of what glory is Jesus here speaking? Well, He is speaking of the glory of the name of which He was given and of which He represents. Then He calls them into oneness. This oneness refers to His Spirit. Since it does, it brings them into oneness with who God is. We know that the Word says that He is love (1 John 4:8), so those who receive this prayer are being brought into the peace of God's love. From that oneness, the believer begins to live life from a different perspective. That perspective is expressed in the Fruit of the Spirit becoming the outward manifestation of the inward work.

> But the fruit of the spirit is love, joy, peace, long-suffering, gentleness, goodness, faith, meekness, temperance: against such there is no law. And they that are Christ's have crucified the flesh with the affections and lusts. (Galatians 5:22–24 KJV)

The crucifixion of the flesh becomes the elimination of outward works that in times past have been related to the nature of the sin that resided within us. The love of God has translated us into becoming a new and better representative of the person that the world knows and identifies by our name. The translation from darkness to light has changed us, and the peace of God has transformed us. But then even a deeper work occurs, and the blood of Jesus transfers to us. Because of His love, we have a new nature, character, and demeanor. What an awesome experience this new birth is!

Love in the Spirit is a powerful peace connection. The Bible declares,

> I will keep him in perfect peace whose mind is stayed on me. (KJV)

What would your mind have to be constantly in remembrance of? The love of God that has brought you into oneness with Him. Now, that will keep your spirit steady! Verse 23 tells us how oneness occurs, and of course, it is shared by love. The unity of the Father, the Son, the Holy Spirit, and the reconnected spirit of man brings a four-pronged cord of peace. This can only be received by locating the Shalom of God. This peace will only be found when one's spirit connects with the blood of Jesus and the new birth is transacted.

> I will that they see My glory and be with Me in that glory.

Those who see that glory will only understand the means to get there and the means to function in that glory by realizing peace. Jesus is in complete Shalom with the Father. He expresses complete Shalom to those of whom the Father gave Him. He includes all that will believe because of their Word in complete Shalom. Any man who ever experiences the glory of God with Jesus in the realm in which Jesus is praying about in John 17 will only experience it through understanding that Jesus Himself is the expression of the glory of God as peace. This expression was received into glory as peace, seated as peace, and anyone who follows will come through the glory of the peace He has provided.

Jesus says so much in verse 26,

> And I have declared unto them thy *name* [peace] and will declare it: that the love wherewith thou hast loved me may be in them, and I in them. (John 17:26 KJV)

> I have declared peace to them, and I declare that this peace may reside in them. I declare that peace resides as deeply and effectively as I reside.

What a concept and what a comfort to every believer! May we look one chapter earlier to see what Jesus had stated concerning this peace issue.

> These things I have spoken unto you, that in me ye might have peace. In the world ye shall have tribulation: but be of good cheer; I have overcome the world. (John 16:33 KJV)

What had He spoken to them?

> First, do not be offended by the fact that there are going to be difficult times ahead. You will have no different treatment as a servant than the treatment you saw given to your Master. These things will fulfill the Word of God. You will be a part of that fulfillment.
>
> Second, when they come, and they will, you will recognize what is happening and not allow the environment of discomfort to inhibit your mission for Me. When I was with you representing the glory of God as the peace of God it was not required for you to know what lay ahead,

> but I personally will not be with you when these issues arise.
>
> Thirdly, I am going to provide for you with My leaving another just like Me. He will serve as your Comforter. He will be the Spirit of Truth who will lead and guide you into the truth because He will only speak concerning Me.

So what is the truth of which the Holy Spirit is being sent to glorify the Son by exposing to the disciples and ultimately every believer? Well, we locate that in John 16:33.

> These things I have spoken unto you, that in me ye might have peace. In the world ye shall have tribulation: but be of good cheer; I have overcome the world. (John 16:33)

The peace of rest, the peace of prosperity, and the peace of the glory of God as shared by the glory that is in Jesus Christ. It is this glorious part of the Son that the Holy Spirit will shed abroad in the spirits of believers. There is a great deal of information that is provided in John 16. The culmination of that information is defined in John 16:33. What you have heard, you have heard for the purpose of peace.

Now, let's look one more step to where that peace comes from.

> Peace I leave with you, my peace I give unto you: not as the world giveth, give I unto you. Let not your heart be troubled, neither let it be afraid. (John 14:27 KJV)

> I am leaving the glory of God that I received as the expression of that same glory within My earthly walk. It is Shalom! I am giving it to you to have in yourselves. I am giving the glory of peace just as I am giving the Holy Spirit to serve in

> you. While He serves as comforter, guide, truth, reproof of sin, righteousness, and judgment, you will live in the quietness and rest and comfort of peace. How will you manage this?

Jesus would say that we would manage it the He same way He did.

> You will express the glory I am giving you. I received it from the Father, and I am giving it to you. Shalom! Peace that will allow you to receive the work of the Holy Spirit as I give Him command to address your life.

This piece of the glory of God is one that Jesus identified that the believer would require if he were to successfully navigate the paths that he must choose to live the Christian life. Therefore, He gave this glory directly to all who would believe upon Him by the words that the disciples would teach concerning Him. Thank God for this revelation! Thank God for the foresight of the Master to give us the glory of God through Jehovah Shalom. I can live in the glory of peace because Jesus gave it to me.

When people struggle, the first area that they must examine is, "Why is the peace of God not expressing itself in my life?" There are many reasons. But none of those reasons eliminate the promise. If you love God and have come by the way of the life of Christ and the life of the disciples, then this peace belongs to you. The reason it is not being appropriated in your life must be determined by a thorough examination of what is going on within your personal spiritual life.

In other words, the issue is not in the promise of peace. It is not in the effectiveness of the promise as it relates to today. No. The issue resides in your ability or inability to order your life in such a fashion to quicken peace into your life. Peace and the truths concerning peace will come into your spirit when you evaluate yourself in view of the Word of God. Then you must eliminate the areas of your life that the Word of God highlights as being contrary to the truth. Finally, keep those areas and any others under the control of the Holy Spirit. If these identified areas rise, put them down. If sin occurs due to them, confess, repent, and move forward.

Remember, this entire cycle is the production of the love of God manifesting Himself to you. Due to His love, the glory of His peace is given to you. Due to His love, the beauty of forgiveness is available to you. His love brings His peace. The more inspection and evaluation of your relationship with the Master, the more love grows. The more love grows, the more peace flows. What an awesome revelation of the glory of God in Jesus Christ as the Jehovah Shalom. Jesus is the peace of God. That glory is directly given to us!

The Glory of God in Jesus as Jehovah Shammah

Jesus was made and revealed as the glory of God who is Jehovah Shammah. This name of *God* means that "God is there." John is speaking concerning the revelation of Jesus in John 1, when he brings out these facts concerning him in verse 14,

> And the word was made flesh, and dwelt among us [and we beheld his glory, the glory as of the only begotten of the Father]. (John 1:14 KJV)

In this New Testament revelation of Jesus, John shows us some most important information concerning this revelation of the glory of God.

First, we see Jesus as dwelling among us. We know this to be true because they saw Him, they handled Him, and they listened to Him teach and preach. The works that He did are not only recorded in scripture but history as well. So there leaves no doubt that He was among them in His earthly ministry. The truth is that He is among us even this moment! Jesus said in Matthew 18:20,

> For where two or three are gathered together in my name, there am I in the midst of them.

I SURRENDER

What name is He referring to? Is He referring to the name Jesus, or is He referring to the name that He represents, which is the glory that is in Jehovah Shammah?

To me, He is referring to the glory of God that is represented in Himself as He is by His Father's name, which is present. Why do I say that? Because Jesus came to represent the Father. When you saw Him, you saw the Father, and that was His consistent message. This is the exact statement that angered the Jews. So clearly, when Jesus referred to His name, He was referring to the name of the Father that was given for Him to represent the glory that was in that name to the people. Certainly, when two or three met, the glory of God was there. His presence was encompassing the people, just as God had encompassed the city in Ezekiel's vision, where the reference to Jehovah Shammah is mentioned in the Old Testament (Ezekiel 45).

This chapter of Ezekiel, we may locate some insight into the possible type of city in which God is located. There are bigger implications for the believer however. When we determine the significance of Paul's writing in Colossians 1:27, it is easy to establish that the eternal relationship of God, who is there in man and for man, who has been reborn, is the connection of Christ in you. This connection becomes our hope of glory. If Christ is in us, then He is there. The glory of His being there is expressed in the way we live and represent His presence.

> To whom God would make known what is the riches of the glory of this mystery among the gentiles; which is Christ in you, the hope of glory. (Colossians 1:27 KJV)

He resides in me, and therefore, I experience the Jehovah Shammah glory of God. I am translated by His blood into his kingdom. Then I am transferred or changed into the glory that is in His name because He dwells in me.

He is not among us presently, but He is in us currently! What an awesome revelation of the glory of God. This concept is the most effective force; it moves men to live in such a way as to surrender in their inner man to the possession of the Spirit of life that is in Christ Jesus. The affairs of their life and their flesh will come under control and into correct order only when this revelation is understood.

Since He is in man through the new birth, and man is transferred into the kingdom, man—because of the glory of God—must crucify the flesh, the world, and the desires that are found in both realms. Because he has come to the knowledge of the truth concerning Jesus, he must also come to the truth concerning the glory that resides in His Spirit. So it comes as no surprise when we meet and His Spirit manifests among us. The real surprise should be the occasion when we meet and there is no manifestation of His glory. This becomes the time when we must examine our relationship.

If we sense no glory and no presence of the Lord when we meet with other believers, then we must ask why. Did the Lord change His methods of operation? Is the person who sits near me blocking the spiritual flow of the presence of the Lord? More than likely, the glory of God that is dwelling within you as a Spirit of life is not being brought alive through prayer, meditation, and time spent mining the Word of God. Our worship life can all to easily be put aside by the cares of this life. No, God did not remove the glory of God. No, God did not decide to pull out and leave you on your own. No, God has not moved on to another church. No, God has not forgotten you or your needs.

The truth is that we have allowed the glory of God to wax cold in our personal relationship. We have not put the priority upon the things that cultivate relationship. How did this occur? The same way that divorce in our culture has reached such a high rate. We failed to cultivate the relationship. We have failed to continue to put the premium on the other party, meaning God, and placed the premium upon ourselves. Let me illustrate. We have a new doctrine that has swept our Christian world called the prosperity Gospel. What does that Gospel place as its core? What God can do for me! Now the question is not if there is a prosperity in the Gospel. Of course, there is! Anyone who knows Jesus Christ is a prosperous man.

But that prosperity resides only when the central theme of the Gospel is Jesus Christ and Him only. Any relationship that places us at the center of, and core of, the relationship's existence is doomed to fail. So when we equate the divorce rate to the relationship of the believer to the Savior, we can see the connection. The marriage becomes selfish—all about me—and the connection falls into complete disarray. Our relationship to Christ is no different. When it becomes about us and not Him, the glory that is from Him goes cold.

Now, you may still go to church, give in the plate, and work in the church. But you are aware that there is a fire on the inside that is lacking. You know that the Word does not affect you as it once did. Even though the Word is the same, the service is conducted the same, and the people who surround you may be the same, you are aware that you are not the same. The time has come for serious self-inspection! The question becomes "Are we satisfied with a cursory walk with the Lord, or are we really interested in experiencing the glory of His presence?"

As for me, I have made that decision. I want the glory of God! I desire to live, knowing that He is there and that the decisions that I make are being inspected by the Spirit of life that resides in me. I desire to live so that the anointing is protected. I desire to live so that I reflect the glory of God that is in Christ Jesus. People have often asked me why I don't preach like others. I respond by, "What do you mean? How am I different?" Their answer sometimes shocks me. They say that I don't preach predeveloped or other preachers' sermons, I don't preach from a liturgy, and I don't stand in one spot while preaching. They also say that I seem so excited and can get loud.

I chuckle at these comments. No, I don't preach off others' messages, and I don't do standard yearly sermons. Nor do I stand behind a pulpit to preach. No, when I come into the house of God, I am excited because I have spent the week doing the things that cultivate my relationship with Him. Worship is easy and enjoyable. I am easily moved by the message in song, prayer, or testimony. Because I have cultivated my relationship with the Master, the service is all about Him. In me, the glory flows!

Preaching is very easy when you are hearing the voice of the Holy Spirit. Living is very easy when you hear the voice of the Holy

Spirit. So can we live under such an anointing all the time? Jesus did. Someone would say, "Yes, but I am not Jesus!" You don't have to be. Your flesh will never be. But it is not your flesh that is in question. It is your spirit!

Any man can prepare his spirit for the glory of God to have complete control. As a matter of fact, it is to this end that man was created.

> There is therefore now no condemnation to them which are in Christ Jesus, who walk not after the flesh, but after the spirit. For the law of the spirit of life in Christ Jesus hath made me free from the law of sin and death. (Romans 8:1–2 KJV)

We have the Spirit of life in Christ that makes our spirit man free from the law that governs sin and death. That fact alone defines how the glory of God has complete control in men, who choose to walk by the Spirit that resides on the inside. They also choose that glory over the immediate gratification of the flesh.

Romans 8:6 then shares with us what occurs in our spirit and how the glory of God that is "there" manifests itself in the believer.

> For to be carnally minded is death; but to be spiritually minded is life and peace. (KJV)

The glory of God in Jesus Christ causes a man to pass from death to life, and then while living, to experience peace. What an awesome place to be. It is no wonder Paul wrote that when Christ resides in you, there is a hope of glory! Because He is there, life and peace abide in us!

It is necessary that I add one more explanation to the New Testament reference to Jesus as the glory of God, Jehovah Shammah. Of course, Jesus referenced this in several places in the Gospels. But the scripture that we identify with that states this fact is found in Matthew 28:20. I did not reference this first, because this reference was after his resurrection. But as we will see, it applied to situations and conditions during His earthly ministry as well as his relationship to the apostles after He had ascended to heaven.

Let's look at Matthew 28:20.

> Teaching them to observe all things whatsoever I have commanded you: and, lo, I am with you always, even unto the end of the world. Amen. (KJV)

Jesus, from Matthew's perspective, is sharing some parting information to the disciples that will be required as the fact necessary to continue the mission and ministry.

In essence, He is telling them that they would now do the teaching of the message that they have heard Him teach and seen Him do.

> This message will be dependent upon your resolve to maintain the truth. It will not be continued without some trouble, trials, and adversity. However, there is one thing you need to be certain of, and that is that I am is with you!

I can see their mind's eye referring to when Jesus sent them out to minister on their own for the first time. I can see their heart disconcerted with the knowledge that He was not going to be there in person. Some no doubt were coming to grips with the reality that Jesus was not going to set up an earthly kingdom on the spot. Nonetheless, in Matthew 10:1, Jesus had given them power. This power did not come from them; it came from Him! They had abundant power to do the works for which they were dispatched. And when He had called unto Him His twelve disciples, He gave them power against unclean spirits, to cast them out, and to heal all manner of sickness and all manner of disease. There was nothing that they would encounter that the power that had been conferred upon them could not and would not be able to come against. They were to operate in complete authority from that power, just as Jesus would if He were present. Jesus provides direct instruction concerning who, where, what, how, and with whom they were to utilize this given power.

> But go rather to the lost sheep of the house of Israel [who and where] and as ye go, preach, saying, the kingdom of heaven is at hand [what] heal the sick, cleanse the lepers, raise the dead, cast out devils: freely ye have received, freely give [what] provide neither gold, nor silver, nor brass in your purses [how] nor scrip for your journey, neither two coats, neither shoes, nor yet staves: for the workman is worthy of his meat. [how] and into whatsoever city or town ye shall enter, enquire who in it is worthy; and there abide till ye go thence. And when ye come into an house, salute it. And if the house be worthy, let your peace come upon it: but if it be not worthy, let your peace return to you [to whom and where]. (KJV)

Jesus was never one to leave cracks for men to have to fill or blanks for man to have to introduce their own thought or answers. He was direct, He was purposeful, and He was intentional. The disciples experience all those in Matthew 10. Then He informs them from what source they will express the power that they have been given.

> But when they deliver you up, take no thought how or what ye shall speak: for it shall be given you in that same hour what ye shall speak. For it is not ye that speak, but the spirit of your father which peaked in you. (KJV)

This is an amazing statement! Men could be given powers, and sometimes those powers were demonic in nature, or at a minimum, not from the Spirit of the Father. But Jesus told them that their personal power would come from the Spirit of the Father. Also, that what they would speak would be given to them in the same hour that they needed it. It was as though Jesus was right there! It was as though they were standing and watching the Son of God, as He was listening to the voice of the Father, and telling the people how not to be poor, captive, enslaved, in bondage, or blind. It was as though they had the Spirit of the Lord upon them to minister to the people.

The Father is there! The Son is there! The glory of the Lord was expressed in twelve men who had no legitimate background in theology. They had no legitimate educational reason to be able to accomplish what had been asked of them. Neither did they have command of speaking and communication with enough polish to be identified as orators. What they had was a given power and a promise of an inner voice that would serve to guide them through the various needs of the people who needed their ministry. Jesus would represent the glory of God in them, while they represented Him to the children of Israel.

> Behold, I send you forth as sheep in the midst of wolves: be ye therefore wise as serpents, and harmless as doves. But beware of men: for they will deliver you up to the councils, and they will scourge you in their synagogues; and ye shall be brought before governors and kings for my sake, for a testimony against them and the gentiles. (Matthew 10:16–18 KJV)

These verses of chapter 10 confirm my earlier statement. They were as sheep among wolves. They were ill prepared in the eyes of the world. Those educated in the ways and means of the world would require answers from these supposed unlearned and uneducated men. The religious would try to beat out of them something that the flesh did not place in them. Those religious men had no clue that physical pain does not overcome what has been placed on the inside of a man who has had a real encounter with God. By the way, they would attempt this severe physical torment with Jesus, as we know. In neither case did it accomplish the desired results. These beatings and questions only served to galvanize the message of the cross.

Someone would respond to that fact with the question why. The reason is that each time the leaders of the world attacked the men whom Christ had set forth to produce blessings by His power and through the guidance of the Spirit, the results were overwhelming! You cannot physically harm an individual who has an "I know that I know" experience with the Lord. This was evident in the statement of the man who was blind from birth.

Here is the way that went from John 9.

> His parents answered them and said, we know that this is our Son, and that he was born blind: but by what means he now seeth, we know not; or who hath opened his eyes, we know not: he is of age; ask him: he shall speak for himself these words spake his parents, because they feared the Jews: for the Jews had agreed already, that if any man did confess that he was Christ, he should be put out of the synagogue. (John 9:20–22 KJV)

The parents were placed in a position where, although they no doubt were ecstatic with what had happened to their child, it had not happened directly to them. They had no relevant experience from which to stand on the table and declare that "they knew that they knew" that Jesus had done the deed, and their son subsequently was healed. They were not there when it occurred. All they had on it was the word of the child and the knowledge of what he was then and what he is now. They were afraid. Fear will make you as vulnerable as a little child with a fist full of candy on a playground with older kids. He may get a piece, but he will not have more than one. He will give away, or have taken away, what belonged to him. What he expected to enjoy does not come to him at all. It goes to those who come and take it. By the way, this analogy is the explanation of the old saying that "it is like taking candy from a baby."

Being put out of the synagogue was far too much of a risk for the parents to take. So taking the path of least resistance, they threw the kid under the bus!

> Therefore said his parents, he is of age; ask him. (John 9:23 KJV)

They now are dealing with the one who has had the encounter and left with the experience. Let's see how he handles the situation.

> Then again called they the man that was blind, and said unto him, give God the praise: we know that this man is a sinner. He answered and said, whether he be a sinner or no, I know not: one thing I know, that, whereas I was blind, now I see. (John 9:24–25 KJV)

The man with the experience becomes a most difficult nut to crack! Here is what I want you to see. He was in danger of being put out of the synagogue as well. He was in danger of being a religious outcast in a society where your entire life revolved around your family, your tribe, and subsequently your national religion. The council states their beliefs and expected this man to adhere to what they had stated as their official position. This statement is a leading statement for the young man and is done with the intention that he would simply comply, and the situation would be concluded. We believe that he is a sinner. Because we believe this, and for you to continue in good standing, you must consent to the same belief.

His response identifies no such agreement. How could it? Those questioning him were in the same condition that his parents were. They had no encounter with God and, therefore, no experience on which to base a belief system. What a sad condition these men were in with relation to knowing God and identifying His Son. So the healed man says, "You call him a sinner and that I cannot tell. But what I can tell you is that I once was blind. I know blind, as I have been that way all my life. You should be rejoicing with me because of what has happened. You are more interested in your religion, your status, and your politics than you are in the reality of the experience that has happened to me. My experience and my reality tell me something that your religion, status, and politics could not give to me." I can hear him say something to this effect. "I have been in the synagogue, I have been in the system, but the system left me without sight. So I don't know sin, except the sin that you all describe for me, but I do know this. I once was blind, but now I see!"

> Then said they to him again, what did he to thee? How opened he thine eyes? He answered them, I have told you already, and ye did not hear: wherefore would ye hear it again? Will ye also be his disciples? (John 9:26–27 KJV)

Now, once they could not coerce him or threaten him, they began to investigate the methods that were used to cause this miracle to happen. But to the man who had received his sight, the methods were inconsequential. It was the result, the experience, and the reality that mattered to him. He could tell them again, and they would not believe, because a person who has no encounter will have no experience and, therefore, no manifestation. When Jesus described this scenario to the disciples, He knew what they had been given and how it would affect their ability to minister and to withstand the issues that they would encounter from the list of religious dissenters. The disciples could only equate the possibilities to those that they had seen Him go through.

The outcome was clear. When problems occur, the Spirit of the Father will give you what to say. Further, He will speak it through you. The glory of God will be with you. Jehovah Shammah will be there to give you the answers that are required of you. Hebrews 4:16 says that help comes in the nick of time. That was the promised word for these men. The Gospel of Mark gives us the outcome of this ministerial service.

> And they went out, and preached that men should repent. And they cast out many devils, and anointed with oil many that were sick, and healed them. (Mark 6:12–13 KJV)

These men went out and preached to the extent that the political leadership was concerned that John the Baptist had raised from the dead. They did exploits under the anointing of the master and the direction of the Father that were of major concern to the religious and the political society. How did they do it? The glory of God was there with them. They went back and reported what they had done to Jesus.

These events would be benchmark moments for the disciples and apostles, as the day would come for them when they would be left to totally rely upon the glory of God that would be Jehovah Shammah—"God is there"—as they turned cities upside down, using this glory in power, and this glory in the Spirit, to do greater things than even the things that they had seen Jesus do.

Jesus told them that this would happen. They could not see it when He said it. They did not know how it would happen. But when they went out to minister under His anointing, it became apparent that greater works lay ahead. The glory of God, given from the one who came as Emanuel, was to be with them. He would be there! He would be closer than a brother. That tells me that He would be with them and identify with them in such close measure, just as the blood of a brother identifies the DNA that makes them look, act, and speak alike.

The Glory of God in Jesus after the Resurrection

Lastly, concerning the glory of the Lord, let's look at the glory of God in Jesus after the resurrection.

> And I turned to see the voice that spake with me. And being turned, I saw Seven Golden Candlesticks; and in the midst of the Seven Candlesticks one like unto the Son of man, clothed with a garment down to the foot, and girt about the paps with a golden girdle. His head and his hairs were white like wool, as white as snow; and his eyes were as a flame of fire; and his feet like unto fine brass, as if they burned in a furnace; and his voice as the sound of many waters. And he had in his right hand seven stars: and out of his mouth went a sharp two-edged sword: and his countenance was as the sun shineth in his strength. And when I saw him, I fell at his feet as dead. And he laid his right hand upon me, saying unto me, fear not; I am the first and the last: I am he that liveth, and was dead; and, behold, I am alive for evermore, amen; and have the keys of hell and of death. (Revelations 1:12–18 KJV)

There are several things we know from reading revelation chapter 1. One thing is that John, the writer, was in the Spirit on the Lord's day, the churches were already established, and John was instructed to write to the churches the things he saw in a book and send them to the seven churches in Asia—and not only these things, but the things to come that he would be shown after this. These things we clearly understand. But then, when John turned to see who was talking to him and he saw him, he literally fainted and fell at his feet. John was so shocked at this man's change of appearance. Still he knew He was Jesus, but he couldn't believe what he saw. He did not look like the Jesus John had formerly known before His death. His hair was white, His eyes were like flaming fire, and His feet were like brass as if He had been in a furnace. Unbelievable! Yet He was telling John things that John could not help but understand that only Jesus could accomplish. He had the keys of hell and death, and He was alive again after being dead. He certainly was resurrected.

Well, this led me to a question. Why in Matthew 28 and John 20 did no one now recognize Him until He spoke? Mary Magdalene, who knew Him so well, thought He was the gardener until He spoke to her after His resurrection. Cleopas and another man walking on the Emmaus road just outside of Jerusalem were overtaken by Jesus. He walked with them as they were discussing the crucifixion. He went home with them, after walking and talking with them, and they did not recognize Him until they were eating and he broke the bread. They knew Him and knew about His death. Why did they not recognize Him?

Then there were His own disciples, huddled in a room where He entered, and must have tremendously scared them, because He had to speak peace to them after they believed they had seen a spirit. He began to talk to them and showed them His hands and His feet and asked for something to eat. Why didn't they recognize Him? There are others who saw Him and didn't recognize Him until He said or did something. Why?

May I suggest that the answer to this lies in the fact that, in the three-day interval between the crucifixion and the resurrection, He had been in a desperate, destructive place, and that it changed His appearance forever. Let me remind you that John saw Him in Revelation 1:12–18 and gave us a horrifying description of Him in

AD 96, sixty-three years after His death. I think this leaves no room for any doubt that Jesus was in hell paying your time and mine, defeating Satan on his own turf, taking back the keys of hell and death. Then He walked out of there and locked the door behind Him! If anyone goes there after that, they're going to fall into it and not go in through the gate—and of your own volition, by the way.

Daniel, in a book bearing his name, called Jesus the ancient of days. He describes Him as having hair like pure wool, His garment white as snow, and His feet like a fiery flame.

> I beheld till the thrones were cast down, and the ancient of days did sit, whose garment was white as snow, and the hair of his head like the pure wool: his throne was like the fiery flame, and his wheels as burning fire. A fiery stream issued and came forth from before him: thousand thousands ministered unto him, and ten thousand times ten thousand stood before him: the judgment was set, and the books were opened. I beheld then because of the voice of the great words which the horn spake: I beheld even till the beast was slain, and his body destroyed, and given to the burning flame. As concerning the rest of the beasts, they had their dominion taken away: yet their lives were prolonged for a season and time. (Daniel 7:9–12 KJV)

He says the thrones are set for the judgment of those who died without Christ, including the beast. According to Revelation 20:6, this is called the second death which follows the second resurrection and does not come until after the thousand-year reign of Christ in the earth in His own kingdom. Here John writes,

> Blessed and holy is he that hath part in the first resurrection: on such the second death has no power. (Revelation 20:6 KJV)

So Daniel in Daniel 7:9–11 describes this change in the appearance of Jesus after a thousand years.

Paul has the answer, I think, to this horrific change in the features of Jesus. He says in 1 Corinthians 15:43–44,

> It is sown in weakness; raised in power, it is sown a natural body; it is raised a spiritual body. (1 Corinthians 15:43–44 KJV)

In both John's and Daniel's visions, Jesus's features were so altered that He was not recognizable. He was only recognized in what He spoke or did. Is this the reason that those who knew Him so well could not identify Him? This only came from being in a place called hell.

Let me be quick to explain that those who die in Christ will never, ever experience the physical change that Jesus bore. Because of what Jesus did for us, we will be spared from going there for ourselves.

Let's look again at a vision which Daniel had. In Daniel 10:4–21, we read,

> And in the four and twentieth day of the first month, as I was by the side of the great river, which is Hiddekel; then I lifted up mine eyes, and looked, and behold a certain man clothed in linen, whose loins were girded with fine gold of uphaz: his body also was like the beryl, and his face as the appearance of lightning, and his eyes as lamps of fire, and his arms and his feet like in colour to polished brass, and the voice of his words like the voice of a multitude. And I Daniel alone saw the vision: for the men that were with me saw not the vision; but a great quaking fell upon them, so that they fled to hide themselves. Therefore I was left alone, and saw this great vision, and there remained no strength in me: for my comeliness was turned in me into corruption,

and I retained no strength. Yet heard I the voice of his words: and when I heard the voice of his words, then was I in a deep sleep on my face, and my face toward the ground. And, behold, an hand touched me, which set me upon my knees and upon the palms of my hands. And he said unto me, O Daniel, a man greatly beloved, understand the words that I speak unto thee, and stand upright: for unto thee am I now sent. And when he had spoken this word unto me, I stood trembling. Then said he unto me, fear not, Daniel: for from the first day that thou didst set thine heart to understand, and to chasten thyself before thy God, thy words were heard, and I am come for thy words. But the prince of the kingdom of Persia withstood me one and twenty days: but, lo, Michael, one of the chief princes, came to help me; and I remained there with the kings of Persia. Now I am come to make thee understand what shall befall thy people in the latter days: for yet the vision is for many days. And when he had spoken such words unto me, I set my face toward the ground, and I became dumb. And, behold, one like the similitude of the sons of men touched my lips: then I opened my mouth, and spake, and said unto him that stood before me, O my Lord, by the vision my sorrows are turned upon me, and I have retained no strength. For how can the servant of this my Lord talk with this my Lord? For as for me, straightway there remained no strength in me, neither is there breath left in me. Then there came again and touched me one like the appearance of a man, and he strengthened me, and said, O man greatly beloved, fear not: peace be unto thee, be strong, yea, be strong. And when he had spoken unto

> me, I was strengthened, and said, let my Lord speak; for thou hast strengthened me. Then said he, knowest thou wherefore I come unto thee? And now will I return to fight with the prince of Persia: and when I am gone forth, lo, the prince of Grecia shall come. But I will shew thee that which is noted in the scripture of truth: and there is none that holdeth with me in these things, but Michael your prince. (Daniel 10:4–21 KJV)

Here he stood by the Tigris River on April 24 and looked up and saw a man clothed in linen whose loins were girded in a golden girdle. His body was like beryl, a yellowish greenish chrysolite, and His face as the appearance of lightning. His eyes are as lamps of fire, His arms and feet are like polished brass, and His voice like the voice of a multitude.

Daniel was in captivity, and when he saw the vision, he was with other men. However, the men did not see the vision. They only felt the effect of the presence of someone. The presence was so extreme that they fled, and Daniel was left alone. The person that he saw had the same effect on Daniel that it had on John. He also fainted. The person that he saw touched him, set him back on his feet, and told him His reason for coming.

Keep in mind that Daniel is seeing a prophecy that he does not understand. The man came to tell Daniel of the future events in the end-time. It is clear, however, from Daniel 7:9–14 that Daniel in his vision is seeing Jesus after His resurrection just as John had.

> I beheld till the thrones were cast down, and the ancient of days did sit, whose garment was white as snow, and the hair of his head like the pure wool: his throne was like the fiery flame, and his wheels as burning fire. A fiery stream issued and came forth from before him: thousand thousands ministered unto him, and ten thousand times ten thousand stood before him: the

judgment was set, and the books were opened. I beheld then because of the voice of the great words which the horn spake: I beheld even till the beast was slain, and his body destroyed, and given to the burning flame. As concerning the rest of the beasts, they had their dominion taken away: yet their lives were prolonged for a season and time. (Daniel 7:9–12)

We have three different records of seeing Jesus after the resurrection by way of visions. We know that He went into hell from other things that are stated in the Word concerning that event. He came back unrecognizable to those who knew Him before the resurrection. Seeing what it did to the Son of God, why would anyone risk going there, when Jesus made a way of escape? After all, hell was not created for mankind. It was created for Satan and his angels.

So we have investigated the three places where God's glory has been made known to mankind. When Jesus came out of hell, He was changed and unrecognizable by those who knew Him prior to his crucifixion. But He came out of hell with what He went to hell to retrieve. At some point during His time involved with the devastation of hell, the Holy Spirit showed up in God's glory to retrieve Him as the Holy Spirit had prophesied through Luke and David.

> Because thou wilt not leave my soul in hell, neither wilt thou suffer thine Holy one to see corruption. Thou hast made known to me the ways of life; thou shalt make me full of joy with thy countenance. Men and brethren let me freely speak unto you of the patriarch David, that he is both dead and buried, and his sepulcher is with us unto this day. Therefore being a prophet and knowing that God had sworn with an oath to him, that of the fruit of his loins, according to the flesh, he would raise up Christ to sit on his throne; He seeing this before spake of the resur-

> rection of Christ, that his soul was not left in hell, neither his flesh did see corruption. This Jesus hath God raised up, whereof we all are witnesses. Therefore being by the right hand of God exalted and having received of the Father the promise of the Holy Ghost, he hath shed forth this, which ye now see and hear. (Acts 2:27–35 KJV)

He was not to be corrupted by His time spent there. Rather, He was to bring corruption upon the regions of the damned. The glory of God went and took Him from the state in which they saw Him after the resurrection. In the meantime, Jesus told us what He would do while He was there.

> No man can enter into a strong man's house, and spoil his goods, except he will first bind the strong man; and then he will spoil his house. Verily I say unto you, all sins shall be forgiven unto the Sons of men, and blasphemies wherewith soever they shall blaspheme: but he that shall blaspheme against the Holy Ghost hath never forgiveness but is in danger of eternal damnation. (Mark 3:27–29 KJV)

He went to spoil the goods of the enemy. While He was there, seemingly under the control of the sin of mankind and in the clutches of the devil, something happened, and Jesus tells us in verses 28–29. He references the Holy Spirit, regarding how the strong man's spoils would be taken. It would be the Holy Spirit that would enter onto the scene and deliver the Son of God. God would show His glory in the place that was relegated to Satan. But Satan never again would be able to show his face in the portals of glory.

The strong man's grip upon the spirit of man was destroyed. Jesus was forever to be in control of the keys of hell and the grave. Man was to find pardon through the blood of the Lamb and the benefits of eternity, due to the glorious resurrection of the Son of

God. Men would see the effects of His tour of duty in hell. Heaven would see his changes from the same. Most importantly, heaven would never forget the cost the Son paid with His life and His blood. Nor would they ever forget the changes in His appearance that would forever be the sign of His dominance over all that hell had to offer while He was there.

Truly, He is the glory of God, and when John says greater is He that is in you than He that is in the world, he is surely informing us of the authority and power that He has in heaven and in earth. He is also informing us of the power that was derived from His descent into hell and the subsequent resurrection from that place. This resurrection is the ultimate show of the glory of God as He is risen with all the essentials required to secure the presence and glory of God for any person who believes in His accomplished work.

Just one more thought on this subject. We need to understand fully the two resurrections. They come a thousand years apart. The first one will include all the saved, the redeemed, and the prepared. That will be a great day for them. The second resurrection will include all who did not receive Christ as their Savior. They will be resurrected to be judged and cast into hell according to the Word of God. What a tragedy!

The Revelation of the Grace in Jesus

There I sat on a Saturday night in a building that seated about fifty people, listening to a preacher who had shown up in our town to preach healing to our community. He was a very large man from the Western part of the United States. When he arrived, he shared his story concerning how the Holy Spirit had led him into our town. He told us how he had driven around the area until he found the location that the Holy Spirit was describing to him. It happened to be a small independent Pentecostal church.

The building was hidden under a hill and located directly above the drive-in movie theater. It had been a hot spot for the movement of Pentecost in the past. But after a while it always seemed to fall off. At this time, there was a very small membership in regular attendance. But the service, which was in day 4 of a revival, was almost full. I sat in the back of the building by myself on this Saturday evening.

As the service proceeded, the preacher began to recount stories of the move and power of God of which he had been a part. The graphic illustrations of the healing power of God were shared for the crowd to be able to identify that this man had been on the inside with God. He shared the reason why, as he revealed that the move of the Spirit that results in healing only comes through prayer and fasting. As he shared his stories of the multiple forty-day fasts of which he had completed, I found it almost unthinkable. How in the world could any man put his body through that sort of pressure and live to share the tale with others?

After he spoke a while, he began to work with the crowd. There were many needs represented in the crowd on this Saturday evening. The people's faith had been activated by the man of God's stories of the presence and power of God from his past meetings. That evening there was a child present who had a leg that was from his birth shorter than the other. He could not run and play as the other children did. His mother through tears explained the situation to the preacher.

He did not blink at the need of this child. He called for a chair, and it was brought. He sat the boy in the chair and pulled up his pants legs to evaluate the situation. Sure enough, the child's right leg was a good inch shorter, maybe more. I remember distinctly how he took his hands and placed them on the boy's calf and on his heel. He looked heavenward and declared, "In the name of Jesus, grow!"

In front of my eyes as I stood to see, the leg grew! This young child began to cry, and the mother began to cry. As the people began to rejoice, the preacher lifted the boy from the chair and cleared the aisle. He instructed the young boy to run down the aisle. He did with a normal gait. The place went nuts!

I went home that night captivated by having been in such an electric atmosphere. During the evening, I had many thoughts concerning what I had just been exposed to. Did I really see what I thought I saw? Could there have been a gimmick of some sort? Was it an optical illusion? Surely there was an answer that I could wrap my mind around that would make physical sense to me.

After meditating on this event for a long time, I went off to sleep. I was living almost two hours from this church and had been in the area visiting. The next day, which was Sunday, I would go to my home church and then make the drive back to my own home. As the Sunday wore on, I began to sense a directive from the Holy Spirit. That directive was to remain and attend the service that evening at the visiting preacher's church. I began to inquire as to why. In a few minutes, I had my answer. My son had developed a naval hernia. We had done everything we could do to help the naval retract, but it was not retracting. It became more apparent day by day that a medical procedure was necessary. That was bad news. I was a college student with very little money. It was a bleak situation.

So I chose to stay that evening and attend the service. I took my son with me as I knew what the Spirit had inspired me to do. It came offering time as it does in all services. I remember looking in my wallet and preparing to present my offering to God. I had a twenty-dollar bill, a five-dollar bill, and two one-dollar bills. In my financial condition, I reached for the ones. The Holy Spirit quickened me that this was not the correct amount. I put them back and reached for the five-dollar bill. Again, the Holy Spirit informed me that this was not the correct offering. At this point, I began to mentally share with God my personal and family needs. I shared how long this amount of money would serve to put gas in the car, feed, and provide for the baby. However, my spirit had hit upon the correct bill. As I placed the money in the offering plate, I had placed myself in that pan. I had surrendered the thing that I seemed to need the most for the potential of something someone else needed more.

As the service went on, great things were happening. People were being healed. I was not able to get the child within arm's reach of the preacher. The service concluded. There had been no point of contact except the money that I had given into the offering for giving my very best and bringing my very best to lay before the King.

After the service, I went to my car. We had sat near the door, so exit was easy. Suddenly, out of another door, appeared the preacher. We were in the lot with no one between us and him. I stopped him. He was tired but kind. I explained the need. He looked at the child and me and stated that he would like for us to come back tomorrow evening. He felt as though the anointing which he was under during the service was not there for such a work. Again, I explained the situation to him.

He looked at the child and lovingly said, "Okay." He reached down and asked to see the hernia. I uncovered a nasty-looking naval area. He, as always, did not flinch. He reached his right hand toward the naval. All of a sudden, and I can hear and feel him saying it even as I write, he declared, "In the name of Jesus, I speak to you, naval, you go in and be normal!" He looked at me and emphatically stated, "The child will heal and be normal." I thanked him profusely, put the child and myself in the car, and began the trip home. I went rejoicing in what the Lord had done and the promise that the man of God had declared over the child.

A few days passed, and I noticed a change in the naval. It went from an abnormal protruding rounded area to a less-angry-looking area. It seemed that as each day or so passed, the area began to improve. Shortly, the area looked normal. God had done the healing that we could not do. He had used a man I did not know, in an environment outside the confines of the church, to produce the miracle that was needed for a little child who did not know the difference. What a great God He is! This taught me an awesome lesson concerning the anointing. The time nor the place plays a role in the utilization of the anointing of God. Only the circumstances and the situation that presents itself before the anointing matters.

When Jesus was faced with seeing the widow of Nane's son dead, He was in a circumstance and a situation that did not require music or the safety of a church house. No, it required the anointing to be released at the moment the anointing was required. When Jesus showed up at Lazarus's after-death party, He did not need to be early or on the time schedule of those in attendance. He functioned in the grace of God. He operated in the favor and influence of God. He brought the function of the Holy Spirit when the function was required. We could go on and on with how the anointing did not require special or specific circumstances for Jesus to minister. This anointing is present, and it prospers in those who walk after the Spirit and not after the flesh.

The ministry today is under the misguided assumption that we can only operate in the anointing while residing in sheltered conditions. This is far from the truth. If the grace of God will save a man on his death bed, on the job site, on a bridge, in a car, or wherever the Holy Spirit locates that man whose heart is open and tender to His direction, then the same anointing will work through any man who seeks and pursues the life of grace that is found through the utilization of the Seven Spirits of God. These, in conjunction with prayer mediation and the Word of God, will produce a man that is "sitting on ready." Or as Paul stated concerning this matter in 2 Timothy 4:2,

> Preach the word; be instant in season, out of season; reprove, rebuke, exhort with all long suffering and doctrine.

We have the ability and the comprehension of the doctrine of grace that allows us to be ready on a moment's notice to be witnesses of what the name of Jesus can do. He, then, is the one who produces the grace of confirming the Word with signs that follow.

Grace is a word that, like most words that have spiritual implications, is used in the natural as well. When used in the worldly vernacular, this word has a couple of different uses. The ease and fluidity of movement is one common meaning. It is then used to describe the athletic ability, or the artistic ability of an individual as it relates to how the eye sees the movement. It also represents the ability to be kind, gracious, and compassionate. All these uses of the term grace or graceful are exercises that have been learned. They express a natural but trained movement pattern. They also express a system of values and morals that are expressed by the means in which you deal with people.

Then there is the real side of grace. This refers to how grace affects the inner man, which is represented by his spirit. This grace is one that must be experienced. Therefore, it is in direct contrast with the grace that affects the flesh. This grace model comes with a divine purpose. In Jesus, this grace was developed within his seven spirits. As he developed the grace that allowed him to be wise and comprehend the divine purpose of God, the other five attributes—counsel, might, knowledge, judgment, and the fear of the Lord—took depth. This allowed him to be identified as grace. Grace is the state in which Jesus resides. It is in Him because He is the embodiment of the spiritual meaning of the word.

When this grace takes effect in the life of a believer, it happens by faith. When faith is expressed by a believer, a change is completed within the spirit of the one using their faith. This faith then leads to the new birth. A believer can remain here and live a life that only reflects the new birth. But that believer will live a shallow and unsatisfied existence as a Christian. This will be so since there would be no depth of training to be able to activate the promises in the Word of God. When the storms of life come, and they will come, the parable of the broadcasting farmer will be reenacted in that shallow believer's life. The outcome will be a life that has every opportunity to become doubtful and fearing.

Then there is the potential that grace offers every believer. That potential is to develop and train our spirit through the means that Jesus taught. This will lead us into the areas that are required for us to live in the good gifts of our Heavenly Father. We can mature into a sanctified or separated life. By grace we can be filled with the baptism of the Holy Spirit. We can, by grace, develop ourselves into the measure of the stature of Christ. This will lead us into the image of his dear Son. The result of grace then is that our bodies are fashioned like His glorious body by the same means that He is able to subdue all things to Himself.

Grace has a few common meanings in the Christian world. One of them is the favor of God. I like to use two more that I think are relevant to the topic of grace. The first is that grace is the influence of God, and the second is that grace is the way God does things. During this chapter of the book, we will look at Jesus through the lens of these three explanations of grace. I think we will see that Jesus was the perfect embodiment of these explanations and that He exhibited all three during his earthly work. Then we will look at Jesus as the provider of many grace works that impact the lives of those to whom they are expressed. These works of grace are given to men to meet the need that is present at the time when the need must be met.

The first premise of the concept of grace that is often overlooked is that the work of grace is a work that occurs upon the spirit of man. It is in this grace that Paul speaks when he defines the grace of unmerited favor in Ephesians 2:8–9.

> For by grace are ye saved through faith; and that not of yourselves: it is the gift of God: not of works, lest any man should boast. (Ephesians 2:8–9 KJV)

This work of grace is completed upon the spirit of mankind. It is this grace when received by faith, transforms man, and delivers him from the power of darkness into the kingdom of the Son. It is a gift that was made available because God so loved the world that he gave His only begotten Son to provide the opportunity for man to reconnect his spirit to the eternal Spirit of the Father.

This grace when applied to the spirit of man changes that man into a new creation. In essence, he is born again. Now, what does that mean? The picture that this phrase paints is one that we must have a firm grasp upon to be able to understand the work of grace and how faith impacts this work. The Holy Spirit is sent into the earth with many divine orders. Three of those orders dramatically impact the spirit of man with respect to the new birth. John 16:8 gives us some insight into this work of the Holy Spirit as it relates to how men identify the necessity of the grace that came in Jesus Christ.

> And when he is come, he will reprove the world
> of sin, and of righteousness, and of judgment.
> (John 16:8 KJV)

This, of course, is the King James reference of this particular scripture. Let's look at the word *reprove*. It means both "to convict and to convince." So when the Holy Spirit begins the work that we call grace within a man's spirit, he first begins by convicting or identifying the separation that man has between himself and God. Then he identifies the reasons for the separation. This convicting is a dynamic activity of the Holy Spirit.

When I was a young lad, I went to a revival with my mother. We had a dynamic communicator holding revival at the church of God in Roanoke Rapids, North Carolina. I happened to be wearing a French Cuff shirt that night. You will see why I mention that shortly. As he preached, I sensed the presence and power of God on and around me. He was preaching that night on the reward for the lost who leave this world without Jesus. I was spellbound by his message. Really, I was deeply under the conviction of the Holy Spirit, but this was something that I did not have the age nor the spiritual maturity to understand.

As he continued, I began to perspire. I could literally feel the heat coming through my body as he spoke of the conditions that a man without a Savior would encounter. I perspired through the cuffs of the shirt. I was ringing wet by the time he gave the altar call. Who could resist such a powerful presence and tender calling of the Spirit of God? Down the aisle I went—a nine-year-old boy who just did not want to go to hell! The convicting power had become the convincing power of the Holy Spirit. I was mesmerized by both. I went and prayed and had my first grace encounter. I was born again at nine. I did not understand it. I did not know that you needed to be trained and developed in this walk. I just knew that I was not going to go to the awful place that man had described. My mother was an awesome Christian, and I learned to pray from her. But to truly identify the need to train myself and develop my spirit man, I was unaware.

This brings me to part 2 of John 16:8 and of righteousness. The newborn work of grace must be developed through the means of understanding by both conviction and convincing, when needed, that this work has made us the righteousness of God. Paul told us this in 2 Corinthians 5:21.

> For he hath made him to be sin for us, who knew no sin; that we might be made the righteousness of God in him. (2 Corinthians 5:21 KJV)

The Holy Spirit, by the work of grace, leads us into the righteousness of God that only Jesus could provide. There are times when we walk into sin on purpose or by accident. The Holy Spirit then must use who we are in Christ Jesus to convict us of the sin that we so easily entangle ourselves with. It is by this means that we are able to recognize that our spirit is out of step with God. This conviction affords us the opportunity to right ourselves and repent, thereby moving forward in Christ.

This same Spirit identifies the righteousness of Christ in us when we need to be convinced that our righteousness in Christ affords us the benefits of the cross. Regardless of the situation in which we find ourselves, the Holy Spirit is constantly enforcing the fact that by the work of grace, our righteousness produces the benefits of the cross, provided we receive those benefits the same way we received grace, by faith. So all manner of sickness, disease, and all manner of unclean things that may come against us are covered in the righteousness that Jesus provided and that the Holy Spirit connects to us.

Then we must look at how the work of grace affects the process of judgment. When the Holy Spirit convicts and convinces in this area, he is providing man the means of escape that Paul referred to in 1 Corinthians 10:13.

> There hath no temptation taken you but such as is common to man: but God is faithful, who will not suffer you to be tempted above that ye are able; *but will with the temptation also make a way to escape, that ye may be able to bear it.* (1 Corinthians 10:13 KJV)

Within each situation that man encounters, is the opportunity to apply the judgment, which means bringing correct decision-making into the equation. We are given our means of escape through our ability to decide for or against a righteous choice. The Holy Spirit is working the work of grace to help you judge for righteousness. If you choose against righteousness, see the part above concerning His work for convicting and convincing you concerning sin.

This cycle is played out daily, and sometimes moment by moment, in the lives of Christians. We have received a work of grace that has saved us. We now must allow the Holy Spirit to execute his work through grace to help us become the person God has called us to be. There is the work of grace that defines the influence of God upon man. This has special significance as we study the grace that was expressed in Jesus. He was a man made by grace for divulging grace to mankind. In order for grace to complete a work upon the spirits of men, men would have to undergo a transformation by grace which we saw earlier. Then men would have to undergo a transfer of grace—which we will look at next.

A few months ago, I found some most interesting information about how Jesus was trained and developed to become the grace of God. I was reading the book of Proverbs when the Holy Spirit revealed something to me that was a revelation concerning what I will refer to as the silent years. These were the years between the time Jesus was twelve years old and the time of which His ministry was manifested to the world. Jesus did not require a work of grace as we know it. He had no sin for grace to have to be the method of interceding. No, He was perfect. But there was still a work of grace going on for the young man as daily He moved toward the ministry and ultimately the cross. Now, bear in mind, by the law, Jesus could not begin His ministry until he was thirty years old. There was a process that Jesus underwent during the eighteen years that Solomon shares with us. Solomon begins the training and development of Jesus with these words in Proverbs 1:2–3.

> To know *wisdom* and *instruction*; to perceive the words of *understanding*; to receive the instruction of *wisdom, justice,* and *judgment,* and *equity.* (Proverbs 1:2–3 KJV)

As I began to ponder these words, the Holy Spirit began to show me the words that I have emphasized. As I began to think on these words, I saw Isaiah 11:2–3:

> And the spirit of the LORD shall rest upon him, the *Spirit of wisdom* and *understanding*, the *Spirit of counsel* and *might*, the *Spirit of knowledge* and *of the fear of the* LORD; and shall make him of quick understanding in the fear of the LORD: and he shall not *judge* after the sight of his eyes, neither *reprove* after the hearing of his ears. (Isaiah 11:2–3 KJV)

As I read through the Proverbs, I began to identify again and again Solomon referring to the elements that make up what we now identify as the Seven Spirits of God. Again, what a revelation! I began to read Proverbs as the training ground and developmental process for how God built the boy Jesus into a man of God who could stand and withstand the wiles of the devil.

Then I saw verse 8 of Proverbs chapter 2.

> My son, hear the instruction of thy father, and forsake not the law of thy mother: (Proverbs 2:8 KJV)

Why did he say it this way? Hear the instruction of thy Father. I was preaching this one Sunday morning in November when I heard myself declare, "Here you can identify that this is Jesus of whom Solomon is writing. We clearly see that there were two distinct sides of the boy. There was his Father's side, and there was his mother's side. Jesus would refer to this passage Himself when He would relate that he did not say or do one thing that He did not see his Father do or hear Him say. He was adhering to the instruction of His Father. It was His Father's teaching of which Solomon was sharing."

As we read chapter 1, it is easy to see that the instruction led the boy away from sin, sinful activity, sinful people and greed. It is also apparent that the same instruction was and would be available to all men. As Solomon says, "Wisdom cried in the streets, and says, 'Hey, Stupid, how long will you be stupid and not listen to Wisdom?'" The words become words of rejection and devastation to those who will not hear.

Then in verse 33, Solomon says,

> But whoso hearkened unto me shall dwell safely and shall be quiet from fear of evil. (Proverbs 1:33 KJV)

He is referring to those who hear the Son. This is spoken to encourage the boy who would see others choose the very ways and the very activities that were prophesied to lead to desolation and destruction. You, young man, will be living and leading others to dwell in safety!

Please allow me to look at the second half of verse 8:

> And forsake not the law of thy mother.

It became apparent to me that this second portion was precisely what Jesus had done. He had gone through the Jewish ritual at twelve. He had lived in the home of his Jewish mother. He had been a good Jew. This, to the extent that Jesus speaking of Himself, said in Matthew 5:17,

> Think not that I am come to destroy the law, or the prophets: I am not come to destroy, but to fulfil. (Matthew 5:17 KJV)

Yes, He did. Why? Because He had to continue in the law of His mother. He was taught to do so. He had instruction from the Father and the law from His mother. He was well armed from heaven to execute the divine commands. He was also well prepared in the religion of the day to be able to understand the customs associated with that culture. He was the perfect man, taught by His mom for one purpose and His Dad for another.

Consider these words from Proverbs 2:1.

> My son, if thou wilt receive my words, and hide my commandments with thee; (Proverbs 2:1 KJV)

Here is the work of grace functioning in the life of Jesus. By receiving the Father's words, He was redeeming the day and taking advantage of His day of instruction. The time of instruction is critical. Many have missed their golden opportunities because they missed the moment of instruction. Here again, we can refer to the work of the Holy Spirit in the lives of men from John 16:8. I want you to notice that in the scripture, the writer seems to pen these words with the message of an option.

> If thou wilt receive my words.

Jesus, like everyone else, could have chosen to be involved in other things. How do we know this? We read it in chapter 1 of Proverbs. But He had declared His loyalty and obedience from a young age. He was here to complete the divine call of God. He was training and developing the grace required to do the job. He was developing within His Spirit the tools required to be able to proclaim, "I have overcome the world!"

We often miss the day of instruction. The various distractions identified in Proverbs 1 keep us from doing the things that would allow us to come the way Jesus came. Here, however, is the truth we can come the same way and be trained by the same methods. We can find the same grace. Here is the truth: If Jesus, through the Spirit, could develop His spiritual side to control His natural side, then any man who chooses to walk in the Spirit can do the same. The question then is not "Can we locate the same training and develop in the Seven Spirits of God?" It is "Are we willing to attend, put in the time, and place our priorities totally upon him?"

Then Solomon provides us with the piece that allows us to be led into good judgment by the Holy Spirit:

> And hide my commandments with thee.

The ability to make this relationship personal is the key to the identification that what is being said is being heard and understood.

When you hide the commandments in your heart, David said that you would not sin against God. That's awesome! But Jesus took it further in John 14:21.

> He that hath my commandments, and keepeth them, he it is that loveth me: and he that loveth me shall be loved of my Father, and I will love him, and will manifest myself to him. (John 14:21 KJV)

Why would Jesus say this? He knew it to be true. How? Because this is the exact relationship that He had with his Father. He loved his Father. He was obedient due to love. His Father loved Him. That was obvious because of the works that He was doing. He also knew that the man who followed the commandments would live in the manifestation of the Father and the Son because this was precisely the life which He led. He lived, walked, acted, and spoke by means of keeping the commandments. We can also. This relationship came as a work of grace. It manifested because He executed verse 4 of Proverbs chapter 2.

> If thou seekest her as silver, and searchest for her as for hid treasures. (Proverbs 2:4 KJV)

The instruction and the law were of ultra value to Jesus. It was the treasure and the priority of His being. This is how the work of grace is completed for both training a man how to live and then developing the man in how to continue to become the man He has been called to be.

Someone would say to me, "Mike, how in the world could this relate to me?" Let's look at Provers 2:9.

> Then shalt thou understand righteousness, and judgment, and equity; yea, every good path. (Provers 2:9 KJV)

Do you see the reference to righteousness? It is an important inclusion for you and me. Jesus was the righteousness of God. Paul said that we were made to be the righteousness of God in Christ Jesus. So when Solomon uses that word to describe the path that the trained and developed lad would traverse, he included you and me in the statement. Since we are by force made to be the righteousness of God, we also can come by the way of the training to be able to live in the rest of this verse.

We, through the Holy Spirit, can use judgment to our advantage. We can become quality decision-makers when it comes to spiritual things. We can expect the guidance of the Holy Spirit to help us use heavenly abilities to eliminate and lay aside any sin that attempts to beset us. The word *equity* means "equal"! It also means "prosperity." Through the work of grace that makes us righteous, we can train ourselves to be equal with the one who was first trained to hear instruction. We can become prosperous and be able to utilize the benefits of the cross for the meeting of our needs. We can develop our spirit man to be like His and come into the image of His dear Son. That was the purpose for which man was created in the first place.

Then Solomon says that we can understand every good path. This is such good news! Through Him and the work of grace that Jesus developed, we can have a clear course laid aside for us to walk through this life. The path has a guide. He is the Holy Spirit of God, who is called alongside to help us experience the work of grace. That work of grace is the same work Jesus knew, and it will accomplish the same result that it did for Jesus. We will live in and under the manifestation of the Son of God. Awesome!

> My son, forget not my law; but let thine heart keep my commandments: for length of days, and long life, and peace, shall they add to thee. Let not mercy and truth forsake thee: bind them about thy neck; write them upon the table of thine heart: so shalt thou find favour and good understanding in the sight of God and man trust in the LORD with all thine heart; and lean not unto thine own understanding. In all thy ways acknowledge him, and he shall direct thy paths. Be not wise in thine own eyes: fear the LORD AND depart from evil. (Proverbs 3:1–7 KJV)

Here we find the scripture that is included in Luke's writing in chapter 2 and verse 52. This part of Proverbs, in my opinion, is the direct correlation to the young life of Jesus. It defines His relationship to His mother by way of the law and the results of living a disciplined life. This life brought about the favor or the divine influence of God upon Jesus. It is the development of the man that the world would see. It is the means of successful living that would result in Jesus fulfilling the divine plan of God. This process was a work of grace developed during the silent years.

As you read further into the book of Proverbs, you will be able to see the Seven Spirits of God surface as Jesus was trained for the task ahead. This work of grace in the life of Jesus was of no little consequence. It was these elements of his person that allowed Him to function as He did. It is due to these spirits that Jesus would say in Luke 4:16,

> The Spirit of the Lord is upon me, because he hath anointed me to preach the gospel to the poor; he hath sent me to heal the brokenhearted, to preach deliverance to the captives, and recovering of sight to the blind, to set at liberty them that are bruised. (KJV)

It is here that the work of grace completed in Him comes forth from Him to every class of people.

Having received the instructions and words of the Lord, and then applying those words to one's spirit, brings about the ultimate outcome of a developed spiritual relationship with God. He is a Spirit, and we are made in the image of that Spirit. And now we have reconnected the two spirits together with our spirit. Paul says in Romans 8:8,

> The Spirit itself beareth witness with our spirit, that we are the children of God (Romans 8:8 KJV)

The influence of the grace of God has developed us until we are the children of God. Mature in Him and prepared to walk in the Spirit.

This brings us to the third work of grace. It is the way God does things. This is easy to see in Jesus. As a matter of fact, Jesus was quick to identify how this grace worked in Him. When it worked in and through Him, the people were translated and transferred into the glory of God. Lives were transformed, and circumstances were changed. It is all done by the dynamic work of the way God does things! The first reference to the way God does things is stated by Jesus in John chapter 5 verses 19 and 20. Here is what He said. Jesus has just healed the impotent man at the Pool of Bethesda. This angered the Jews, who began to question the man. He had done this on the Sabbath, and of course, this was against the law.

In verse 17, Jesus makes a statement that to them is unacceptable; to us, however, it is a blessing.

> But Jesus answered them, my Father worketh hitherto, and I work. (John 5:17 KJV)

Here, in my opinion, is one of the greatest sayings in the scripture. Jesus is saying to them this is what He was instructed to do. Look at verses 19–20.

> Then answered Jesus and said unto them, Verily, Verily, I say unto you, the Son can do nothing of himself, but what he seeth the Father do: for what things soever he doeth, these also doeth the Son likewise. for the Father loveth the Son, and sheweth him all things that himself doeth: and he will shew him greater works than these, that ye may marvel. (John 5:19–20 KJV)

Jesus clearly identifies the instruction of which He was given. He clearly identifies the source of the instruction, and He clearly relates why he is the one with the instruction. This is completed by this means because it is a work of grace. It is the way God does things!

Where did He learn this? He was eternal, He was personal to God, and He was designated to operate in the office of Creator. He was life, He was light, He was illumination, He was salvation, and He was the glory of God. But there is more. Look at this passage from Proverbs chapter 8. Here you will clearly see that Jesus was there and watching the Father as He orchestrated the future works that were to come forth as the heavens and the earth kissed and grace and mercy materialized.

> The LORD possessed me in the beginning of his way, before his works of old. I was set up from

> everlasting, from the beginning, or ever the earth was. Solomon here is referring to Jesus. He was prophesying concerning his state and position. When there were no depths, I was brought forth; when there were no fountains abounding with water. Before the mountains were settled, before the hills was I brought forth: while as yet he had not made the earth, nor the fields, nor the highest part of the dust of the world. When he prepared the heavens, I was there: when he set a compass upon the face of the depth when he established the clouds above: when he strengthened the fountains of the deep: when he gave to the sea his decree, that the waters should not pass his commandment: when he appointed the foundations of the earth: then I was by him, as one brought up with him: and I was daily his delight, rejoicing always before him. (Proverbs 8:22–36 KJV)

I see Jesus watching and working the divine plan with God and rejoicing with Him as each piece of the plan was revealed. He, in His position within the Godhead, had access that was to be used in the very system of which He was a part of creating.

> Rejoicing in the habitable part of his earth; and my delights were with the sons of men. Now therefore hearken unto me, o ye children: for blessed are they that keep my ways. Hear instruction, and be wise, and refuse it not. Blessed is the man that heareth me, watching daily at my gates, waiting at the posts of my doors. For whoso findeth me findeth life and shall obtain favour of the LORD. But he that sinneth against me wrongeth his own soul: all they that hate me love death. (Proverbs 8:31–36 KJV)

Now Solomon comes from this prophetical utterance where he had identified the one to whom the prophecy is concerning and begins to go back to the instruction of the son. The most important information is to connect this prophecy and this teaching to why Jesus was able to act in the grace of God or the way God does things. He was there and working with God from the beginning. Nevertheless, when Solomon identifies the Son as having two distinct parts, that of the Father and of the mother, the requirement for instruction upon His Spirit was necessary. Since He was to do works from His Spirit while in the flesh, He must be taught and developed in both domains. Now we can tie the scripture in John 5 with His instruction in Proverbs 8. By doing so, we can understand how Jesus could say that He only did what He saw His Father do. He had been not only involved in the work and spoke the creation into being, but He would subsequently bring that ability by grace to man. He would express the way God does things while ministering to people.

Then there was the next statement that Jesus made concerning how He accomplished the works that mankind witnessed. Jesus said in John 8:28,

> Then said Jesus unto them, when ye have lifted the Son of Man, then shall ye know that I am he, and that I do nothing of myself; but as my Father hath taught me, I speak these things. (John 8:28 KJV)

Jesus simply did as He was taught. His instruction had taken Him to a place in his development where He operated in the Seven Spirits of God. He did this to such an extent that the material world obeyed His words. When He spoke, it was as if the Father had spoken directly to the situation. The silent years brought the instruction to the man Jesus Christ that allowed Him to infuse His spiritual side with his earthly side. This combination brought out of His flesh the things that His Father had spoken to Him. The world would not recognize this because they were too influenced by the human side.

Jesus had that side also, but due to the training at the feet of his Father, He could operate on a different plane.

Notice this with me please: The Jewish home was one wherein the mother played the prominent role in the training of the children. So when the scripture says that the Son should not forsake the law of the mother, it is showing us the necessity of both sets of instructions. The child, to be a good and well-learned Jew, had to know and understand the law. This is most relevant, because when Jesus's ministry was presented, it was presented to the Jews. In order for Him to navigate the landscape, He had to have command of the law, the culture and the customs of that day. He had to be able to function in the way God had done things under the law that was essential to the people as He ministered to them in the temple.

He also had to bring about the ministry of miracles for the Jews to identify his relationship to the God of the law. There would not be a day of the dispensation of grace for Israel until they saw the God of the law intervening in the lives of the people. It is for this purpose that Jesus sent his disciples in Matthew 10 only to the children of Israel. They could relate the God of the law to so many relationships that Jesus was having with them. There was no one in Israel with the power or presence of God to do the things Jesus was doing. Do you remember the blind man that Jesus healed? He had been blind from birth. He and his family had been good Jews with respect to training and attendance in the temple. But he was not healed until he had an encounter with Jesus.

We can trace this very story to the Hebrew teachings concerning the creation of man. We know that Adam was made of dust and DNA. In their presence, Jesus had taken the same products and healed a man that they knew well. Again, the Jew was being led to correlate the works with the God of the law. Therefore, Jesus said in John 14:11,

> Believe me that I am in the Father, and the Father in me: or else believe me for the very works' sake. (John 14:11 KJV)

"If you identify the works, then you can clearly see the relationship between Me and My Father. He is your God of the law!"

When Jesus healed the leper, that was not new in Israel. God had done that for Naaman. When Jesus raised the dead, that was not new; God had done that for the Shunamite woman. When Jesus said that He was going into the strong man's house and spoil his goods, that was nothing new; Abraham, David, and Israel had conquered people and lands doing that. He was connecting Himself with the God of the law. He was doing things that He had seen done and that He had heard God say to do. He was simply operating in the way God does things in the natural world. This was the connection that the priests, Sadducees, and the Pharisees refused to relate to the people. Therefore, the connection, because of the reality of who they were and the power that they had taken, would be lost. The people, on the other hand, who stood in desperate need of a spiritual encounter with the God of the Law flocked and followed Him everywhere He went. They were amazed at His words and His power. When He walked on the water and called Peter to Him in Matthew 14, those on the boat identified Him as the Son of God for the works that they had seen Him do.

When He healed the mute, the lame, and the diseased, the people present saw the correlation in Matthew 15 and began to praise the God of Israel. They had connected Him to the God of the law because they saw Him do the exact same things they had been taught concerning the God of the law. What a wonderful revelation this was to the people! They got their needs met; the connection was made between the Father and the Son, and Jesus continued to do these works from city to city. The grace of God that was in the man that came from the instruction of the Father was expressed in Jesus's relationship to mankind. The work of grace that God did in Jesus has a pattern that I want to share with you. This pattern is one that any man who chooses to see it and pursue it can follow and ultimately work the works Jesus worked.

I know that sounds way out there, in an age where the church has become so weak that manifestations of the Holy Spirit rarely occur. I have heard preachers declare that all we need is Jesus. That is awesome. But Jesus did not teach that. Jesus included the work of the Holy Spirit in His teaching. The Holy Spirit would serve to be in a believer, on a believer, and upon a believer. He would accomplish two works for the believer. First, He would be the agent who would convict us and lead us to be saved. Second, He would fill us with Himself for service and witness.

Jesus said in John 14:12,

> Verily, Verily, I say unto you, he that believeth on me, the works that I do shall he do also; and greater works than these shall he do; because I go unto my Father. (John 14:1 KJV)

The genesis of these works are shared with us here in this verse. Peter alluded to it in Acts 2:32–33.

> This Jesus hath God raised up, whereof we all are witnesses. Therefore being by the right hand of God exalted and having received of the Father the promise of the Holy Ghost, he hath shed forth this, which ye now see and hear. (Acts 2:32–33 KJV)

Because He went to his Father He sent back the Comforter, the Paraclete, and the one to whom He would give command for the completion of the greater works which He promised. This was to be the way God does things in the life of a believer. Jesus told us this in no uncertain terms in Acts 1:2,

> Until the day in which he was taken up, after that he through the Holy Ghost had given commandments unto the apostles whom he had chosen. (Acts 1:2 KJV)

So as we look at the way God does things, we need to find the methods of instruction that were used to develop Jesus.

Let's look at Proverbs 1:2–5.

> To know wisdom and instruction; to perceive the words of understanding; to receive the instruction of wisdom, justice, and judgment, and equity; to give subtilty to the simple, to the young man knowledge and discretion. A wise man will hear, and will increase learning; and a man of understanding shall attain unto wise counsels. (Proverbs 1:2–5 KJV)

When I was a student in high school, I was not really math-oriented. I did not enjoy the courses. I could not for the life of me identify how geometry or algebra was going to impact my adult world. They said I needed it, so I took them. I did not have a great focus on these courses. In my adult life, I have become a math teacher. Do I teach geometry and algebra? No! I have no use for them. I teach basic computational mathematics. These are useful and important in our everyday lives. The point I wanted you to see is this: we will never focus ourselves to learn or be taught anything that we do not realize as being important.

Now let's look at the methods the Father used to train and develop the Lord. To know this comes from identifying the importance of what it is that you are trying to know. Solomon used the word *perceive*. This is a great word as it means "to become aware of, conscious of something, or come to realize or understand." Jesus perceived the importance of the Father's instruction. Since this was His pervading attitude, is focus was solely upon His training. How do we know this? He said so. He was aware of the significance of the instruction of His Father and His mother. Without the understanding of both worlds, He would have risked becoming a cultural misfit and be understood by the society as out of place. But notice that for thirty years, He was strictly a practicing Jew. His mother knew better, and His Father knew better, but the surrounding world was clueless as to who the man was who was hammering and nailing with Joseph. By the way, they would say as much in Matthew 13:55.

Then Solomon wrote that He had to receive the instruction from the Father. This is a crucial piece of information. The word *receive* is used to describe "how something that was given is taken from the giver and is put to use by the receiver." So when Jesus was provided with the opportunity to learn understanding and wisdom from the words of the Father, He did not become obstinate or disinterested in the gift. No, He took what was being offered as a priority in His growth. How do we know that? Solomon and Luke told us so. They shared how He grew physically and spiritually.

> So shalt thou find favour and good understanding in the sight of God and man. (Proverbs 3:4 KJV)

> And Jesus grew in wisdom and stature, and in favor with God and man. (Luke 2:52 KJV)

Here we see the result of His perception and what it was that He received from the instruction. He received the principle thing of wisdom, He was growing physically, and He was favored by man and God due to what He received from defining the need for it. So the first two areas become clear.

Thirdly, He gave something of Himself into the process. To give subtilty to the simple, to the young man's knowledge and discretion. He gave Himself to the teaching by using the good sense to pay attention to the instruction. That is what *subtilty* means. It refers to good sense. Jesus, by using good judgment, which is one of the Seven Spirits of God referred to in Isaiah 11:2–3, was able to give Himself to the requirements of the course. He studied, attended, and made a priority of all the instruction that was offered. He used discretion, which means He chose to perceive and receive the teaching as a treasure. So He gave intentional purpose to the things He needed to know to fulfill His calling. Now, how do we know this? Solomon told us so.

> If thou seekest her as silver and searchest for her as for hidden treasure. (Proverbs 2:4 KJV)

> She shall give to thine head an ornament of grace: a crown of glory shall she deliver to thee. (Proverbs 4:9 KJV)

Then lastly, when we discuss how He was able to reconcile Himself to the instruction of His Father and His mother, we come to the need for the area that men in general lack. We will find this in verse 5 of Proverbs chapter 1.

> A wise man will hear, and will increase learning; and a man of understanding shall attain unto wise counsels. (KJV)

Can you see the word in this verse that will place men and women of God at the feet of the teacher? "A wise man will hear!" Jesus surrendered Himself to listen. Surrender is the most difficult of all the works of God for man to comprehend. Jesus did it, and for Him it accomplished three crucial areas in His development.

First, He increased his learning. So because He surrendered, He could hear the teaching and allow what was said to Him to inhabit His mind and then be translated into His Spirit. When Paul says, "Put on the mind of Christ," we can now connect the reason. I heard a man once say, "When you are talking you are teaching, but when you are listening, you are learning." Jesus was learning well under the influence of God precisely how God does things. He was learning this in a form that was new to Him as he was encumbered with the body of clay which had the nature of His mother.

Second, He surrendered to learning to become a man of understanding. He exhibited the first two distinct areas of the Seven Spirits of God, which are wisdom and understanding. In other words, He comprehended the teaching and was able to demonstrate comprehension by the completion of designated behaviors that expressed understanding. It is of little use to teach without checking for understanding. Comprehension can be demonstrated in many ways, but for the instructor to be sure that what he is teaching has reached its target, there must be testing. How was this accomplished?

Do you remember when Solomon instructed the Son to hear the instruction of the Father and to forsake not the law of the mother? Jesus could immediately go to the book of the story of the Hebrew history and identify the works of the God of the law. He could read it and meditate upon it. He could correlate and allow it to coincide with the instruction of the Father. It was all there for Him to see and understand. Now how do we know that He did this? Because He consistently quoted the scripture, referred to the prophecy of the scripture, and related Himself to the old scripture. This was exactly how He demonstrated understanding of what He had heard. He found the way God did things, understood it, and related it to the scripture.

Thirdly, He surrendered to wise counsel. He was willing to be instructed by those who knew more than He did. This, my friend, is a lost art. But Jesus surrendered to the teaching that would develop His Spirit for the work that lay ahead. The only method that Jesus had while under the burden of the flesh was to utilize the wise counsel of His Dad. The Father knew the places and people that Jesus would encounter. He knew the men and women that would approach Him. He knew the needs that would be exposed for Jesus to have to deal with. Therefore, the preparation had to be focused, intense, purposeful, and it had to be most intentional by the learner. The Father had sent Him. His Spirit was full of the Holy Spirit, but His mind and flesh had to perceive, receive, give attention to, and hear the instruction for Him to, under the weight of the flesh, accomplish all the goals set forth by divine mandate. His Father was His wise counsel. His mother served to be the method of checking for comprehension. It was beautifully designed and orchestrated for the development of the young man.

There are three more parts of hearing that must be added to this verse. First, when one is hearing, that person has dedicated a time for the completion of the activity. He is listening intently to what is being said. His entire being is focused on the topic being shared, because that person realizes the importance of the information. Beyond that, he realizes the implications of missing or misunderstanding the information. When one invests time into anything, that person, through the investment, is placing an emphasis on the information. Due to this, that person is expecting a reward. It may be the recall of the information for comprehension purposes, it may be a test that must be passed, but more than likely, the information is being shared so that it may become of practical use for the hearer. This is precisely the reason for which Jesus invested His time in training and developing His Spirit. Time is the single factor that shows the teacher that the student is invested, engaged, and interested in what the instructor is sharing.

From God's perspective, there is little difference. When a man so prioritizes his life to ensure that time is spent in the presence of the Father, God will embrace the investment and manifest Himself to the investor. Jesus said it would be so in John 14:21.

> He that hath my commandments and keepeth them, he it is that loveth me; and he that loveth me shall be loved by my Father, and I will love him and will manifest myself to him. (John 14:21 KJV)

The life of intimacy takes work. The life of relationship must be nurtured and cultivated. The life of communion, however, must be quickened with time. Time is the agent that defines the investment. We will never keep the commandments unless we invest these three precious pieces into knowing God. We cannot express genuinely the love of the Father, the Son, and the Holy Spirit unless we intentionally pursue Him. The only means to do that is through, as my players would say, "doing work."

The Father manifested Himself to the Son and instructed Him. The mother instructed Him through the lessons of the law. He spent time under both instructions. This made Him who he was. But at no point did He think He had reached the pinnacle of learning and listening. No, He often got up early to spend time with the Father. He would take the inner circle of Peter, James, and John to accompany Him while this was being done. Yes, time is critical for any man to spend with the Father if one intends to legitimately dwell in the secret place of the Most High.

Will He manifest Himself to you and me? Friends, if we believe that what Jesus said in John 3:16 is real and if that experience has happened to us, then we must accept the fact that the same man is speaking in John 14. He is telling us the methods that will cause Him to manifest Himself to us. Since we receive His words in one place, we must also receive His words in every place. We do not have the right to determine what parts of the Gospel we select as our own personal belief system or doctrine. No, it is there for us, and it is written there for us. If we are willing to place the emphasis in being in the throne room and speaking and communing directly with the God of the universe as Paul describes in Ephesians chapter 2, then we must invest in our spiritual life and in the promise of His manifestation to us.

Secondly, there is the more difficult part of this triad. It is the waiting upon the Lord. David spoke to us concerning this subject.

> Wait on the LORD: be of good courage, and he shall strengthen thine heart: wait, I say, on the LORD. (Psalms 27:14 KJV)

Time is the investment that must be made for the process of instruction to be given. Waiting is the next step that must be done before the instruction can and will manifest. Jesus began this process at an early age. There was a lot to learn and a lot of material to cover for Him to be prepared to complete the mission of ministry and sacrifice. The thirty years of preparation was in keeping with his mother's law. But it also had significance in the Father's instruction.

There would be plenty of opportunity for Him to fail in ministry and on his way to the cross. Without the Seven Spirits of God being completely operable, He risked the conflict that could occur within His flesh. He waited and heard from the teachers. He waited and learned the required lessons. Then and only then could He come forth with the good courage that preparation instills. He could be strengthened in His heart to know that He had been exposed to the lessons, that He had learned, the lessons that He had proof from God's dealings with Israel as He studied the law, that the lessons worked and being armed with the Seven Spirits of God, He could overcome every adversary. The opposition was to appear to Him as disarmed and defeated. This made His journey to the cross a walk of calculated control. He knew where He was headed and how He would get there. The negative for Him was the time of separation from the Godhead, not the act itself.

Then the last part of this triad is what time and waiting does for the one who invests in this procedure. It creates a dynamic in the believer that we know as faith. Paul said in Romans 10:17,

> So then faith cometh by hearing, and hearing by the Word of God.

Ultimately, the purpose of intimacy, relationship, and communion resides in faith. Faith is a dynamic that God has designed in man by measure. This measure can be developed and must be developed for a believer to train his spirit man. This is the ingredient that man develops to express to God his comprehension of the instruction provided. When God sees this spiritual part of man grow, it pleases Him. He knows that the required lessons for living the life that He designed for the believer to be prosperous in the image of Christ is happening.

> Now faith is the substance of things hoped for, the evidence of things not seen. (Hebrews 11:1 KJV)

Faith is an activity in the believer that is built upon something. It is built upon the instruction of the words spoken by the Father and the Son and commanded to the believer by the Holy Spirit. Faith has a foundation that is created by something that has been quickened within the spirit of the believer. That foundation is persuaded that what it has been taught is correct. The substance or confidence on which the foundation is built is the direct instruction that the Holy Spirit is providing to the believer's spirit. An expectation arises in the spirit of man. This expectation is an understanding that finds its basis in the wisdom of God. Then faith becomes. It is manifest. Jesus manifests to you the spiritual ingredients that the instructor said were available. It first manifests in the believer's spirit, then it manifests in his life. Please look into my YouTube cite under the titles of "Substance and Evidence" for a deeper understanding of faith—what faith's beginning is, what substance is, what hope means and how do you use it, what faith's evidence is, and how faith is released. Lastly, these messages will show you where faith takes you and how faith appropriates the promises of God for your life. This all occurs due to the grace of judgment that is available for man when he locates the presence of God.

We can go back to the day we were saved to see how this cycle unfolds. It is no mystery. Everything we receive from God comes the same way the born-again life comes. We hear it. It takes root in our spirit and builds a substance for a foundation. We take it by being persuaded of the need for a Savior. We then grow to manifest the new nature in our flesh. The world sees a new creation because of new methods, actions, and priorities. The plan of living by faith is a universal plan. It does not have different approaches for different needs. One God, one Lord, and one faith.

These are the expressions of how Jesus developed to become the grace of God. He was trained to do so. We as believers can do the same. The phrases that state that we can be fashioned like His glorious body and that we can be in the image of His dear Son were stated for a reason. Those reasons have heavenly implications for a newborn experience in the world. Any man who completes the prescribed training can and will live his eternity from the moment of the new birth. Eternity now is the lifestyle that I choose…and that Jesus provided for every believer.

To close this section, please allow me to discuss for a minute why Jesus responded as He had to the woman with the issue of blood. Jesus was on His way to heal the daughter of Jairus, who was a ruler of the synagogue. En route, as often happened, a crowd thronged Him. The story in Luke chapter 8 now begins to include the story of a woman with an issue of blood. It describes her condition and what it had done to her resources. It shares with us that none of these had helped. But when she saw Jesus, she identified Him as the healer.

He was the one who had gone around Israel doing good for the people. She had evidently seen the garment that He was wearing and recognized it as a garment of the priest. It had the borders in blue, which represented the divine element that was in the garment. But the crowd was large and attempting to speak with Him concerning her condition would be impossible. She determined to somehow and someway break through the crowd. If she could just touch the divine piece of His garment, then, she said in her heart, she knew she could be healed. She did exactly that. With faith in what she knew was in the garment and determination, she reached for what it was she needed. When she touched Him, immediately the blood flow ceased! She was healed!

Jesus now responded to this, knowing that healing had gone out of him, and said, "Who touched me?" You know the story as they attempted to reason with Him, "The throng was touching you, how could we know who it was?" Why did He respond this way? Because He knew what it was to live a surrendered life to the instruction of the Father. He also knew when and where the Father had sent Him to work the works that glorified the Father. But there had been an occurrence that had come from His body that was not on the radar for that day. No, He had cast out devils, taught on the Word, talked about how His family members would hear and do the Word of God, walked on the water, and challenged the faith of the disciples. Then on to cast the devil out of the man named Legion and on to Jairus's house to heal his daughter.

He had talked about what the Word would accomplish and where it needed to be located in order for it to produce. He had challenged the faith of the disciples as they feared for their life in the storm, and now this woman exhibited the location of the seed as forming faith in her heart. She was ready for a miracle. Jesus, on the other hand, was ready for a miracle at the ruler's house. When she touched Him, He knew that surrender had occurred in Him. He had produced, by the touch of another, the power that had always in the past been disbursed by His word or His touch. When one is surrendered to the anointing in such a way as this, that person knows and comprehends when someone has come by the paths of instruction.

She perceived in her heart. She took the blessing by faith. She gave herself for pursuing the answer that met her need. She had heard of the divine measure in this garment. She reached out, and she took it. He was immediately alerted to the flow of anointing.

"Who touched me?"

He could have said, "Who has come by the way of the instruction of the Father? Who has sat under the tutelage of the words of wisdom? Who has comprehended the grace that flows from the lips of the Father?"

When she identified herself, Jesus said something that is as good today as it was when He said it. In verse 48 of Luke chapter 8,

> Daughter, be of good comfort: thy faith hath made thee whole; go in peace. (Luke 8:48 KJV)

"You have perceived, received, given, heard, and surrendered! You can have good comfort. What you have done has made you whole."

Now this is not just relegated to healing. It is complete wholeness—spiritually, physically, emotionally, and financially. She could be well in whatever area in which she needed to be well. Further, she could live a life full of peace.

This is most important for you and me. What she did was to take the step required to show competency, comprehension, and understanding. If a sick, broke, tired woman can accomplish such a dynamic feat through using her faith, then we can also. If we look at this scripture through the correct lenses, then we can readily see why it caused Jesus to respond as He did. She had come to her miracle the same way He came to the wisdom and understanding of the instruction of the Father. He developed and trained the Seven Spirits of God. She had used faith to draw out of Him the element that the instruction of the Father had placed in Him. She has a spot in the hall of faith for doing so. We can also.

> My son, attend to my words; incline thine ear unto my sayings. Let them not depart from thine eyes; keep them in the midst of thine heart. For

they are life unto those that find them, and health to all their flesh. (Proverbs 4:20–22 KJV)

Jesus did exactly as these verses from Proverbs suggest. He kept the commands of the Father and was the grace that the Father exposed to the people. Jesus accomplished the goal of the work of grace in His life. We can trace the work in Him through the instruction of his Father and the comprehension of the law. These developed the essential Seven Spirits of God.

We can also trace in His mission how the three works of grace were present in His earthly work. The favor of God was in Him. The influence of grace was on Him as he moved among the people. Lastly, the grace of God that expressed the way God does things was operating upon Him as He ministered to the needs of the people. These grace evidences began the process of turning the world upside down.

The Revelation of the Truth in Jesus

There have been times in my life when it felt as though I were attempting to jam a square peg in a round hole. Those times seemed to be the troubled patches in which I found myself. It was those times that led me to identify some truth concerning myself, the profession that I loved, and how all that impacted my spiritual life.

I was elated by having just won the biggest game in our school's recent resurgence in the football program. Shepherd College was the flagship program of our league. My school had not beaten them in thirteen seasons. The year before they had throttled us 56–6. Not this time however; we dominated the game. From start to finish, we were on them like a cheap suit. Wherever they went on offense, we were there waiting on them. Our offense scored thirty-eight points, and the game was really decided by half time.

Our school and community were going nuts on the field after the game. The media was all into our win as well. There had been few postgame celebrations of this nature on the turf at Martin Field. We had gone toe-to-toe with a perennial power in our league and not only won but done so convincingly. Our president seemed pleased. The athletic director was elated, and the head football coach was thrilled. Of course, I was the AD and the coach, but nevertheless, I was pleased.

I went home after the excitement died down to relax a bit. What a great day! However, it all changed with one phone call. The phone rang, and I answered. It was my biggest booster on the line. Naturally, he congratulated me on the win. We shared a few pleasantries, and then he dropped a bomb. He began to share with me an encounter that had occurred during the game.

He and the president were watching what would be the biggest win in thirteen years for our school when he said to the president, "Look at this place. This is electric. Your school and your team are doing something no one ever thought possible. We have been laughed at and mocked for more than a decade, but look at what you have made happen. The stands are full, people are excited. This is what you have made happen!"

You can read and envision the pride in his voice. As a former player and alumni of the institution, he had lived through the decade of the '90s when the school won five games. What was going on down on the field was long awaited.

Her response, however, was most unexpected. She coolly looked at him and responded, "What you see down there means no more to me than horseshoes or badminton. I really could care less. The only reason we keep it is because you alumni want it."

He was devastated. He had put his money into the program. He had purchased coaches' gear when there was no money provided for us. He had given to our program and was far more instrumental than the president in our success. As he told me the story, I could hear his spirits drop. Then he concluded our conversation with these comments:

"I am done with Tech. I will not give another dime to that school as long as she remains the president. You need to find yourself another job and get out of there. They don't value you or the job you have done. They certainly don't value the money that I have worked for. You know I and the alumni love you, but I have had enough."

I thanked him, but I knew what he was telling me in all areas was true.

The truth about the thing that I was addicted to had surfaced. I was neglecting my wife, my health, and my spiritual life to do something that those in charge really did not care about. That was a stark reality to face. The truth is a difficult bed partner. I went from elation to a posture of what do I do now. We had more games to play, so I went back to work and told myself that I would have to ride it out for the sake of the players.

Later that year, we had another dramatic win at West Liberty. We came back from a twenty-point deficit in a five-minute span to win the game. We recovered two on-side kicks and a fumble to secure the win. It was what we would now call an instant classic. As I looked out at the extra point that would win the game for us, our sideline was in euphoria. At about five seconds before the kick, it hit me that the three kids responsible for the outcome were two walk-ons and a kicker. It has been said by some coaches that in football, there are two groups on the field that you never trust, and one of them is on your team. The first are the officials, and the one that is on your team is your kicker! However, this group had functioned efficiently all year. This moment of history would be no different as the results of the snap, the hold, and the kick were flawless. We won the game by that single point. That game is still a topic of conversation in West Virginia.

But again, the truth reared its head. We had lost a player to injury, and we had lost a player to an unfair decision by an official. We were not deep enough to absorb such losses. We lost our next two of the next three games against inferior completion. The first because we could not replace the critical players we had lost, the second due to a horrible rain storm that caused us to lose the impact of our speed in the mud.

Here was the truth: I was trying to put a square peg in a round hole. The institution did not want football. Six years after I left, they dropped the sport. I had made such a deep commitment of time, energy, and emotion into building a winner that my spiritual life was depleted. I was asked to preach at a church at one point during that season. I was exhausted. I had attempted to prepare, but my focus was so fragmented that when the time came, I had no anointing, and nothing of any consequence to share. I had run aground due to my devotion to my job.

The truth is, as much as I knew and know to this day about the game, it really was a process where the devil was deceiving my mind, will, and emotions with the possibilities of a bigger payday, a bigger school, and more resources to work with. This deception caused me to allow the candle of the Lord in my spirit to go on an extremely low burn. I was saved, and I still lived a Christian lifestyle, but I had no intimacy of my relationship with God. My intense desire to prove my ability and to win games had served to diminish the real me that was on the inside.

I did not finalize this lesson at Tech. No, I moved on to another job. I worked harder and went deeper into the deceit of the devil. I spent more time and found more roadblocks than at any time in my career. It was less fun than ever at the new job, but I continued to push myself to perform. The truth hung in the air like smoke. I coughed and continued to fight. All the time I was doing this, I was thinking that I was doing God's service. These players needed me and my influence. I was the only one who can lead them toward Jesus. That was me placating me. Eventually, I came to grips with the truth.

God had never called me or endorsed me to be a football coach. He had called me, just as He had called the Tribe of Levi, to be a priest, a servant, and a minister to Him. He had called me from the laver of separation into the Tabernacle of service. I was privileged to be able to walk in the smoke that comes from the blood of the slain Lamb and to worship at His lampstand. I was one who could hear the instruction and direction of the Rhema Word of God at the table of show bread. My calling would take me to the altar of incense, where I would see God in all His wondrous names. I would be allowed to approach the Holy of Holies and communicate with God through His Covenant. The cherubim would watch over our interaction and ensure that there would be no interference as we speak. I could leave His presence with the power and authority that reside in the Living God. I had the privilege to share Him and His name with His people.

I missed these truths for forty-plus years. My life was spent attempting to gain something that I was never really able to obtain. All the time I thought God was in my plans. What a tragedy! I did everything I could do to reconcile my professional goals with my spiritual goals. Unfortunately, my professional goals always seemed to be more enticing. The truth is, if I had died, I would have gone to heaven, but I would have never known the life of prosperity, health, welfare, wholeness, soundness, and what real anointing was.

This is the life I refer to as "eternity now." It is the life that Jesus promises us when we come to the knowledge of the truth that is in Jesus Christ. It encompasses the peace that Jesus provides and the joy that He gives to us. Couple this with Jesus as the person of salvation, and you have the dynamic life that produces eternity in the moment. Now, that is great living!

> And the word was made flesh, and dwelt among us [and we beheld his glory, the glory as of the only begotten of the Father] full of grace and truth. (John 1:14 KJV)

Jesus is the truth for several reasons. The first reason, of course, is that this is how John referred to Him and it is how He referred to Himself. In John 14:6, Jesus, speaking of Himself to the disciples, referred to Himself in three distinct ways. All these ways were identifiable by the Jews.

> Jesus saith unto him, I am the way, the truth, and the life: no man cometh unto the Father, but by me. (John 14:6 KJV)

When He referred to Himself as the way, they could identify with that, as they understood the process of Tabernacle worship. He was, in fact, the entrance into the gate of the Tabernacle. When they stood outside the gate of the Tabernacle, they saw the colors of the gate that represented the way to the outer court. To get into the outer court for the execution of the sacrificial system, they had to pass through this way.

This way was formed by a tapestry of material that had colors that all identified Christ. There righteousness was the white linen, which represented Him as being the Son of Man. There was the blue, which represented Him as being the Son of God. There was the crimson, which represented Him as being the Sacrifice. And there was the purple, which represented Him as being the King. So when a man came under the process of the law to complete the business of the Tabernacle as God required, he had no alternative but to come to that process through the gate that represented Jesus. So when Jesus referred to Himself using these words, it left the hearer with no choice but to ask the question, "What is this? Is He speaking of the process of the Tabernacle worship? Is He speaking and identifying Himself as the only way into the worship of God?"

The answer is yes and absolutely!

Then He refers to himself in a second way. This is that He is the Truth. The entrance into the holy place was referred to as "the Truth." When the priests came to this entrance, they had to have themselves in the correct spiritual condition. They were about to enter the tent of the blessing of God. Their entrance had to be done through thorough preparation at the laver. This preparation sanctified them and made them acceptable to come into the presence of God, which resides in the Holy Place.

The truth concerning their personal relationship would eventually be revealed by the ways God dealt with the success and prosperity of the people. If those that entered in were doing so without having made the proper preparation, the result of their efforts would be unacceptable, and Israel would struggle. If the priests came to and through the gate with acceptable sanctification and preparation, the offering would be accepted, and the people would prosper. The offering was never the issue; the offeror was! The priest, who became worldly in his thinking and behavior, became a stench in the nostrils of God. His lack of spiritual care for himself and reverence of the God behind the veil would cause the people to fall under the condemnation of judges and kings from other nations. This was never the intention of God for the people. However, it became the intention of man when he chose to operate in the flesh and become disobedient to the instructions of God.

So the truth had two distinct different sides, as it related to the people. Both had at its core the same basic tenant. That tenant is judgment. As I have described, if the Holy Place was entered without proper preparation and cleansing, the outcome would be unacceptable, and the people would be left without the covering of the protection of God. Not because God did not do what He had promised. It was the representatives of the people that were offering themselves to God without managing and controlling themselves according to His instruction. This brought judgment to the people.

Further, the people were unaware of the impending problems. Why? They had done what they were instructed to do. They had sacrificed according to the prescribed methods. Beyond the outer court, however, there was no more access for them. They had to rely upon the tribe God had identified as the ones who would minister directly to Him. The breakdown occurred right here. The people suffered due to the spiritual depravity of their own ministers. Judgment of the people then was defined by the behavior of those who entered the Holy Place. If they came in a correct fashion, their work was accepted. If they came with stain in their lives, the work was not accepted. Hence, judgment was coming.

Then there was the priest that entered their work with their personal life purged and cleansed from any stain or sin that could bring a negative response to the offering of the people. Because this area was a place of judgment, as we explained, it also was a place where the judgment of acceptability was present. When the offering and the offeror were in obedience to the prescribed methods that God had given for approaching Him, the result was prosperity and blessing upon the people. The truth of the activity that was being brought forward would ultimately be seen by the people. God is a God of judgment. His judgment is sure and pure. He knows with precision what it is He is looking for. But at the same time, He knows what He is looking at.

Can we consider the nation of Israel, under the reign of King Uzziah, as providing us a look at how the ministry dealt with reverence toward the Tabernacle? This same story will give us insight into how God protected His sanctuary when the priests functioned under the prescribed methods of operation that God had designed for the Tabernacle.

In 2 Chronicles 26, we read an interesting story of King Uzziah. Israel had taken him to be king at a young age. At sixteen years old, he had been made king from his father Amaziah's lineage. This man held power in Israel for fifty-two years. Initially, he was an accepted king because he did the correct things before God. He followed the paths and training of his father. His prosperity strictly revolved around his intimacy with the Lord. If he maintained intimacy, God blessed his actions. In war, building, and the development of mighty men, God caused Uzziah to prosper and be blessed.

Due to his relationship and posture of seeking God, the activity in the Tabernacle was ongoing. God was blessing the nation with growth, prosperity, and influence among other nations. The priests were free to operate in the Tabernacle in a way that pleased the Lord. This Tabernacle worship extended to the understanding of the people as they invented new means of defending the city and the nation from outside attacks. Uzziah, the Bible declares, was tremendously helped by God. Everything was good until Uzziah reached an insurmountable obstacle in his life. His own heart deceived him. As he became strong, he forgot the source of his strength. When this occurred, his destruction was imminent.

Uzziah, being strong in his own eyes, made a disastrous move against God. He knew the temple process and the role of the priests. This was not just a role for the priests, as their God-directed ministry in worship was the source of the strength that Uzziah had been prospered with. This prosperity was shared by the children of Israel. But Uzziah began to operate from his own strength, and by his actions, he declared that he no longer had a need for the priesthood or the ministry, as God had defined it. He walked into the temple with his own censer to burn incense before the Lord.

This sounds benign to the reader, but it is in direct violation of the procedures that God had given Aaron in Exodus 28. The worship was to be completed in the Tabernacle only by a priest from the Tribe of Levi. This king was usurping the authority of the priests and in turn, with his actions, declaring that he was capable of executing worship on his own and within himself. This was done with intent to diminish the priests and exalt himself.

Azariah, the priest, took four other priests and stopped their king from completing the desecration of the Temple. His position outside the Temple had no standing inside the Temple. In God's house there was the God of Israel, and the priests served and ministered to that God. There was no provision for anyone from outside to serve or minister.

In this instance, the priests stood their ground and protected themselves and the Temple of God from the King and his desire to place his strength above the strength of God. Naturally, in himself, Uzziah protested and no doubt threatened them with his capabilities. The priests also understood the capabilities of the God of the Tabernacle. As they spoke while the priests protected their position and God's commands, a disease began to come upon Uzziah. Leprosy was seen to appear in his forehead. God had struck the man with a disease that would ultimately result in his being removed from the palace and having to spend the rest of his days in a several house. He would be put out of the palace, to live among the lepers until he died. Most importantly, his sin would cause him to be put out of the Tabernacle of the God of his nation. That separation is worse than leprosy.

Why did the leprosy appear in his forehead? This is my opinion, but it is in the mind that Uzziah had determined to receive the strength that his heart said he possessed. His mind bought into what he perceived as the fact that he could do it now on his own. Therefore, the mind was the first area that God broke. The flesh that sides with the soul, which is man's mind, will, and emotions, instead of allowing the Spirit to lead the way, will ultimately make decisions that will cause their own destruction. I wonder, if Uzziah had stopped to consider how God would respond to his raising himself above the God that made him, would he have remained in the palace and left the service in the Tabernacle alone? Somehow, I think he would have made the choice to let the spiritual be handled by those appointed to do so. But he did not, and like many, he fell under the weight of a weak mind.

In this case, we clearly identify the following:

1. When a man seeks God, he can be blessed.
2. When a man allows the system of worship to continue as it is commanded, both he and his people prosper.

3. When a man who is prosperous under the hand of God identifies and acknowledges who his source is, he can continue to prosper.
4. When a man lifts his soul and his flesh to supersede the God of the universe, rest assured that evil is on the way.
5. When a man attempts to make himself and his desires more important than the commands of God, eventual collapse will be the result.
6. When a man steps over the ministry to promote himself as larger than the commandments of God, there will be a reckoning for that behavior.
7. The ministry must protect the place of worship.
8. The ministry must place the commandments of God above any other allegiance.
9. The ministry must be strong enough to stand and withstand attacks that are in opposition to direct instruction.

Now the question is, "How does this relate to us?" The answer is clear. God is not overlooking the desecration of the Gospel any more today than He did in the Old Testament. He deals with it through the means of grace that we described in the last chapter. But do not deceive yourself into thinking that God is not in the business of judgment. You would be wrong. God is judging people today in ways that we refuse to see as the judgment of God. Look at the outcome of the lives of those that waste themselves upon the rocks of personal satisfaction. They desire to have and consume themselves upon their desires. Often it leads to premature death, lives of depravity, and tremendous pain. These outcomes are viewed as the result of their decisions. Exactly. The same thing happened to Uzziah. He made the decisions that caused the ruin of his life. Is this not what is happening today?

Men have attempted to counterfeit the process of God. It would appear that they have done this with some success. To the naked eye, this looks as though the activity of the individuals associated with the counterfeit must be doing acceptable works. It looks like they are being blessed. It appears that they are growing. It has a ring of success. There are good feelings that say to us that what is happening is being judged by God as the truth. It looks good, it feels good, so it must be good. This is common human response to the physical senses. But is it the common response in the spiritual world?

This process of disobedience and self-centered leadership was prevalent under Ahaz and Hezekiah. Saul would also come under such undesirable character traits. These men caused trouble for the people, because they created a division between themselves and the God that had given them a kingdom. This caused judgment to fall upon Israel. The truth for Israel was clearly defined and described by God for the people and the priests, but men who chose themselves over God defined the conditions under which the people would be forced to function. These activities brought defeat, death, and captivity to the people. These were felt by the people in actual reality. Today we deal with these results with spiritual defeat, spiritual death, and spiritual captivity.

So look at the legacy of three kings mentioned. Uzziah, as we shared, became a leper and died having lost the kingdom from the effects of leprosy. Ahaz was a king that had Israel in wars consistently. He did wrong in the sight of God, and it resulted in consistent turmoil. Hezekiah restored the temple worship, but the priests were unclean. The response to the truth then must be understood with respect to the results that we can identify in the world in which these activities are occurring. There must be an honest evaluation of how what we are doing is impacting the direction of the people. The truth is that what Jesus died to produce and secure is failing. The church and the people associated with the church are not being reproduced in the form or fashion that the Word of God teaches. We are a labile people with a shallow relationship with God. There could be volumes written concerning the failure of the church. We will look at a few.

Church attendance is declining. The necessity of a coordination of spiritual life that includes church attendance is no longer a priority. Media churches circumvent the scriptural process of assembling together for the benefit of worship and the benefit of encouraging one another. There is a general dysfunction of spiritual beliefs that have divided the church upon doctrinal lines. This dysfunction drives people from the church. People tend to flow with what is easiest so alternative spiritual dimensions, ideas, and concepts cloud the truth. People then make choices with little research or biblical understanding and accept as foundational approaches that there may be relations to the scripture. Those relationships at their core are in opposition to the scripture.

There are many more that could be mentioned that has produced a culture where religion is accepted as long as it is not Christian in nature. We have a society where there are many ways to find God, but none of those ways come through the Truth, Jesus Christ; therefore, none of them bear legitimacy with transforming the men and women who espouse their beliefs. This brings us to an inspection of the current state of the society. Now, I do not think that I have all the answers to the breakdown of our culture, not at all. What I will do is to identify the visually apparent and common things that are easily seen within our community. These things will then identify a couple of significantly important insights into the truth of God. It is the common things that the devil uses to deceive, destroy, and kill those who fail to identify what he is doing. Paul taught these common things in 1 Corinthians 1:13. He also taught the way of escape that only came from God.

First, the society is operating in general without the influence and impact of the God of the universe upon the nature of men. Due to this lack, man finds life and the importance of life irrelevant. We abort children, we gun down in the street, and we celebrate a life that is fortunate enough to reach the tender age of eighteen. This is a far distance from the reason for which Christ came and died, as this death made him to be the Spirit of life that would transform people and teach them to operate after the spirit of love.

The society has placed a badge of rejection on holiness and righteousness. We have determined that man can create his own decisions concerning what is right and what is wrong. We can produce our own definitions of what wrong is and to what extent we choose to determine if it needs to be addressed, corrected, overlooked, or punished. For instance, bumping into someone. For some people, it may be an act that is so egregious that death is deserved. Along with that, a driving mishap may be of such a serious nature that death on the spot is the answer that two humans may choose because of their encounter. We could continue to give the many instances of personal interpretation of wrong, right, and degrees thereof that result in the validation of man as God and life as inconsequential. Holiness and righteousness are not taught or understood by the people. My rights and your infringement upon me supersede anything that makes you important.

As we have mentioned, the school system has deteriorated to the extent that learning is frequently not occurring. However, countercultures are exploding upon the scene to disrupt, discourage, and dishearten both those who work in the system and those who are legitimately attempting to use the system to their personal benefit.

The home environment has deteriorated to the place that life within the home is extremely difficult. Excessive work, money, alcohol, drugs, free sex, and the influence of the counterculture have made the home a zone of uncertainty. There is a fear factor as well as a pride factor that makes the home an unstable and, in some cases, an unsafe place for all those present. Domestic violence and divorce seem to be prevalent. The result is an environment where those caught in these unstable situations seek shelter in others, other places, or in other groups. Instability breeds instability, if the person locates shelter with those who have no foundation of care to legitimately help that person into a stronger environment.

Once this spiral is identified, people may, due to a faulty environment, find themselves engulfed in several social issues that can continue the downward spiral. These social and cultural issues may produce involvement in vices such as human trafficking, prostitution, theft, and ultimately jail. These are sad truths, but they are truths nonetheless. Good people are destroyed. Good kids are lost to a life of decay and depravity.

This vein of defining the flaws in the culture could obviously continue. There are ample illustrations of what is wrong in our society. I want you to consider, however, what is the root cause of all of this. We can trace it to sin, and that would be a good start. We can trace it to the pride of life, the lust of the eye, and the lust of the flesh, and that would also be good and correct. We can trace it to the seventeen works of the flesh, and we would again be on target. We can trace all these to Adam and Eve; this is surely the ultimate answer to our need to be able to point the finger at our downfall. Of course, this would include the devil and his role in our societal implosion. All true, all correct, and it seems all-encompassing. But it is not!

Judgment has come to the people for the same reason it came to Israel. It has come due to the weak position of the church. The truth is we are where we are, because the church has failed to do what it was established to do. We no longer make prayer our way of life. We no longer place the emphasis for instruction upon the Word of God. We no longer place the Tabernacle, which is the church, as the point of importance within our communities. Our ministers do not revere the position of ministry, to the extent that the Word of God, and the preaching thereof, is the single thing that is worthy of our complete attention. The church has become a social club. It does not hold as its clear focus the ministry of equipping the people for the work of the ministry.

Judgment has come due to the shortcomings of the men and women who name the name of Christ. We want to be entertained, laugh, make off-color jokes, and expect the people to filter out the elements that are not spiritual for themselves. It is obvious that this is not occurring. We should have known this would not work. God showed us the outcome of such behavior in the Old Testament right through the Tabernacle.

We have made the choices we have made and justified our current state by saying that God has blessed us doing it this way. We have glorified those who, through their fallen nature, have located a means to find their niche of success. We have attempted with great success to clone those methods. During this process, we did not inspect the impact of our own deeds upon the people and the communities in which these activities were imposed. Though it surely looked good, the outcome had been disastrous. The indictment lay at the feet of the church, its ministry, and its mission. Judgment has not been perceived by these two entities, meaning the church and the ministry, probably because they have been too busy to inspect the community and society in which they live. Without inspection, there is no reason to have expectation. Until we inspect what we expect, we really have no legitimate expectations. Therefore, we operate on a mission with no direction, no purpose, and which has no expected outcome. Can you see how this loss of focus is really the judgment of God upon the people?

Then there is the other side of judgment. It is the side where judgment brings the acceptance of blessing. The truth is that, when we come into Jesus, the truth about who we are and what we were designed to become is released unto us. I refer to this as the fourth part of the grace of God. It is the grace where all the promises of God are in Him. Yes and amen. It is the part of grace that we currently live under. Heaven is opened for God to give us the promises that His Word describes belong to us. We are compelled to follow the appropriate instructions in order to come to and be in the throne room of God to receive those judgments and take them so that they can manifest in our world.

God made man to function and to prosper in His Spirit. The truth is, we are a spiritual being. We function best in the realm of the flesh when our spiritual self is strong and vibrant. It is the divine design of man. He was made first a spirit. He was made second a soul with flesh. When the three sides work in the correct order, truth is found. When the spirit is the dominant factor, man functions on a heavenly level. When man attempts to order his life under any other conditions, he will fail.

Jesus's inference to "the Truth" in John 14 gave us the understanding that when we locate the truth, we locate all the blessings of God. Look at the holy place, as this area will show us how Jesus, the Truth, blesses his people. Now that we have defined where the society appears to be and have taken our foundation from the judgment that always must begin at the house of God, let's look at how this same process occurred among the people during the reign of King Hezekiah.

For that we will have to look at 2 Chronicles 29. Hezekiah was an older king as he did not become king until he was fifty-two. He reigned in Israel for twenty-nine years. He was a man who did right in the sight of the Lord, as his father David had done. He challenged the priests of his day to begin to execute their respective job correctly. He was well trained in the worship of the people, as he understood the inner workings of the Tabernacle. He also understood the importance of the Tabernacle following the commands of God. In verses 8 and 9 of 2 Chronicles, Hezekiah makes a declaration that shows how the prosperity of the nation was tied to the worship of God. This worship would then produce a prosperity among the people, as God showed His acceptance of their service. But under faulty leadership, Hezekiah shares that trouble, astonishment, and ridicule has resulted among the people. He tells them that death and captivity has come to the people. Notice that these results were the truth concerning a people that were God's chosen. They had gone a direction by fleshly choice that had ended in national tragedy.

Hezekiah, having the training of his father, realized the necessity of the covenant with the God of his father. The challenge is cast to the ministry to return to the commandments of the Lord. The critical issue that faced Hezekiah was that the priests were so unclean that the kingdom had fallen into complete spiritual disarray. This was, in fact, the reason that Hezekiah had to show the people and the priests how their unholy and ungodly behavior had brought ruin to the nation. The priests had to be stirred back to the reality concerning the necessity of their position. They must serve, minister, and burn the incense that declared to the people that God was in the house. The words seem to rejuvenate the priesthood, as they arose with intention to get themselves in the correct spiritual state to complete their calling for the welfare of the people.

They began the process of sanctification. They washed themselves to separate themselves for the service inside the Tabernacle. This washing was commanded as the step to be completed before entering the house of blessing and judgment. This process included the priests identifying their personal relationship to each of the Ten Commandments. They studied themselves to ensure that the commandments of God through Moses were being followed in their own lives. They were sanctifying themselves to the revealed truth of the day. When they looked into the water, the reflection that appeared had to be one that only reflected the glory of God through the application of the known law. They were priests by lineage. They were sanctified by the law. If they were to complete the instructions of Hezekiah, they must be completely cleansed of anything outside of the commandments. All sin had to be accounted for and surrendered, so the glory of God could rest upon them. The process of recovery took eight days. Only when purged and cleansed by the commandments of God could they begin to enter the Tabernacle to complete the start-up procedures.

The priests came by the way of the words of the Lord. In other words, they got back down to the business for which they had been called to do. When the ministry redirects themselves to doing what is required, the people are changed and transformed. The blessings of God begin to flow, as we will see from this scripture. Due to following the words of the Lord, they are ready to begin to rededicate the Tabernacle. It took sixteen days for the ministry to sanctify themselves and the Tabernacle for the continuing of service and worship. The place of God must have been in a dreadful condition. All the disrepair and lack of use had caused the place of God to need intense attention.

This is a clear example of the condition of the church today. We have kept the edifice recognizable, but the condition of the spiritual content on the inside is in desperate need of an intense purging and an intense cleansing. Our churches look good to the naked eye, but the experiences coming from our Tabernacles leave us in trouble, astonished, and mocked for all eyes to behold. The spiritual death that ensues, extends beyond the parishioners, and infiltrates the eyes of those who look on from the outside. Notice the writer stated that this is seen with your eyes. It is no secret that the church has done damage to its reputation and its own message. At some point, we must purge the uncleanness and get ourselves back to the design of God. This is what Hezekiah saw and ordered to be changed.

The priests paid the price to reestablish the Tabernacle's holy place and the Holy of Holies. They made themselves and the Tabernacle ready for the worship and service that it was intended to offer Israel. It was a glorious awakening for the children of Israel and its leadership. Hezekiah brought his leadership with the sacrifice, to begin the process of the burnt offerings that represented the people's surrender to God. Once again, the process of a blood sacrifice was presented for and by the children of Israel, for worship and connection to God. What a hallelujah moment for the people. They were once again moving toward the prosperity and blessing of God. More importantly, they were moving away from the judgment that was caused by a lack of care, concern, and intentional service had caused.

Let's look at the offerings that Hezekiah brought to the brazen altar to be sacrificed. This will provide us some insight into the truth concerning the spiritual condition of Israel. First, he brought seven bullocks. These were strong animals that had strong wills. They had to have a yoke around their necks to get them to perform a task in unison with one of their own species. These animals could labor, but only under the condition that their abilities be harnessed, and that there was a whip available to enforce the labor upon them. I see Israel in this animal. Strong, rebellious, a wandering nation and subject to drift toward the gods of other people! So when these bullocks were offered, Israel was saying, "We surrender our inability not to work together and constantly require Your judgment in order to learn how to relate to You."

The rams are the next offering. A ram is recognized as an animal that is made with a hard head. He rears up and butts his head upon his foe time and time again. He is born with a nature to fight and defend himself with this method. I again see Israel in this animal. They would rise, murmur, and complain about anything that they deemed as unsatisfactory in their own eyes. To blame and to complain must have been as natural as breathing for this group. The ram signified Israel's defiance and hardheadedness as they dealt with God's ways. They failed to understand the way God does things, and this caused a consistent butting of heads with God. They always lost in this deal. So when the ram was sacrificed, the concept was that we surrender our hard to listen and hard to learn attitude.

The goats were offered to signify the offering for the sin that had come into the kingdom as a wandering goat. This goat represented the ever-searching soul who, for a desire to fill himself, would take part in anything that looked appealing. This goat was an animal that could be satisfied with almost anything. He had no limits on how he satisfied his needs. This represents the children of Israel's availability to be involved with colors, creeds, races, and religions that would serve to supersede the God of the nation. Israel must surrender their wandering eye and their insatiable appetite for disobedience in order to reestablish the blessings of God.

The lamb, of course, was offered as a sin offering for the people. This lamb would represent the Passover Lamb for Israel. They related this to the original lamb, whose blood was sprinkled on the doorpost. We now know that this blood was sprinkled on the door post as the signal of the cross which was to come. These lambs would represent the sacrifice of the Lamb of God. Israel, by this animal, would surrender their lives to a substitute. In that substitute, deliverance was assured.

As each of these offerings were presented, the truth about Israel unfolded in front of the people and the priest. They laid hands upon the animal and sacrificed it. In doing so, they committed themselves to the surrender of the character traits within that caused them to come under the judgment of God. What a wonderful outcome for the people. They could again come back to the God of their covenant. This would reinstate the prosperity of the people! When the sacrifice was done with open understanding of what the reason for judgment was, God responds in acceptance.

When the presentation of the offerings took place, the song of the Lord began to play. Worship was enacted to the God who had satisfied Israel with the salvation of deliverance, safety, healing, perseverance, and soundness. They played with instruments that David had commanded for this purpose. This was an awesome display of service, worship, and repentance that Israel was giving to God. Worship was commanded and given. All that was left was the living within the confines of the consecrated lifestyle, to which they had sought God to pursue.

After this awesome display of surrender, the priests could rejoice in the faithfulness of God. They could offer thanks to God and begin to fulfill the other types of offerings that were a part of the Tabernacle sacrificial process. The people had a revival of Truth. The outcome was an overwhelming result of rededication to the methods of worship that were significant to the people in that day. The Levites were those who God had designed for this service. Israel had fallen so far from the instructions of God that the ministry was ill prepared to do the work. There were too few available, too few sanctified, and too few who had maintained their position to complete the job. But the call was still upon the tribe. The Levites knew why they were. They knew what they were called to do. The abandonment of the work of the Tabernacle had not meant that they abandoned the work in their heart. They stepped in and completed the consecration of Israel. This allowed the "house of the Truth" to be set in order.

As I write this it is apparent to me that we today are in a similar situation. I have attempted to define from my perspective the state of our culture and society. The answer seems clear to me. Get our leadership turned back toward God. Get our ministry reequipped with the Word of God and the sanctification that is required to help the hungry people to reconnect with God. This was done in Israel, so God has produced the blueprint that will give us access to the methods required to bring about a repentant attitude.

It is there in the Book and in front of us. Will we continue in the ways of Uzziah and die an outcast? Can we live and survive under the thumb of Ahaz and be at war inside of ourselves and outside in the world? Saul was a king who totally lost the kingdom due to his wickedness. Is that what we are legitimately after? Can we consider a return to the methods that Hezekiah brought to reestablish Israel? Under this kind of leadership, we rekindle the flame of the Gospel. We rebuild the Tabernacle within us. We execute true repentance and surrender ourselves to God. Then worship him for his faithfulness and serve him with our entire being. The truth will be visually apparent. We will be able to look no further than the church to determine our choice. Here is the line that defines our decision. Is the church flowing in spiritual prosperity, or is the church prospering in everything or anything else? Should we conclude that we are operating under the second scenario, then we are operating under judgment, and the end will be one of destruction. The truth will always and at all times reconcile itself to the efforts of the people.

So we look ahead now to the life of Jesus Christ. God designated him to be the truth. The writer of the book of Hebrews substantiates that claim in Hebrews chapter 8, when he refers to Jesus as the High Priest of the true Tabernacle. Here is why He is the Truth. When Jesus was crucified, the Bible declares that the veil in the Tabernacle that was designed and operated according to the law was divided from top to bottom. This signified that the truth concerning the means and method for man to come to God has appeared and died for the sins of the world.

> Hath in these last days spoken unto us by his Son, whom he hath appointed heir of all things, by whom also he made the worlds; who being the brightness of his glory, and the express image of his person, and upholding all things by the word of his power, when he had by himself purged our sins, sat down on the right hand of the majesty on high: being made so much better than the angels, as he hath by inheritance obtained a more excellent name than they. (Hebrews 1:2–4 KJV)

In these last days, God has spoken to us by the dynamic of the birth, life, ministry, death, resurrection, ascension, and seating of his Son in the Tabernacle of and for the true High Priest. He is the one for whom the entire creation was made. He is also the one for whom the entire creation seeks according to Matthew's writing. His Truth appeared in the express image of His Father. This book defines what that image looked like, how it operated among men and the impact that it was to have in, on, and upon men. The truth is that he upheld the standard of heaven, because he was the representation of that standard. He was the righteousness of God that appeared among men. His righteousness would become our righteousness, because the truth of God bore our sins and by the force applied to his person destroyed death, hell, and the grave. His ability to overcome the force of sin and the force of death allowed him to have the authority to secure the keys of eternity for every individual.

From that point forward, no man upon whom the truth is applied will ever again walk into the hell through the gates. No, they are eternally secured if the truth truly brings a born-again experience. Should the truth, God's image, God's man, the Creator of the earth, the appointed heir, the bearer of all sin, and the one who sits at God's right hand as the High Priest over his own sacrifice locate any individual who does not possess the force of his righteousness applied to his life, that man, because of the Truth, will be cast down. Over the gate and above the perimeter and into outer darkness for eternity. So if man goes to hell, he will go over the very best efforts to save, restore, and forgive his fallen nature. The God who created him has designed a way of escape.

As we described concerning the Tabernacle in the wilderness that has both blessing and judgment within the borders of the Tabernacle, the same exists in favor of mankind. When man locates Jesus Christ the Truth, he begins an eternity that is in him and functioning from him at the moment his heart becomes fixed on believing the Savior. The benefits of eternity belong to you. Those benefits are encompassed in Jesus as salvation.

Lastly, on this subject, I want you to notice the Levites who worked with the priests to finish the work of the ministry for the people during Hezekiah's return to the Tabernacle and worship of God. These Levites, according to scripture, were men whose hearts were more upright concerning the sanctifying or separating of themselves for service than the priests of their day.

> For the Levites were more upright in heart, to sanctify themselves than the priests. (2 Chronicles 29:34)

Is it possible that you are one of those whose heart is well after the same depth with God? Is it possible that while reading this chapter, the Holy Spirit has opened your heart to understand and comprehend the truth about Jesus? I pray that these statements can be directed to your life.

He is all that we have described Him to be in this chapter and in this book. The key element is left in John's defining of Jesus until last. He will be the Lion of Truth on the throne, as He brings judgment to the people, or He will be the Truth of the Lamb upon the cross, as He brings deeper blessing and deeper truth of eternal communion. In either case, the results of the condition in which you personally face, the truth will be an eternal encounter. I pray that we realize that our eternity has already begun. The span of life dictates our opportunity to locate the truth of eternal blessing or choose the truth of eternal separation. This we know concerning that same span of life as the Bible tells us: men die. We know this piece of scripture to be true. Then the real truth concerning the real you is told.

How to Relate the Revelations of Jesus Christ to Yourself

During a recent midnight prayer session, the Holy Spirit began to deal with me concerning the worship and praise of His people. I quickly realized that this was something that I only understood topically. So I asked the Holy Spirit to teach me concerning these two important issues. I am going to share with the reader what He shared with me. I think when you conclude, you will be able to identify how to relate your worship and your praise to the revelations that are occurring in your life as you reflect upon the events of your life.

So what is worship? Worship is the sacrifice that an individual makes while developing His opportunity to approach God and to live in His presence. First, we worship due to the substitute that we found in Jesus. He was the one who took our sin and placed them upon Himself. He died in our place in order for us to be redeemed and be free from sin in the sight of God. The reader who is saved can relate to this concept because they have been cleansed of their sin. They can identify how the cross impacted their lives once they believed. They can remember their own stories of the journey, which they came through to know the saving grace of God. These stories are remarkable. They are humbling, they are personal, and they are life-changing. When you consider the eternal Jesus, and the eternal blessing of everlasting life, then each of the ten revelations revealed in this book resonates with you.

For the reader who has not made the expression of repentance and faith in Jesus, if you have read up to this point, you certainly have an interest in the subject matter that has kept you coming back to the text. How do you relate to these revelations? In reality, your relation to each revelation is the same. He can be your Savior, He can be your burden-bearer, He can be your peace, and He can be the prosperity that you so desire. So when you think of Him, you see the salvation of God specifically prepared for you in every revelation. Once this conclusion is drawn, you can then begin to look at when, where, and how God has delivered you to bring you to this moment in time. The question now is, "Why have these events occurred, and why must I reflect upon them at this particular time?" I contend that "why" for you, and every individual, is to believe, know, and love the one who gave Himself to relieve you from the burden and bondage of sin. Unfortunately, the enemy of the soul of man has deceived many who have gone into eternity earlier than they expected. That does not have to be the case for you or your loved ones as you can know him and begin to experience the blessings of eternity immediately.

So you can order your stories and allow those stories to have the intended impact. Your life can change. The prosperity of peace will belong to your life, and your steps, which have not always been ordered by the Lord, will begin to be ordered in such a way that your inner person changes, your friends and activities change, and the promise of Psalms 75:6–7 becomes a reality for you. Look that scripture up as it has a word that will have a dramatic impact on your life. It will show you how God influences the life of a believer. You will live under the revelation of Jesus Christ. My friend, that is a place and position of victory, especially during the storms of life.

At this minute, while the Holy Spirit is impacting and influencing your spirit, pray with me.

Lord, I am a sinner. I repent of my sin. I desire that You save me. I accept You as my substitute. I now believe with my heart and confess with my mouth the Lordship of Jesus Christ over my life. I believe my spirit is connecting with the Holy Spirit to bring into my spirit the abiding Christ Jesus. I am saved, and I will serve You! In Jesus's name. Amen!

If you prayed that prayer from your heart, now you are all in. Glory to God!

Second, now that our readers have become one, which means that they are saved and the unsaved have gotten saved, there is a deeper place of worship. The next step is the sacrifice of surrendering yourself to Him by being crucified with Christ. This surrender affords the opportunity to pick up the cross and follow Him. It allows the individual to come into the image of Jesus by the standard of righteousness that is in Him. This standard will cause the development of a new nature and character that will bring out of you the fruit of love, joy, peace, kindness, gentleness, meekness, and faith. Your worship in this area will open the gateway for your inner man to connect with the Holy Spirit and together with Him build in you a new heart. What a blessed understanding of the opportunity to simply surrender your thoughts, desires, opinions, and ideas which affords the Holy Spirit in roads that uplift your spirit.

Paul showed us this concept in Romans chapter 8:16–17.

> The Spirit itself beareth witness with our spirit, that we are the children of God: and if children, then heirs; heirs of God, and joint-heirs with Christ; if so be that we suffer with him, that we may be also glorified together. (Romans 8:16–17 KJV)

When we worship efficiently and effectively, the outcome is the strengthening of our spirit man as the Holy Spirit comes alongside to bear witness to the work that is developing in us. It is this worship that brings the revelation of the fact that we are made children of God. More importantly, because we are children, we are instantly identified as heirs to the kingdom, which includes the kingdom's dominion. The suffering portion may be no different than any growing child. We may make mistakes, slip, and skin our knees with life's many twists and turns, but ultimately, our consistent pursuit of the character and nature of God will result in our understanding and being able to live in the glory, which God intended for us.

Someone may be thinking that this scripture has implications for our future life. It does—of that there can be no doubt. The thought must go deeper. When does the glory of God's blessed assurance of eternal life begin? Paul, again, gives us insight into what the status of the child of God is and the heirs place in the current economy of God. Look at Ephesians 2:5–7.

> Even when we were dead in sins, hath quickened us together with Christ [by grace ye are saved] and hath raised us up together and made us sit together in heavenly places in Christ Jesus: that in the ages to come he might shew the exceeding riches of his grace in his kindness toward us through Christ Jesus. (Ephesians 2:5–7 KJV)

We are alive in the Spirit now! Our acceptance of the grace of God has ensured our life in Christ. This same quickening has raised us now to sit together with him in heavenly places. This position gives us the right to show forth in the ages in which we now live the riches of his grace and kindness that was given to us by Christ Jesus. My friend, this is the purpose for which we surrender to Christ. For as we surrender in worship, His glory that has manifested to us through grace becomes the wealth and prosperity that equals that of the glory that exists in heaven. It all resides on the inside of you and me. I draw it out through my own worship of the God who gave it to me.

Thirdly, we worship him in and with our service. We find our position and office within the framework of the church. Paul shares thoughts on the outcome of the worship of the saints with respect to their potential work for the kingdom of God in the earth.

> And he gave some, apostles; and some, prophets; and some, evangelists; and some, pastors and teachers; for the perfecting of the saints, for the work of the ministry, for the edifying of the body of Christ: till we all come in the unity of the faith, and of the knowledge of the Son of God, unto a perfect man, unto the measure of the stature of the fulness of Christ. (Ephesians 4:11–13 KJV)

Paul declared Jesus to be the head over the church and us to be His body. If we are to know how to relate to the revelation of Jesus that has occurred in us, then we must locate our position of service to Him. Once located, we must be dedicated to the cause of witnessing for Christ through our calling of the life that now reigns in us.

There are many possible positions that one can complete in ministry. Rest assured there is one for you. Seek it and find what God has called you to do. This worship will minister to you as well as it does to the ones to whom you may minister. It will also motivate you to accomplish the meditation, prayer, study, and attendance at church that will afford you the opportunity to deal with life as it comes. Remember these words. Being a Christian does not stop the troubles and issues of life from coming your direction. It does, however, provide you with the ability to have a comforter, encourager, and a family to support you as you locate the revelation of God meant for you during your times of training.

Lastly, on this worship issue, I want to share two thoughts with you that are critical to your development and growth in the revelations of Jesus Christ. First, it is the importance of forgiveness. This forgiveness is that which you do for yourself. Listen, up to this moment, life may have dealt you some tough blows. You may have made some poor decisions that have brought hurt and difficulty into your life. These self-inflicted wounds of bad decisions and faulty judgment is not just something that belongs to you. You are not the first, nor will you be the last, that has made errors that seem to be so destructive.

Generally speaking, in most situations, when people tell you they know how you feel it is a difficult thing to wrap your mind around. But when it comes to a severed relationship with God through sins, deception, and ravaging, every Christian can relate to that. We were all there. The successful Christian learns to forgive himself. That involves the total acceptance of the love of God that is expressed in the grace of His favor. It includes you, your past, and it also includes the faulty decisions that may come in the future. The process of repentance is the act of identifying where you were wrong, confessing your attitude toward the wrong done, and then stepping over it and going on. There is great news at this point. John wrote in 1 John 2:1 the following:

> My little children, these things write I unto you, that ye sin not. And if any man sin, we have an advocate with the Father, Jesus Christ the righteous. (1 John 2:1 KJV)

He, as the High Priest of your confession, receives your repentance and supports you in the high courts of heaven. The restoration of relationship is revealed in the revelation of the position of the advocate. What a great plan God has for us!

Then the second part of this forgiveness process is the conscious act of forgiving those who have hurt, offended, denied, or mistreated you. This can be difficult, but without the completion of this action on your part, you cannot be free to operate in the faith in which you desire to grow. Jesus taught us this in Mark chapter 11:25–26,

> And when ye stand praying, forgive, if ye have ought against any: that your Father also which is in heaven may forgive you your trespasses. But if ye do not forgive, neither will your Father which is in heaven forgive your trespasses. (Mark 11:25–26 KJV)

As you can see, unforgiveness is a deterrent to your personal breakthrough. The term *trespasses* includes the unlawful act of violating ones' person, place, and rights. In order for you to have the satisfaction of pure worship and the relation of your revelation to God, you must forgive the ones who trespassed against you. The blessing of God awaits your placing these people and events at the feet of Jesus. When weighed against your personal trespasses and the debt of payment made for you, that should come rather easily.

I have explored worship through these brief words to add some insight into how to export your personal revelation into the manifestation which God can accept so that you can become blessed.

May I close this book with the final requirements for your continued success on the journey of the revelation of Jesus Christ. Never forget! The concept I want to bring you to is the instrument of praise. When I asked the Lord to define *praise*, this insight was given. Always remember and always open your mouth to express the things that God has done for you. Just as Israel built altars to remind themselves and to teach their children, we must place mental altars at the critical moments of our lives where we found God faithful. While doing this, we must never grow weary of recognizing verbally and outwardly the content of what we know God has done to show His strong side on our behalf.

We praise Him for who He is, for what He has done, for where He has brought us from, and for where He is taking us. We praise Him for safety, our health, our homes, our families, and so much more. There is no end to your personal mileposts of the revelation of the mercy and blessings of God that can be expressed in any and all of your praise sessions. Utilize your praise time for these purposes, and you will see the Spirit of God arise within you like never before. When David brought the Ark back to Jerusalem, he danced shamelessly before the Lord. He did this because of the joy of praise that was in his heart as he remembered the effects, strength, and power that was in the Ark. It caused him to forget himself and forget those who may be watching and praise God. This angered his wife, but it blessed him and showed the people of Israel how important this Ark was to the life of their leader.

For too long we have allowed the music to engulf us during our services. We have become akin to the atmosphere of a rock concert. We bounce to the beat of the music and lose sight of the purpose of the portion of the service that is supposed to be designed for remembering and praising the acts of God that have been on display in our lives. So in our services before we sing any song, we relate that song to the scripture. We place the Word of God as the preeminent source that directs our thinking toward the ways and acts of our God. This gives us a basis to praise God. I challenge you to do the same. As you relate the music to the scripture, the mileposts of life become clear, and praise is the result. Make the music a visual sign post for the documentation of the glory of God as it has been exposed to your life. Form words that say to God how worthy the Lamb of God is for His personal relation and revelation to you. In this the Spirit of God will find joy, and the most precious verse that I can leave you with will become real on the inside of you.

> He that hath my commandments, and keepeth them, he it is that loveth me: and he that loveth me shall be loved of my father, and I will love him, and will manifest myself to him. (John 14:21 KJV)

Lord, bless Your people with the revelation of Yourself. We can do no better nor have any greater than You. We receive You and the manifestation of You in our spirit to express Yourself in our lives. Thank You! In Jesus's name. Amen.

Blessings!

Works Cited

Glass, Arthur. 2019. *Yeshua in the Tanakh*: The Name of Jesus in the Old Testament, www.messianicliterature.

Endorsements

If Mike Springston is going to write a book, I am going to read it. I was led to the Lord by watching him live his life. He is the most genuine, authentic follower of Christ that I have ever met. His insight into the Word has been powerful throughout some troubling times in my life. Can't wait to dive into what he has written.

—Dean Hood
Head football coach, Murray State University

I would like to enthusiastically recommend to you the preaching ministry of Rev. Mike Springston. Mike began attending Winston-Salem First Pentecostal Holiness Church about seven years ago. Since that time, Mike has preached for me numerous times as well as speaking at a variety of church functions. He always leaves his audience challenged, motivated, and encouraged. Sometimes when people recommend a preacher, they say, "He won't hurt you." Let me say that Mike Springston will positively help your church.

This book is very engaging. I love the way Mike has blended his autobiography with the teaching.

—Pastor Tim Wolfe

It is with great pleasure that we introduce and recommend to you the ministry of Michael R. Springston, a man who is outstanding in many arenas, i.e., educator, coach, singer, but most importantly, a man with a great anointing and message to lift the Lord Jesus Christ. We have known Mike for many years and have found him to be a man "after God's own heart." He is a marvelous speaker and communicator with a word for today that reaches all generations. It is on this premise that we highly recommend Mike to your church and ministry. I have thoroughly examined the information written and find it to be interesting, informative, touching, and eye-opening. Many of my questions concerning the Bible were answered while I read this book. This book will open the revelation of Jesus to the reader.

—Dr. and Mrs. R. L. Treadway
Retired ministers and educators

Mike Springston is a man of belief, and he lives his beliefs every day. In coaching young men in football, and in life, his beliefs guide him. We are all better men by having spent time with Mike. Seeing him as he prepares for games, prepares for life's daily ups and downs, prepares for his battle against cancer, or prepares young men for life—this book will impact you in a big way.

—Ron Crook
Offensive line coach
University of Cincinnati

Ways to Visit the Ministry of Mike Springston

Website: MikeSpringstonMinistries.com
YouTube: Mike Springston FFC
Podcast: Spotify, iTunes, and iHeartRadio: Mike Springston FFC
Contact: MikeSpringstonMinistries.com using the contact tab

CPSIA information can be obtained
at www.ICGtesting.com
Printed in the USA
LVHW050907100523
746522LV00001B/8

9 781647 732288